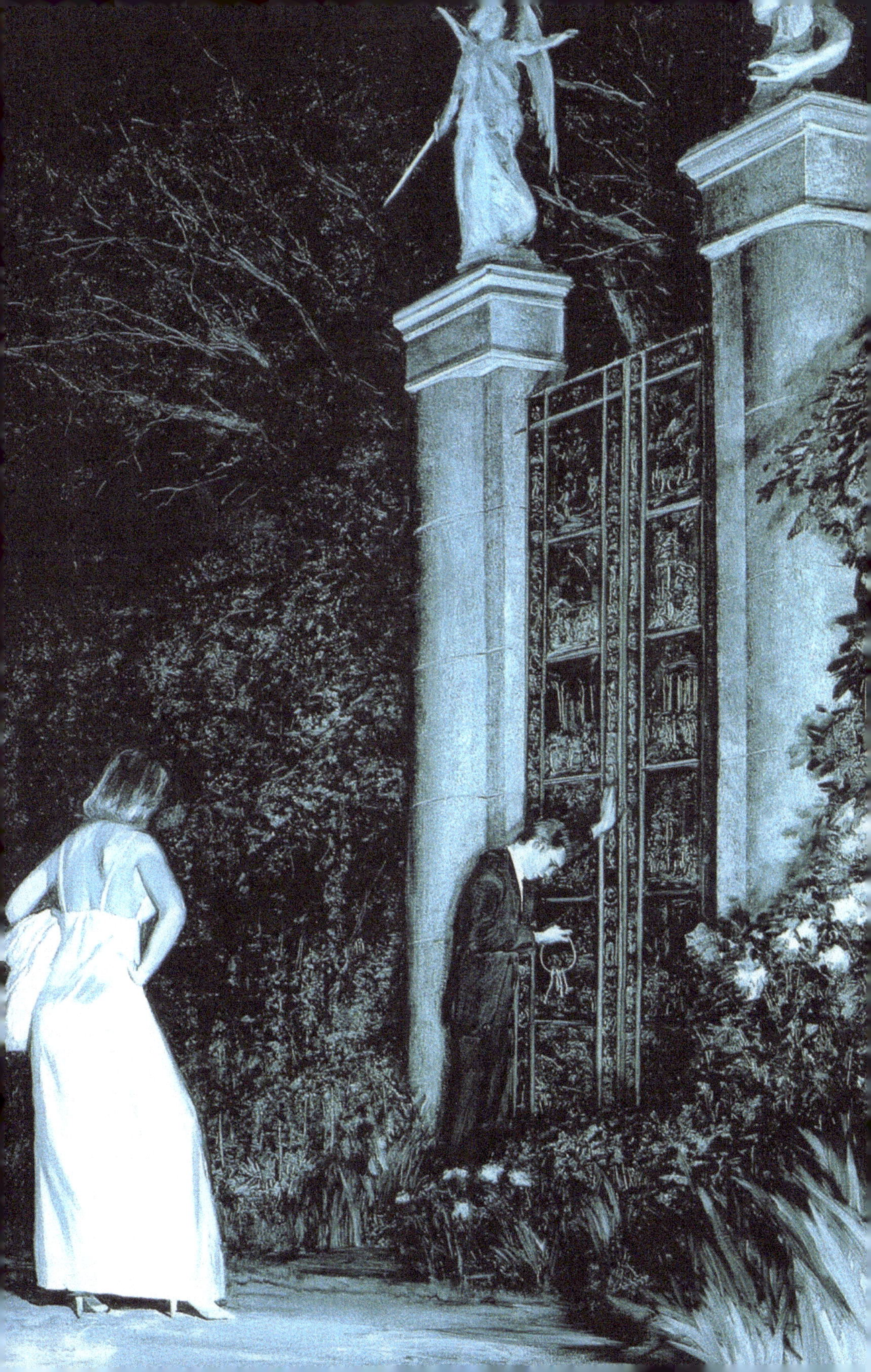

THE RENAISSANCE *of* IMAGINATION

THE MARRIAGE OF HEAVEN AND EARTH IN FLORENTINE RENAISSANCE ART

SAM HILT

Interior cover image:
Mark Tansey, *The Key* (1984)
Private Collection

Cover design and layout:
Julius Broqueza
jbfisherkingdotcom@gmail.com

Digital conversions:
ManishaPagare
pagaremd@gmail.com

Reviewers' Praise for
Sam Hilt's Guidebook:

THE UFFIZI GALLERY

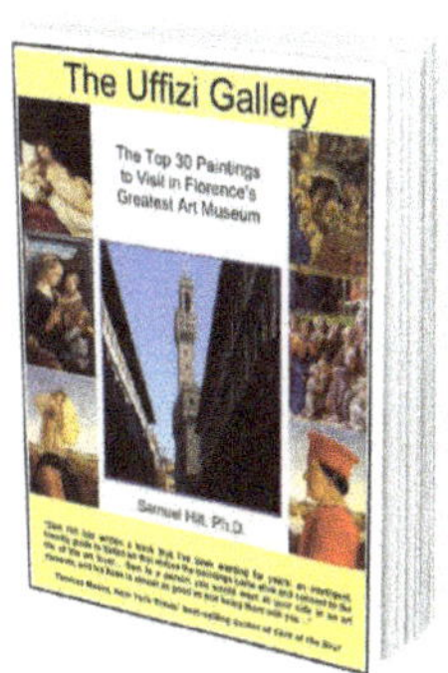

"Sam Hilt has written a book that I've been wanting for years: an intelligent, friendly guide to Italian art that makes the paintings come alive and connect to the life of the art lover. He quickly passes through the usual historical and technical aspects to help a viewer see and appreciate the images. So simple, and yet so radical. Sam is a person you would want at your side in an art museum, and his book is almost as good as him being there with you… Sam's book reveals the heart and soul of the art. Its tone is just right—informative and insightful."

~ Thomas Moore
New York Times' Best-selling
Author of *Care of the Soul*

What Amazon.com Readers Have To Say:

"The Uffizi is overwhelming. Where to start? Start with this gem of a book. Sam Hilt has selected paintings that are not necessarily "the usual cast of characters". This book is not a dry or boring art history text. You can tell the author adores the subject matter and wants the reader to love it as well. Makes me want to jump on a plane and go back to Italy!"

~ Beth Kucera

"Excellent, well written description of major art in the gallery. Perceptive, with few wasted words. A delight."

~ John Mannion

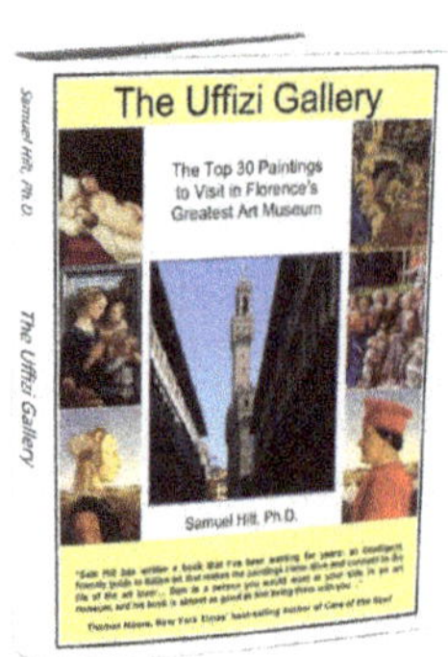

"Great tour of the Uffizi! Better than any of the tour guides I heard over there... It will open your eyes to a different way of looking at paintings and maybe the world. Not only highly recommended, but must have."

~ Paul Rodriguez

"With a sense of humor and a fine sense of art, you'll find this guide to be a perfect accompaniment to your tour of the Uffizi Gallery. Hilt makes what could be an overwhelming experience, a wonderful walk through the museum."

~ Ann Abrams

"As someone who knows very little about art, I found Sam Hilt's ability to explain the significance of the Uffizi collection fascinating. I was lucky enough to tour the museum with Sam, and his background and knowledge is unsurpassed. I would recommend this book for art lovers and travelers alike."

~ Jersey Guy

"The Uffizi Gallery is an overwhelming art experience and for anyone without a degree in Art History, it can be almost boring! Sam Hilt makes it personal because he is sharing his preferences, knowledge of the inside story and love of the collection....just as if he is walking along side you, explaining as he goes. It makes all the difference in the world!!!!!"

~ M.F. Kelly

Reviewers' Praise for

TURNING TUSCAN
A Step-by-Step Guide to Going Native

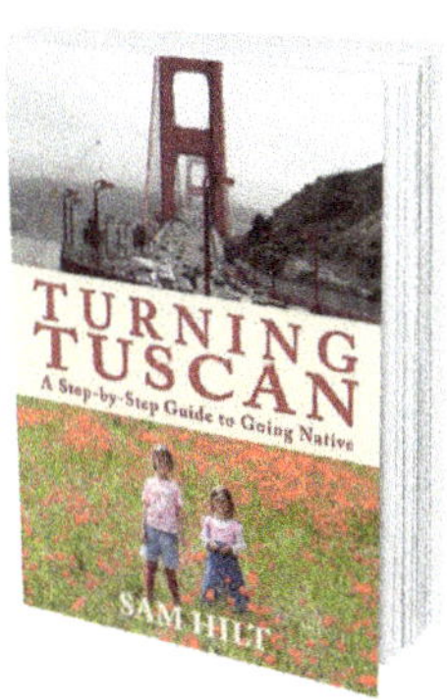

"If you read Sam Hilt's book carefully (and you should!) you'll come away with a cultural roadmap to the heart of Tuscany, the potholes marked, commented upon, and many times even celebrated."

~ James Martin
GoEurope.About.com
http://abt.cm/1ABwR3M

"He provides hilarious reportage on mind-boggling bureaucracies, the frustrations of customer service, and the little cultural quirks that become apparent when you actually live and work in a foreign place."

~ Walt Sanders
SimpleItaly.com
http://bit.ly/1cqflnx

"Overall, the success of a book like this very much depends on readers' empathy with the writer. If you like his or her voice and world view, you'll like the book. I was charmed by Hilt's openness to new experiences, his wide-ranging knowledge and his sense of humour, so Turning Tuscan held my interest from beginning to end."

~ Laura Byrne Paquet
FacingTheStreet.com
http://bit.ly/1QijRlh

""Turning Tuscan is literate, gracious, and touching at times and feels like a very well-written, nuanced journal."

~ Mark Damon Puckett
TheDailyMeal.com
http://bit.ly/1EJOo6t

"I found this book on my kindle in the middle of a sleepless night and never went back to sleep. We are planning to go to Tuscany in three weeks and this book gave such a wonderful picture of life in Tuscany covering everything from driving, to the people, to bits of history, bits of art history, to the frustrations of customer service, to the warmth of nurses in the hospital. Sam Hilt's writing style is like talking to a friend who just can't wait to share all he's learned along the way. He's funny and engaging and a font of information. I am about to read his others."

~ Ginny D.

"I knew Sam and Pam from our long-ago California days when we studied Archetypal Psychology in grad school together. It's been a pleasure to keep track of their adventure of weaving their love and passion for Italy into a fruitful and intriguing lifestyle. And Sam captures it all so eloquently in his book. I suggest it for anyone who is interested in Italy, its fineries and foibles, the Renaissance, psychology, art, and a family's experience of turning Tuscan. You will find the journey very interesting. Whether or not you are planning to follow along in his footsteps, Sam's sense of humor and penetrating insights will take you there nonetheless."

~ Ann Marie Molnar

"This is one of the best books on an expats life in Italy I have seen. I laughed and laughed... in part because most of these things happened to me when I lived there. An excellent read!"

~ Margaret Warren

"I sort of did it the wrong way round. I booked a tour with Sam and his wife Pam's Tuscany Tours, in Tuscany of course, and then ordered the book... I can safely say the book just made me look forward to my holiday all the more... I laughed out loud many times, it is easy to read and keeps you compelled to keep turning the page, an ideal read for outside in the sunshine which is exactly what I did and read it almost all through in one go. I lent it to my mother to read and she felt just the same. In fact writing this has reminded me to go and read it again."

~ Karen H.

"This book was a quick, easy read...so fun, entertaining and interesting!... I laughed out loud as I read parts of it...Sam shares his love of the country equally well with his frustrations. This has certainly wet our appetite and we can't wait to visit Tuscany to experience it on our own."

~ Marie Dobson

ACKNOWLEDGMENTS

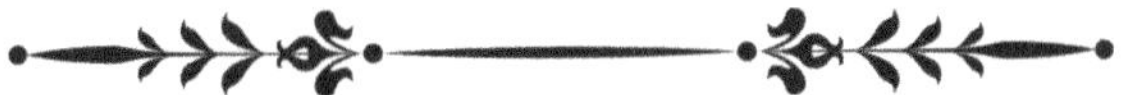

I would like to offer my sincere appreciation to Noga Emanuel for her meticulous wordsmithing and her general editorial guidance. Thanks are also due to my academic mentors and colleagues, notably Susan McKillop, Alicia Forsey, Steven K. Levine, Russell Lockhart, and Joe Meeker, for their comments and critiques when the themes explored in the present work were first taking shape.

Last but not least, I want to express my warm appreciation to the many travelers who have visited the shrines of Renaissance art in Florence with me and my wife, Pam Mercer, on our "Best of Tuscany Tours" over these past 18 years. Your observations and insights have enhanced our understanding of the art immeasurably. (www.TuscanyTours.com)

"Art Therapy in Renaissance Florence" originally appeared in *C.R.E.A.T.E, The Journal of Creative and Expressive Arts Therapies*, published by ISIS Canada, Fall Issue, 1994.

Earlier versions of Gentile da Fabriano's *Adoration of the Magi* and the three essays on Botticelli's paintings appeared in 2012 in *The Uffizi Gallery*, the author's guidebook to the paintings in the Uffizi collection (available on Amazon).

"David's Penis" first appeared in 2012 in my memoir, *Turning Tuscan: A Step-by-Step Guide to Going Native* (also available on Amazon.)

CONTENTS

Introduction | xvii

Table of Figures | xxiii

Openings: Art Therapy in Renaissance Florence | 1

Quattro Santi Coronati: The Mission Statement of the Sculptors' Guild | 17

Donatello's *St. George*: Man and Superman | 25

The Brancacci Chapel: Many Hands at Work | 37

Gentile da Fabriano's *Adoration of the Magi* | 55

David's Penis | 71

Annunciations | 83

Fra Angelico: Three Stages of Annunciation | 89

Fra Filippo Lippi: The Monk and the Madonna | 105

Piero's Pregnant Madonna | 129

Botticelli's *Primavera* | 139

Botticelli's *Birth of Venus* | 145

Botticelli's *Annunciation* | 151

Appendices | 155

Image Work: Art History vs. Art Appreciation | 157

Further Notes on Image Work | 161

Imaginal Dialogue | 167

Transcript of the *Trinità* Dialogue | 177

Bibliography | 183

About the Author | 187

INTRODUCTION

I magine that you are visiting an art museum in Italy. As you look at the painting before your eyes and begin to sigh with admiration, your guide begins to tell you all about it. "The painting before us is a characteristic example of the late Gothic style, probably done by Buggiardo, a relatively minor artist of the early *Quattrocento*. No signed documents support the attribution to Buggiardo, and some critics consider the work to be merely Buggiardesque. But there are certain stylistic elements that this work has in common with his signed paintings that have led several important scholars to conclude that this painting is a true Buggiardo. In any case, the painting entered the museum's collection in 1687, prior to which it was a part of the personal collection of the Duke de Camargues-du-Point-Sevin who is believed to have purchased it directly from Buggiardo's immediate heirs. During the recent cleaning and restoration, the painting was found to have some over-painting on the faces of three of the angels and some light abrading around the aureole of the Madonna. Do you have any questions? If not, we can move on to the next painting."

Now imagine that you are a young woman who has been invited to dinner at a stylish seafood restaurant by a handsome admirer. As the waiter delivers your entrée, he informs you that the restaurant now buys its fish from a new supplier who is considerably cheaper, that the fish was carefully tested for parasites and that none were found, and that although it's not today's catch, it was refrigerated overnight and you shouldn't be able to tell the difference. While you are gagging on your mouthful of fish, your date tells you that you look lovely and begins to ask you a few questions: What brand of mascara do you use? What do you use for your makeup remover? Do you worry about aluminum in your deodorant?

Hopefully you have never had a meal in a seafood restaurant like the one above, but you probably have experienced a museum visit that was quite similar to what I describe. While we carefully cultivate the sensuous, pleasurable aspects of dining, we seem to be oblivious to these values when we step into the realm of art. What's often missing on the part of our guides (live, text or online) is any awareness of an emotional and spiritual dimension to our encounter with works of art. Instead, the professional discourse of art historians, the shop-talk which should rightly remain behind the scenes in these contexts, intrudes and overwhelms the encounter of the viewer with the work of art.

The present muddle has to do with the failure of art historians to distinguish between the objectives of the scholar or researcher and the needs of the amateur, the lover of art without professional aspirations. So, the casual museum visitor who reads a guidebook or takes a docent tour is often presented with a slew of facts that do nothing to facilitate and enhance his or her appreciation of the work of art: disagreements over attribution or about its probable dating, what movement it belongs to, discoveries made by recent X-ray analysis, anecdotes about the artist's life and his mental illness or his stormy relationship with his brother or his wife, and so forth. The net effect of this kind of presentation of facts about the painting is to cover the canvas beneath a blizzard of Post-It Notes until the viewer can no longer see it at all, and no longer feels any need to try because he or she now "knows" all about it.

Before you come to the conclusion that I want to shoot all the art historians, let me assure you of the contrary. To appreciate images from another time and place with any depth and seriousness, we require the knowledge gained through art historical research. While we can enjoy a Monet landscape or a Renoir still-life just by looking, we can't do the same thing when we stand in front of the works of Renaissance masters. If you don't know about the Virtues or the ways in which Charity was typically represented, and you're unfamiliar with the symbol of the pelican piercing its breast with its beak to feed its young, and you don't know that Battista Sforza died in childbirth delivering an heir, it's unlikely that you will be unduly impressed by Piero della Francesca's portrait of her. With the benefit of this background knowledge, when you suddenly understand what Piero has done, you might feel as if you've been struck by lightning.

* * *

In approaching the various Renaissance images considered in these essays, I have tried diligently to respect and utilize the known facts while avoiding entirely the academic side-discussions that contribute marginally or not at all to the appreciation of the work of art: disagreements over attribution, probable dating, historical importance, and so forth. When we approach Renaissance paintings solely in this way, we utterly ignore the purposes for which such images were originally created. The works of the Renaissance masters were never intended to become objects of study but, rather, to open the eye, mind, or heart, to stir religious sentiment, to seduce us into a dream of unearthly beauty, to protect us, to memorialize and to honor, to waken us to the cosmic mysteries, to enrapture and enthrall us, to enliven our souls.

While striving to remain scrupulous in scholarship, my effort has been to re-establish the power of certain fifteenth century images to engage and inspire a modern audience. To this end I've brought certain insights and perspectives born in the world of psychology to the present encounter with paintings from the Renaissance. In particular, I have drawn upon the innovative work James Hillman has done with dream images and the psychological hermeneutic which he has articulated throughout the course of his writings.[1] From the discipline of archetypal psychology I have borrowed an approach to imagery that stimulates psychological engagement and appreciation, and a methodology that empowers images to tell their stories in ways which, not coincidentally, we have not seen in the West since the time of the Renaissance.

Perhaps the most interesting aspect of this experiment has been to learn from

---

1   Most relevant among James Hillman's writings for present purposes have been *Re-Visioning Psychology* (New York: Harper, 1977), *The Dream and the Underworld* (New York: Harper, 1979), *Healing Fiction* (Barrytown: Station Hill Press, 1983), and three articles published in the journal *Spring*: "An Inquiry into image" (1977), 62 88, "Further notes on images" (1978), 152 82, and "Image sense" (1979), 130 43.

the images themselves that the story of the Renaissance in which they have been embedded is not one that suits them. So, as a last stop before venturing into the essays, a few words are necessary about our popular conceptions of the Renaissance and the alternate universe that you will find constituted in these pages.

* * *

The dominant voice in influencing modern conceptions of the Renaissance was that of the Swiss historian Jacob Burckhardt. First published in 1860 his *Civilization of the Renaissance in Italy* has largely defined the parameters of all subsequent discussion of the Renaissance.[2]

Burckhardt sharply stressed the profound differences between the Middle Ages and the Renaissance. He argued that the medieval worldview compounded of "faith, childish prejudice, and delusion" gave way during the Renaissance to a newfound curiosity about the natural world, an objective, investigative attitude. To summarize Burckhardt we might say, "After long centuries of darkness and ignorance, the light of reason began to emerge and the shackles of medieval superstition were gradually cast off."

The problem with this view of the Renaissance is that the new, rational approach to exploring the world coexisted throughout this period with the "superstitious" traditions of the medieval and ancient worlds which continued to thrive. More recent scholarship, particularly the work of researchers at London's Warburg Institute like Frances Yates, Edgar Wind, and Erwin Panofsky, has established incontrovertibly that an abiding interest in Christian religious themes, in pagan "mysteries", in alchemy and astrology and Hermetic philosophy, was as typically characteristic of the Renaissance mind as was its fascination with measurement, perspective, and natural science.

So long as we cling to the belief that nascent objectivity defined the Renaissance mind while medieval mysticism intruded unhappily upon it, we do violence to the historical record in its true complexity. When we encounter

---

2 Jacob Burckhardt, *The Civilization of the Renaissance in Italy*, trans. by S.G.C. Middlemore, in 2 vols. (New York: Harper & Row, 1958)

both mystical and rational, or spiritual and empirical interests joined in the soul of the same artist, we are forced by the narrative to assign such a figure to a "transitional" phase. When we turn to almost any critical treatment of Fra Angelico's work, we are reassured that the artist's technique was progressive *despite the fact* that his subject matter was still informed by a medieval worldview. Historians faithfully study Alberti's formulae for perspective construction as an important key to the art of the period, yet, because they don't fit with our notions of the essential rationality of Renaissance art, we ignore Alberti's explicit statements that the purpose of his method was to empower images to move the soul.[3]

The work of the Warburg Institute scholars notwithstanding, Burckhardt's paradigm has imposed upon us an evolutionary fantasy of the Renaissance that we have yet to cast off. With a different narrative through which to see the essential contours of the period, I am persuaded that many of the images of the Italian Renaissance can be perceived in new ways, that they can be released from the places to which they have been mentally fixed along the axis of the progress fantasy. Those who would argue that a history of the technical development of pictorial representation offers a more objective approach to this period simply mistake a particular story-line for the territory itself. Since I believe that he understood these matters better than most people, I will rest my case with William Blake's judgment in *The Marriage of Heaven and Hell*:

> So the Angel said: "thy phantasy has imposed upon me, & thou oughtest to be ashamed."

> I answer'd: "we impose on one another, and it is but lost time to converse with you whose works are only Analytics."

The new story that the reader will find in these essays is one which explores the remarkable capacity of Renaissance genius to work creatively with opposing forces and to bring them into fruitful relationship. There are bold efforts to reconcile pagan and Christian themes; rational techniques of rep-

---

3   Leon Battista Alberti, *On Painting*, trans, J.R. Spencer (New Haven: Yale Univ. Press, 1971), p. 77.

resentation serve to exalt mystical states of perception; eternal themes are dramatized in the realm of daily life in the quest for a marriage of heaven and earth. By working with the images in novel ways, I also try to reveal the spirit of the times in ways that the images proclaim in compelling terms. I am hopeful that the essays which have emerged from my own enlivening encounters with these Renaissance images will prove to be of interest both to new students as well as to readers long familiar with Renaissance art.

Buon viaggio!

Sam Hilt
Siena, Italy

TABLE OF FIGURES

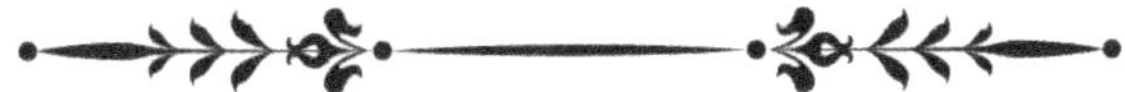

Figure 1 — Ghiberti; *Competition Panel*. Bargello Museum, Florence.

Figure 2 — Brunelleschi; *Competition Panel*. Bargello Museum, Florence.

Figure 3 — Ghiberti; *Competition Panel*, detail. Bargello Museum, Florence.

Figure 4 — Brunelleschi; *Competition Panel*, detail. Bargello Museum, Florence.

Figure 5 — Nanni di Banco, *Four Crowned Saints*. Orsanmichele Church, Florence.

Figure 6 — Nanni di Banco, *Four Crowned Saints*, predella. Orsanmichele Church, Florence.

Figure 7 — Nanni di Banco, *Four Crowned Saints*, detail. Orsanmichele Church, Florence.

Figure 8 — Donatello, *Niccolo da Uzzano*, right profile. Bargello Museum, Florence.

Figure 9 — Donatello, *Niccolo da Uzzano*, left profile. Bargello Museum, Florence.

Figure 10 — Donatello, *St. George*. Bargello Museum, Florence.

Figure 11 — Donatello, *St. George*, predella detail. Bargello Museum, Florence.

Figure 12 — Masaccio et al., *The Tribute Money*. Brancacci Chapel, Church of Santa Maria del Carmine, Florence.

Figure 13 — Masaccio et al., *The Raising of Theophilus*. Brancacci Chapel.

Figure 14 — Masaccio et al., *The Raising of Theophilus*, detail. Brancacci Chapel.

Figure 15 — Masaccio et al., *St. Peter Leaving Prison*. Brancacci Chapel.

Figure 16 — Masaccio et al., *Crucifixion of St. Peter*. Brancacci Chapel.

Figure 17 — Masaccio et al., *St. Peter Preaching*. Brancacci Chapel.

Figure 18 — Masaccio et al., *St. Peter Baptizing*. Brancacci Chapel.

Figure 19 — Masaccio et al., *St. Peter Healing*. Brancacci Chapel.

Figure 20 — Masaccio et al., *St. Peter Distributing Alms*. Brancacci Chapel.

Figure 21 — Masaccio et al., *The Raising of Tabitha*. Brancacci Chapel.

Figure 22 — Masaccio et al., *The Expulsion*. Brancacci Chapel.

Figure 23 — Venus Pudica. Rome National Museum, Rome.

Figure 24 — Gentile da Fabriano, *Adoration of the Magi*. Uffizi Gallery, Florence.

Figure 25 — Gentile da Fabriano, *Adoration of the Magi*, detail of the horses. Uffizi Gallery, Florence.

Figure 26 — Gentile da Fabriano, *Adoration of the Magi*, detail of The Three Magi. Uffizi Gallery, Florence.

Figure 27 — Gentile da Fabriano, *Adoration of the Magi*, detail, left gable. Uffizi Gallery, Florence.

Figure 28 — Gentile da Fabriano, *Adoration of the Magi*, detail, central gable. Uffizi Gallery, Florence.

Figure 29 — Donatello, *David* (early). Bargello Museum, Florence.

Figure 30 — Donatello, *David* (later, frontal view). Bargello Museum, Florence.

Figure 31 — Donatello, *David* (later, side view). Bargello Museum, Florence.

Figure 32 — Michelangelo, *David*. Accademia, Florence.

Figure 33 — Fra Filippo Lippi, *Annunciation*. National Gallery of Art, Washington, D.C.

Figure 34 — Leonardo da Vinci, *Annunciation*. Uffizi Gallery, Florence.

Figure 35 — Fra Bartolomeo, *Annuciation*. Duomo, Volterra.

Figure 36 — Fra Angelico, *Annunciation*. Diocesan Museum, Cortona.

Figure 37 — Fra Angelico, *Annunciation* (corridor). San Marco Monastery, Florence.

Figure 38 — Fra Angelico, *Annunciation* (cell). San Marco Monastery, Florence.

Figure 39 — Fra Filippo Lippi, *Coronation of the Virgin*. Uffizi Gallery, Florence.

Figure 40 — Fra Filippo Lippi, *Coronation of the Virgin*, detail. Uffizi Gallery, Florence.

Figure 41 — Fra Filippo Lippi, *Coronation of the Virgin*, detail. Uffizi Gallery, Florence.

Figure 42 — Fra Filippo Lippi, *Barbadori Altarpiece*. Louvre Museum, Paris.

Figure 43 — Fra Filippo Lippi, *Annunciation*. Church of San Lorenzo, Florence.

Figure 44 — Nicholas of Verdun, *Annunciation to Mary*. Klosterneuburg Altarpiece, Klosterneuburg Monastery, Austria.

Figure 45 — Nicholas of Verdun, *Annunciation to Sarah*. Klosterneuburg Altarpiece.

Figure 46 — Nicholas of Verdun, *Annunciation to the Mother of Samson*. Klosterneuburg Altarpiece.

Figure 47   Fra Filippo Lippi, *Adoration of the Child*. Uffizi Gallery, Florence.

Figure 48   Piero della Francesca, *Madonna del Parto*.
Museum of the Madonna del Parto, Monterchi.

Figure 49   Piero della Francesca, *Madonna del Parto*, detail, left angel.
Museum of the Madonna del Parto, Monterchi.

Figure 50   Piero della Francesca, *Madonna del Parto*, detail, right angel.
Museum of the Madonna del Parto, Monterchi.

Figure 51   Arnolfo di Cambio, *Tomb of Cardinal de Braye*, detail.
Church of San Domenico, Orvieto.

Figure 52   Sandro Botticelli, *La Primavera*. Uffizi Gallery, Florence.

Figure 53   Sandro Botticelli, *La Primavera*, detail. Uffizi Gallery, Florence.

Figure 54   Sandro Botticelli, *La Primavera*, detail. Uffizi Gallery, Florence.

Figure 55   Sandro Botticelli, *The Birth of Venus*. Uffizi Gallery, Florence.

Figure 56   Sandro Botticelli, *Annunciation*. Uffizi Gallery, Florence.

Figure 57   Sandro Botticelli, *Annunciation*, predella. Uffizi Gallery, Florence.

Figure 58   Piero della Francesca, *Sigismondo Malatesta Before St. Sigismondo*.
Tempio Malatestiano, Rimini.

Figure 59   Masaccio, *Trinità*, Santa Maria Novella, Florence

Openings:
ART THERAPY IN RENAISSANCE FLORENCE

One of the most profound mysteries of the Renaissance is the sense of sudden and explosive energy that accompanies its birth. The period which will occupy us initially are the early years of the fifteenth century, as it is almost immediately after the turn of the new century that we witness that unprecedented flowering of artistic genius which heralds the Renaissance. While there is certainly much in the preceding period which prepares the ground for what is to follow, and historians continue to debate what truly demarcates the Renaissance, it is in the opening decades of the fifteenth century that men like Donatello, Brunelleschi, Alberti, Masaccio, Filippo Lippi, Fra Angelico, and Piero della Francesca appear on the stage of world history in a town about the size of Santa Rosa, California (approx. 100,000 souls).

What adds to the mystery of this sudden birth is that it occurred during times of extraordinary duress. And though misery and disaster are not uncommon in human affairs, the decision of a community to respond to them through organized artistic activity in the way the Florentines did is rare, if not unique, in human history. What we see at the dawn of the *Quattrocento*, I would suggest, is a collectively sponsored program of art therapy for an entire people.

The story of these artistic undertakings, along with speculation as to their relation to ongoing political and social events has been memorably recounted by Frederick Hartt in an essay entitled "Art and Freedom in Quattrocento

Florence."[4] In telling the outlines of the story I will be relying on Hartt's researches both into the events of the day as well as into the art and building campaigns which accompanied them. My present objective is simply to draw out more fully the psychological implications of what transpired.

* * *

For the reader who may be unfamiliar with contemporary practices in the creative arts therapies, let me state briefly what I take to be the central assumption that informs this work: *Given the opportunity to express itself in images, the psyche will spontaneously generate figures which mirror its present state of being.* In discussing his early investigations of this key principle of psychic life, Carl Jung described an experiment which he conducted during the period of his military service in the first World War:

> I sketched every morning in a notebook a small circular drawing, a mandala, which seemed to correspond to my inner situation at the time. With the help of these drawings I could observe my psychic transformations day by day... My mandalas were cryptograms concerning the state of the self which were presented to me anew each day. In them I saw the self--that is, my whole being--actively at work.[5]

In early clinical applications of art therapy, as, for example, in the attempted treatment of psychopathology, the patient was encouraged to produce images so that the therapist could read them diagnostically and determine appropriate therapeutic interventions. But in recent years there has been an important shift of emphasis among several innovative practitioners in the field.[6] In the new conception of this work, the therapist's role shifts to that of a facilitator and the patient's to that of a human being engaged in a ritual

---

4   Frederick Hartt, "Art and Freedom in Quattrocento Florence," in L. F. Sandler, ed., *Essays in memory of Karl Lehmann* (New York, 1964), pp. 114-131

5   Carl Jung, *Memories, Dreams, Reflections*, ed. A. Jaffe, trans. R. and C. Winston (New York: Vintage Books, 1965) pp. 195-196.

6   Further discussion of theory and practice may be found in the writings of two leading practioners of this new style of creative arts therapy: Stephen K. Levine [*Poiesis: The Language of Psychology and the Speech of the Soul* (Toronto: Palmerston Press, 1992)], director of the Isis-Canada expressive arts program in Toronto, Ont., and Shaun McNiff [*Art as Medicine* (Boston & London: Shambhala, 1992)], founder of the training program at Leslie College in Cambridge, Mass.

of self-healing. The patient/client/person is encouraged to create images as part of an ongoing process of dialogue between conscious awareness and the deeper reaches of the soul. By working reflectively and responding to these images—with dialogue, with movement, or with other images—we begin to "move the energy" and allow the psychic configuration to shift. When these processes are used in an effort to facilitate recovery from trauma, the psyche typically begins to constellate images of the traumatization before healing breakthroughs occur.

But what is it exactly that makes the process "work?" Why does this imaginative, contemplative work with images seem to have such therapeutic value? Or, to put it another way, why should the imaginative representation of one's trauma itself be a healing ritual?

A plausible approach to this question in terms of the release of imaginative energies is offered by Greg Mogenson in his provocative essay on religion and psychology, *God Is A Trauma*:

> When events defy the imagination's capacity to differentiate between them, they assault the soul... When the soul is unable to make differences between itself and a huge jumble of events, the soul-making process becomes crippled.[7]

Mogenson suggests that when we are overwhelmed by traumatic events, we lose the psychic suppleness to discern patterns and make sense of life's events. We experience a paralysis of our capacity to situate ourselves meaningfully within our life's story. So, we seize upon a simple explanation and make a correspondingly simplistic, ineffective, and repetitive response. In short, we find ourselves stuck in a rut, telling the same old story, and unconsciously enacting the same patterns. If we have the sense, as well as the time and money, we might seek to engage in some form of therapeutic work at such a juncture in our lives.

For therapy to be successful, we have to break the hold of the trauma over our psychic life. And I think that Mogenson insightfully identifies the principle

---

7   Greg Mogenson, *God Is A Trauma* (Dallas: Spring Publications, 1989), p. 29.

at the heart of this work:

> ...in order for a trauma to break free from the spell in which it is trans-
> fixed, the imaginative process which it has unconsciously literalized into
> compulsive behavior must be mirrored back to it in imaginative ways.[8]

In other words, we need to begin by externalizing the images of pain or shame or violence which have traumatized us. By creating representations of these internalized traumatic images, we put them out in front of us where we can see them, and they no longer exercise the same absolute power over our perception and behavior that they do when they live entirely behind the scenes, beneath the threshold of our awareness.

As soon as we start to work with them or, even better, to play with them, we break their power to unconsciously dominate our ways of imagining the events of our lives. Newly freed and set in motion, the imaginative energies are empowered anew to make a meaningful story out of the circumstances of our lives. Regarding the work of myth-making which engages therapist and patient, James Hillman has suggested that: "Some of the healing that goes on, maybe even the essence of it, is this collaborative fiction, this putting all the chaotic and traumatic events of a life into a new story." [9]

I am suggesting that during the dawning period of the Renaissance we can see this sort of a healing and empowering process taking place on a collective level. So, with these notions of the therapeutic power of image-making as a backdrop to our investigations, let's turn back to our story of the Florentines' finest hour.

* * *

Our patient is the Republic of Florence at the dawn of the fifteenth century. The optimism and prosperity of the early decades of the 1300's, reflected in the undertaking of large-scale architectural projects, had abruptly vanished. In 1348 the Black Plague carried off nearly half of the population; in succeeding decades, flood and drought led to major crop failures and widespread famine; an econom-

---

8   Ibid., p. 12.

9   James Hillman, "A Note on Story", in *Parabola*, Vol. IV, #4 (1979), p. 44.

ic depression caused the ruination of many of Florence's international banking houses and many families were left destitute.

The response to such world-shattering trauma, as reflected in the arts of the latter half of the century, was regression and a loss of psychic energy. The innovative and speculative energies which had characterized Giotto's and Andrea Pisano's artistic accomplishments in the early decades of the 14th century were abandoned; in their place we find somber images like Orcagna's *Strozzi Altarpiece* and the tedious frescoes which Andre da Firenze painted for the Dominicans' interrogation chambers at Santa Maria Novella. In these images the efforts of Giotto and his followers to humanize the face of God are abandoned. We see a return to hieratic principles of composition (bigger, full frontal = more holy), and we see a renewed emphasis upon ecclesiastical hierarchy, clear lines of divinely sanctioned authority, fear and awe in the face of the transcendent Otherness of inscrutable deity. Apart from those few major works which affirmed a return to "traditional values," patronage in the final decades of the century was virtually absent, major civic undertakings remained suspended, and the arts generally languished.

At the dawn of the fifteenth century, the Florentine community was suddenly confronted by the threat of disaster from yet another quarter. Florence's political rival, Milan, had grown increasingly powerful under the leadership of the warlord, Giangaleazzo Visconti, and Florence was now being directly threatened by the Milanese imperialist expansion. One by one, all of Florence's allies came under Milanese control. With the fall of Pisa, Florence lost its access to sea routes and became subject to economic as well as military siege. What to do? In the face of this utter extremity, the guild officials in charge of the ancient Baptistery in the heart of the city decided to hold an open art competition!

Of all the possible responses one might make to the presence of the enemy at the gates, the declaration of an open art competition (the first in recorded history, no less) for an extremely costly set of gilded bronze doors for the Baptistery is certainly a remarkable one. Yet I believe that it is with this bold stroke that the Italian Renaissance truly begins.

The theme which each artist was asked to illustrate in a single panel was the Biblical story of the Sacrifice of Isaac. This dark tale of God's command to Abraham to sacrifice his beloved son and Isaac's last minute reprieve has haunted the Western imagination for millennia. Rabbinic commentators in every generation pondered the moral complexity of the narrative; Christian artists from the early centuries of the Church saw the death and resurrection of Christ prefigured in Isaac's redemption. The site of Isaac's ordeal, Mt. Moriah, was the location where Solomon chose to build the Holy Temple.

One possible explanation for the Florentines' selection of the story of Isaac requires that we consider the element of sacrifice itself and its presumed magical efficacy. The sacrifice of the firstborn is a ritual that was apparently widespread in the ancient world, and we find echoes of it throughout the Old Testament (Micah 6:7; II Samuel 21:9; Judges 11:34-40). In his reflections on the ritual of the sacrifice, Northrop Frye has offered the following explanation for the phenomenon:

> The original motive behind human sacrifice was doubtless a *do ut des* bargain: I give that you may give. It is assumed that the god, like the ghost in Yeats, lives off the smell of offerings. So if the god is fed by sacrifices he will respond by giving good weather for crops or increased fertility among animals. And he must be fed first, with the "firstfruits" of vegetable and animal produce.

> ...the eldest son, whenever born, and whether naturally or miraculously born, is in either case the first gift of God, and so is technically a "firstfruit" to be given back to God along with other firstfruits.[10]

As the sacrifice of that held dearest, the sacrifice of the firstborn son was considered to be the most powerful of rituals for attracting the support of one's god. There is a story in II Kings 3:27 which describes recourse to this ritual in a situation much like that faced by the Florentines. When the kingdom of Moab was under siege by the Israelites, the king "took his eldest son that should have reigned in his stead, and offered him for a burnt offering upon the wall." Fol-

---

10 Northrop Frye, *The Great Code: The Bible and Literature* (New York: HBJ, 1982), pp. 182-183.

  OPENINGS: ART THERAPY IN RENAISSANCE FLORENCE

lowing this act the Israelites abruptly abandoned their siege, and we are forced to conclude that it was because they feared the magical efficacy of the ritual.

The narrowly averted sacrifice of Isaac and the consummated sacrifice of Jesus are both stories which find their place against the background of this ancient ritual of blood sacrifice. Both Judaism and Christianity sought to curb the continuing literal enactment of this practice while simultaneously invoking its mysterious potency. For Christians, the sacrifice of Jesus is a world-transforming act that need never be repeated. For Jews, it is paradoxically Abraham's initial willingness, in faith, to carry out the sacrifice that makes its repetition forever after unnecessary. In the aftermath of these primary, archetypal enactments, it is only necessary for subsequent generations to make reference to them in order to avail themselves of their original power. The original act continues to resonate potently in the background.

The scholar of Judaic history, Joseph Gutmann, in an essay on medieval Jewish images of the Binding of Isaac cites the Rabbinic commentator Rashi who states: "The Lord [on account of the Binding of Isaac] will forgive Israel every year and rescue them from trouble." [11] And he notes that during the yearly *Rosh Hashanah* (New Year) services, there is a Jewish prayer which reminds God of Isaac's ordeal and implores him to act "according to Your oath, and reverse your decree from stern judgment to mercy." [12] Jewish references to this original enactment, in seeking to avert misfortune, clearly demonstrate their apotropaic function.

For Christians, it is the Crucifixion which serves this function of providing a defense against evil. In fact, Jesus (John 3:14) specifically compares his own Crucifixion to Moses' paradigmatic act of creating an apotropaic device: his mounting of a brass serpent upon a pole so that those who would gaze upon it would be protected from fatal serpent bites (Numbers 21:8-9). (In modern film and fiction, inspired by Bram Stoker's *Dracula*, we still see the Crucifix used in this manner to ward off vampires.)

Returning to Florence from this brief excursion into the psychology of reli-

---

11 Joseph Gutman, "The Sacrifice of Isaac in Medieval Jewish Art" in Artibus et Historiae vol. 8/16 (1987), p. 70.

12 Ibid., p. 67.

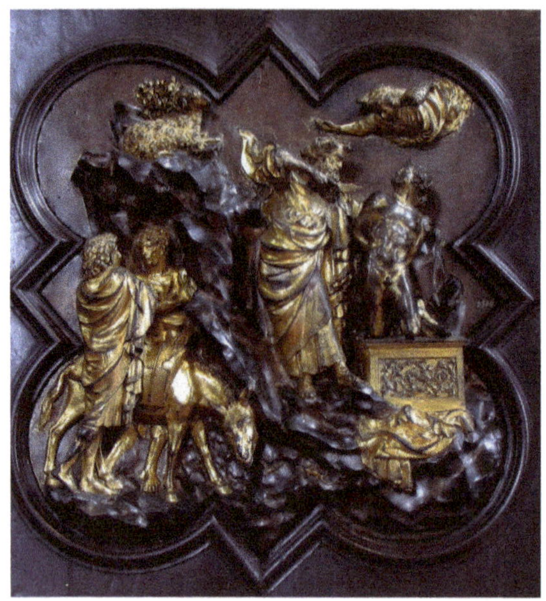

gious sacrifice, we may speculate that by invoking through images the archetypal power of the original enactment, the Florentines may have been trying to appropriate this story's power to deliver them from evil.

* * *

Of the seven panels depicting the Sacrifice of Isaac submitted to the judges of the panel competition, only two have survived—one by Brunelleschi and the other by Ghiberti.[13]

Fig. 1: Ghiberti; *Competition Panel.*
Bargello Museum, Florence.

Ghiberti's panel was chosen by the judges as the winning entry, and he was awarded the contract to cast twenty-eight additional bronze panels for what were to become the North Doors of the Florence Baptistery. Brunelleschi, on the other hand, essentially gave up sculpture after the competition and devoted his extraordinary talents primarily to architecture.

Critics and art historians have generally tended to side with the original judges in regarding Ghiberti's as the superior work.[14] But these judgments have typically been based on criteria such as technical mastery of materials, elegance of line, luminosity of surface, or even more abstract stylistic considerations, such as balance and harmony. Rather than applying "the eternal and immutable laws of aesthetics" toward a critical evaluation of these two works, how might we contrast them in terms of *psychological value* as meditations

---

13   The two surviving panels are currently displayed, side-by-side, in the Bargello museum in Florence.

14   Ghiberti's account of the proceedings protests a bit much by insisting that the decision of the judges was unanimous in his favor. Another account of the affair (in an anonymously published life of Brunelleschi possibly written by his friend Manetti) suggests that the jury was deeply split and had offered a joint commission to both men--which Brunelleschi declined. Since Brunelleschi was later saddled with Ghiberti in precisely this way in the project of constructing the cathedral dome, Manetti's account seems highly plausible.

          OPENINGS: ART THERAPY IN RENAISSANCE FLORENCE

on the theme of the Sacrifice of Isaac? How successfully does each image work in the therapy of the imagination? Which one moves the soul more deeply into story?

In looking at Ghiberti's panel we cannot help but acknowledge the elegance and poise of his exquisitely modeled figures. Yet we might fairly ask whether such harmony and grace are, psychologically speaking, the most appropriate qualities for an image

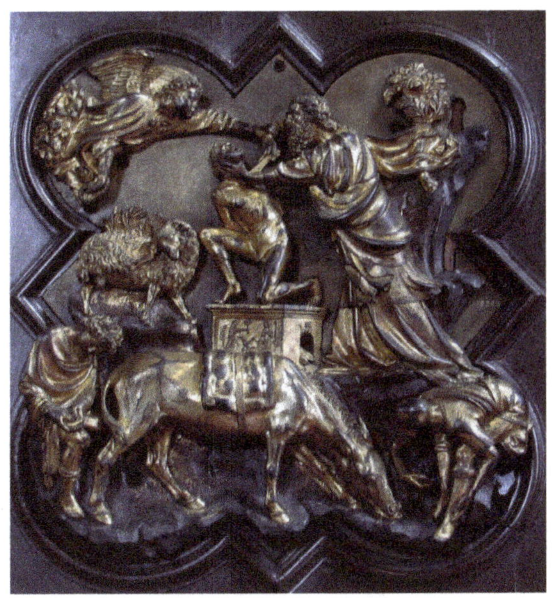

Fig. 2: Brunelleschi; *Competition Panel.*
Bargello Museum, Florence.

which depicts a father engaged in the slaughter of his child. In place of Ghiberti's balanced figures, everything in Brunelleschi's image is deliberately and *thematically* off-balance. Abraham leans forward at nearly a forty-five degree angle, the ram stands awkwardly on three legs, the first servant balances on one leg while the other servant and the ass bend down to drink, the angel lurches forward, and Isaac squats on one knee, his head pushed to the side by his father's hand around his throat. The psychological chaos and raging inner conflicts are mirrored in this bizarre landscape where everything is off-center, in motion, out of balance.

Ghiberti's panel makes a clean division—by means of the rock-face running through the center of the image—between the events on the mountain top and the life of the servants below. The servants engaged in casual conversation are clearly set apart from the high moral drama being enacted at the top of the mountain. And in representing the servants' obliviousness to events on high, the image clearly shows the lack of relationship between what is above and what is below.

There is also a hierarchical order present in Brunelleschi's image, but it is of a different type. The quatrefoil's lateral border divides the action into three planes: a topmost level showing upper torsos and conscious struggle; a

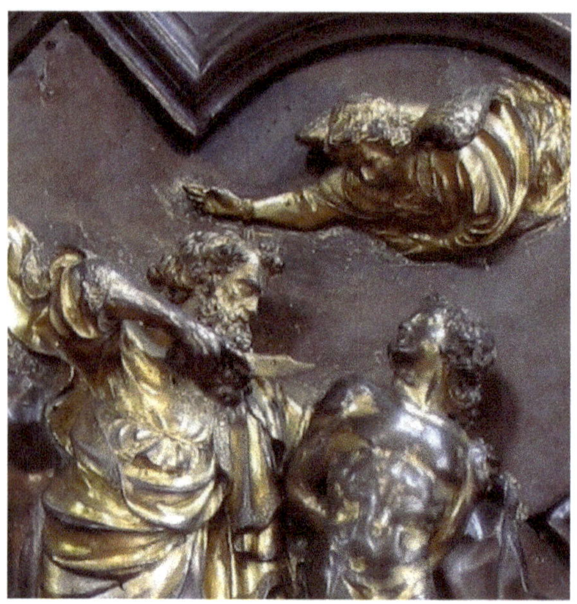
Fig. 3: Ghiberti; Competition Panel, detail.
Bargello Museum, Florence.

midplane of ram, sacrificial altar and the lower bodies; and a ground level depicting the quotidian life of the servants and their donkey. Yet Brunelleschi's image manages to avoid Ghiberti's upstairs/downstairs, high/low split. The image is rich with internal echoes which carry the eye and the mind from one plane to the next. In lifting its leg and exposing its genitals the ram mirrors Isaac's nakedness and vulnerability; the lifted leg also mimics the servant below who is pulling a thorn from his foot; the positioning of the ram's forelegs is identical to that of the ass beneath him; Isaac's ungainly posture is reflected in the squatting of the servant who drinks below, and so forth. All levels from angel to ass are implicated in the event, share in the collective imbalance, and are bound by Brunelleschi into a unified field. Even the rock-face which had cloven Ghiberti's fiction in two is here moved behind Abraham to suggest the extremity of the abyss and the condition of a man on the edge.

As a final point of comparison between the two images, let's look at the particular moment in the story which each artist has chosen to illustrate. Ghiberti has chosen the moment just *prior* to rescue. Isaac bravely awaits his fate and Abraham is still intent on slaughter, entirely unaware of the angel who has just appeared. Ghiberti's Abraham stands, paused, forever ready to kill, as his son is forever ready to be killed. And this static quality in the image leaves us standing just shy of resolution.

Brunelleschi, on the other hand, shows us a world out of balance, but one in which everything is moving. *Brunelleschi has insinuated himself psychologically into the scene and brought it to life in a way that gives convincing expression to the emotional experience of the scene's participants.* He has chosen to depict the precise moment when Abraham moves to slay his son, when the angel acts to stop him, when Isaac screams out as Abraham lays hold of him. Resolved finally to kill his son, lurching forward and finding himself suddenly blocked, Abraham's face betrays only horror and bewilderment. We are invited

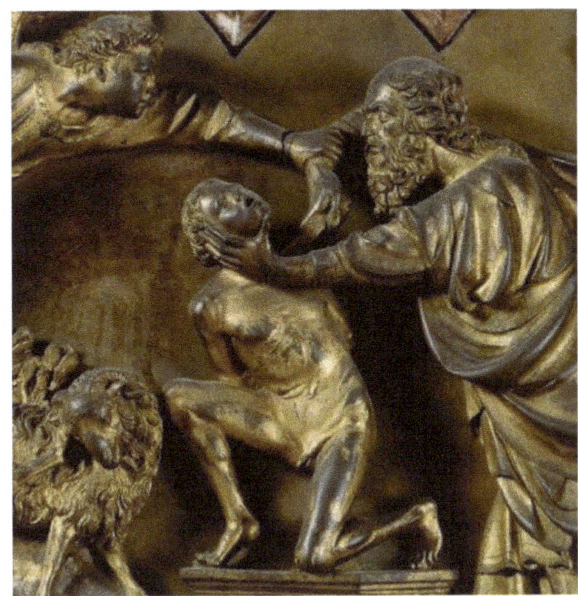

Fig. 4: Brunelleschi; *Competition Panel*, detail. Bargello Museum, Florence.

to ponder with him the dark mystery in which he has been ensnared. There is no piety here, only an unflinching imagining of the soul's journey through nightmare. And by daring to imagine and present the very moment of murder and redemption, of terror and pity, it is Brunelleschi's vision which powerfully sets in motion the forces of the enantiodromia, the sudden transformative shift which will lead from trauma to psychological redemption.

* * *

While we can only guess about the images created by the five remaining entrants in the competition, we can be certain that the attentions of Florence's foremost artisans and civic leaders were occupied for long months in considering the theme of the Sacrifice of Isaac and its different possible renderings. And at the darkest hour the luck of the city indeed suddenly seemed to change. While the art competition was still under way—either through pure luck or divine intercession—a miracle occurred. The warlord, Giangaleazzo Visconti, unexpectedly dropped dead, his mercenary troops lost morale and wandered back up north, and Florence was delivered from an evil fate.

Did the Florentines believe that their redemption had anything to do with the apotropaic power of their representations of the Sacrifice of Isaac? There are hints that at least some Florentines understood the course of events from this perspective. The magnitude and haste of the effort of the guilds to complete certain artistic projects suggests that there may well have been an operative belief in the talismanic potency of these images to protect the city from harm. Frederick Hartt informs us that:

> The fourteen...niches at Orsanmichele had been assigned to the various guilds since 1339, with only two statues completed before 1400. But immediately after the collapse of Giangaleazzo in 1402 began the march of the statues. In 1406 the council of the Republic quickened the pace by giving the guilds ten years to fulfill their obligations at Orsanmichele. After a lapse of nearly two generations the statues were suddenly recognized as a civic responsibility.[15]

In the course of less than three decades, thirty four larger-than-life figures of Saints, Prophets, and other Biblical and historical personages appeared on the facades of the buildings which functioned as the religious, civic, and commercial foci of the city. In 1425 during another period of acute financial crisis and political disaster, one of the guilds abruptly decided that it needed to replace its statue of St. Stephen and commissioned Ghiberti to make a new one in bronze at ten times the cost of marble.[16] It is, indeed, difficult to make sense of this kind of massive, ongoing expenditure of talent and resources throughout trying times unless we recognize that the Florentine sense of "civic responsibility" differed fundamentally from our own with regard to the perceived value of statues on the exterior walls of public buildings.

* * *

In the aftermath of the panel competition there is evidence that the city came to claim the story of the Sacrifice of Isaac as a new vision of its fate.[17] Yet this narrative was only one among several new stories of mission and destiny that

---

15 Hartt, op. cit., p. 123.

16 Ibid., p. 123.

17 Hartt (p. 124) informs us that in a history of the events of the war written shortly after its conclusion, "the hand of God is constantly discovered intervening for the Republic."

suddenly appear. After their deliverance from the armies of Giangaleazzo, the mythopoeic powers of the Florentines seem to have been liberated to an unprecedented degree.

It is during this period of "the march of the statues" that two of the images which we will look at in succeeding chapters were commissioned: Nanni di Banco's *Four Crowned Saints* and Donatello's *St. George*. Both of these images function simultaneously on multiple planes of meaning. We will see that one of their purposes seems very clearly to be an apotropaic function: they stand as sentinels who protect us from external, as well as internal, threats to our freedom. At the same time, they conjure new narratives, new myths of identity for the city and its guilds. Indeed, when we look at the works of art created in the early decades of the Renaissance, we find that both these perspectives are often interrelated in ways that are challenging for us to imagine. The external potency of magical function and the internal power of psychological transformation appear strangely connected, as if they are simply two aspects of a single reality which in our own time has become wholly separated into inner and outer worlds.

* * *

A final question remains: If the art competition was the cure, what exactly had been the problem? If the invitation to the community and its artisans to reflect upon the trauma of Isaac played its part in exorcising the images of dread, what, then, was the unconscious narrative, the imaginative process which had been literalized by trauma, the spell which had held psyche transfixed?

I would suggest that it must have been the venerable "the gods must be angry with us" narrative. Within the realm of religious stories this is certainly the oldest and deepest of ruts, and the one with the most remarkable degree of tenacity. Things have not been going well: clearly it must be time to kill the king or toss another maiden into the volcano to appease the gods' anger. If we experience disaster, we certainly must deserve it; we must have brought it about ourselves by a failure to be sufficiently pious and observant. We hear this line of reasoning in the Bible from Job's would-be "comforters" as the explanation of the cause of his misfortune. And we continue to hear the same neurotic narrative today whenever our contemporary fundamentalists suggest that AIDS is God's punishment for deviant sexual behavior or that some unusual sequence of natural disasters is evidence of God's great displeasure with our collective mores.

During the Florentine panel competition the act of imagining and imaging Abraham and Isaac's traumatic ordeal in various ways broke that spell of blind fear of omnipotent wrath. It offered a clear alternative to the "God is angry and is punishing us because of our evil ways" narrative which informed the bleak images of late Trecento art. The story of Isaac invited a reading of Florence's disasters as *divine trial* rather than *divine retribution*. Seen through the new metaphor of trial and tribulation, these disasters required of the populace neither guilt nor expiation, just faith and endurance. Like Isaac, the city had been (and was still being) forced to endure extremity, but this was as a test of faith and as a preparation for a great destiny. As Isaac was spared so that he might become a patriarch of the Hebrew people, so Florence was challenged to endure hard trials but saved by God's grace so that great things might come to be.

And if this was their reading of their fate, who can argue that they failed to fulfill its promise? The artistic competition and the salvation of the city heralded an explosion of creativity greater than any the world had seen in at least a thousand years; the works of Florentine artists in subsequent decades soon grew as numerous and brilliant as the stars of heaven. And by creating images of such extraordinary beauty and imaginative power the Florentines played their role as a chosen people: Florence became as a beacon among nations, sending forth the light of its genius to influence artists throughout Italy and the rest of Europe and to forever change the world's sense of what was possible in the realm of art.

Meanwhile, a young Donatello who had lived through the tense years of the art competition and the siege seems to have had some essential insight, perhaps through Brunelleschi's work, into the nature of images that recreate the world in their wake. Before the end of the decade of the competition, Donatello would invoke a new story with his first statue of *David*. This image of the young giant killer shows him standing tall and brave, but with hand placed awkwardly on hip in the ungainly posture of an adolescent trying to appear relaxed, much like the new Florence which was finding itself catapulted to prominence after its sudden victory.

As the memory of the knifepoint at their throats receded into history, it became possible to substitute the heroic, young giant-killer for the naked, altar-bound youth as a symbol of the city and its drama. In the years that followed, there were different visions of David, each carrying its own subtle implications for a reading of the image in relation to the life of the city. But there were also St. Georges and Judiths and Hebrew prophets wrapped in Roman togas, and all manner of imaginary beings whose existence bore witness to the soul's ability to situate itself in a multitude of stories. From the one story of Abraham and Isaac came many stories; but the freedom to imagine was won at the original competition for the bronze doors which would open to the glory of the Italian Renaissance.

Quattro Santi Coronati: THE MISSION STATEMENT OF THE SCULPTORS' GUILD

I n the early years of the fifteenth century, immediately following Florence's deliverance from the siege by the Milanese, the decision was made to resume work on various projects which had lain dormant since the previous century. Having successfully asserted its autonomy and independence, Florence began to explore its new identity, its sense of having a destiny, of being "chosen."

Specifically, a mandate from the City Fathers was given to all the guilds to fill their niches on the walls of Orsanmichele.[18] In one these niches, along the north side of the Church of Orsanmichele, we find a somber group of four figures who stand in a semi-circle. The subject of the sculpture is based on a legend from early Christian times: four Christian sculptors are ordered by the Roman emperor Diocletian to make a statue of the god Aesculapius: they are martyred when they refuse to create a pagan idol and betray their faith.

The guild of workers in wood and stone, the *Arte di Pietra e Legname*, originally commissioned *Quattro Santi Coronati (Four Crowned Saints)* to fill the niche which had been allocated to them on the outer walls of Orsanmichele. They entrusted the execution to a brilliant young sculptor, Nanni di Banco, who died in his twenties and left behind only a handful of works that give us some indication of his genius. Although it remains undocumented, the

---

18 Frederick Hartt, "Art and Freedom in Quattrocento Florence," in L. F. Sandler, ed., *Essays in memory of Karl Lehmann* (New York, 1964), p. 123.

sculpture is generally dated to approximately 1413.[19]

Nanni di Banco's *Quattro Santi Coronati* takes its place in "the march of statues" that were created in these decades following Florence's delivery from the Milanese imperial threat. While certain of the guilds were modestly compliant, others went far beyond the simple mandate to fill their niches on the walls of Orsanmichele. Particularly in the guild statues created by Donatello and Nanni di Banco, we find nothing less than new narratives of identity, revised "mission statements," carved in stone.

* * *

Four Crowned Saints is neatly divided into three sections: a predella which shows the artisans at their work, a niche above them which contains the statues of the saints, and a gable overhead in which God the Father appears. These three sections may be contemplated as references to three distinct levels of reality.

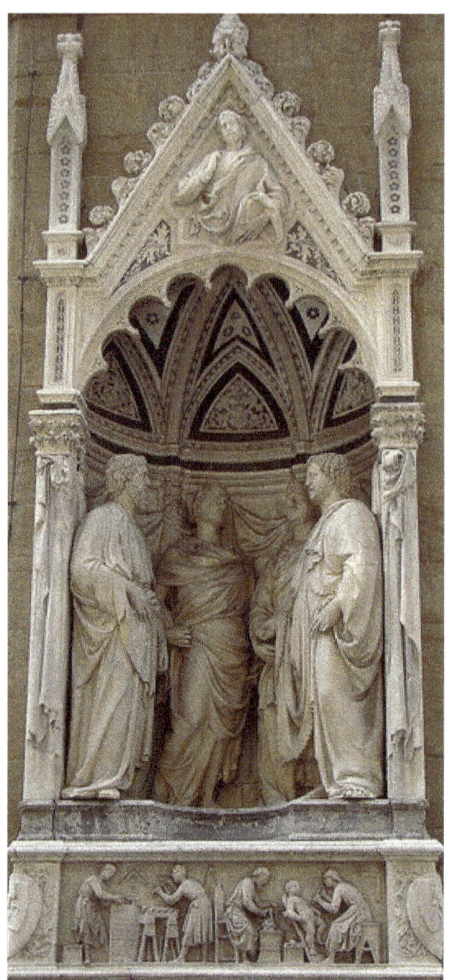

Fig. 5: Nanni di Banco, *Four Crowned Saints.*
Orsanmichele Church, Florence.

It is the lower world of the predella that meets us at eye level, at our level, when we stand before it in the street. Here we get to see the sculptors in contemporary garb at work in their element: we witness the sawing and hammering and measuring that are the accoucheurs of the birth of the art object.

---

19   Hartt, *History of Italian Renaissance Art* (New York: Prentice Hall, 1987) p. 169.

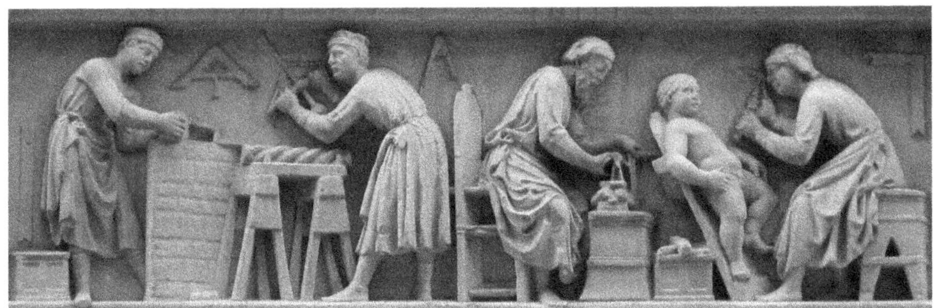

Fig. 6: Nanni di Banco, *Four Crowned Saints*, predella. Orsanmichele Church, Florence.

In the middle section we find an intermediate realm of being; we encounter images of those who live in our collective memory, men whose lives were of such significance that their memory is held sacred by later generations. These figures are placed in such a way that we look up to them, literally and figuratively. And above all, far overhead, God looks down, sending forth blessing or inspiration.

In the grand scheme of things, it's this intermediate realm—located midway between the industriousness of the craftsmen's workshop below and the benediction descending from the Lord above—that receives primary attention. It's in this middle realm that the sculptor is able to invoke the spirits of the noble dead, to represent them for their memorialization, and to give form to values that will edify and inspire his community. On the walls of the church of Orsanmichele, Nanni's Four Saints occupy their symbolic dwelling place in a niche of the edifice built by the faithful.

* * *

When we look at the statues of the saints themselves, we see four men in Roman garb who stand closely packed in a semi-circle. They appear to be of comparable stature, both physical and social. Although they share a seriousness of mien, each man looks off into space along his own line of vision, and their gazes do not converge. The tension, the drama of the image consists in this: four figures stand in such close proximity, yet each experiences his world and his fate in a profoundly individual manner.

The differences between the men's gazes and stances is echoed in the differ-

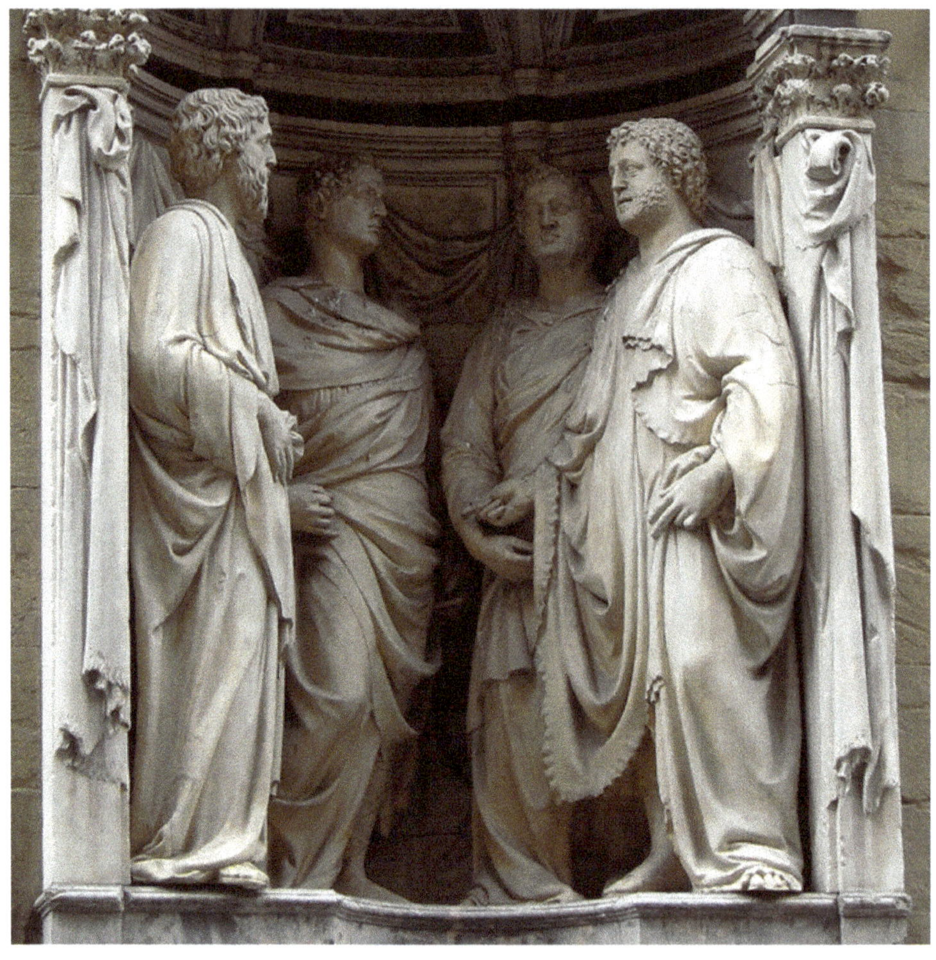

Fig. 7: Nanni di Banco, *Four Crowned Saints*, detail. Orsanmichele Church, Florence.

entiation of their togas. Even the folds of the cloth in each saint's robe are rendered in very distinctive ways: here fabric is gathered and bunched, here it balloons freely, here it looks almost pleated and falls vertically. At the level of moral exhortation the image appears to say: "Let us wrap ourselves in the virtues of our Roman forbears, but let each man wear his toga in his own way."[20]

---

20   This independence in manner of dress actually seems to have been the order of the day. Burckhardt tells us that: "by the year 1390 there was no longer any prevailing fashion of dress for men at Florence, each preferring to clothe himself in his own way." In Jacob Burckhardt, *The Civilization of the Renaissance in Italy*, trans. by S.G.C. Middlemore, in 2 vols.(New York: Harper & Row, 1958), p. 144.

The columns themselves on either side of the niche are also draped in folds of cloth, each quite distinctly. All of which alerts us to the fact that clothing itself—the clothing of the workers, the clothing of the Saints, the clothing of the guild's niche—carries thematic significance in this image.

Nanni's sculpture invites—and also attempts to answer—the following question for the *Arte*: What, as a guild of stone and wood workers, shall be our new imaginal clothing? In what images shall we wrap ourselves as we present ourselves, our work, and our role in society to our fellow countrymen?

As artisans, the guild members acknowledge that they wear the everyday clothing of their fellow citizens. As artists, however, the members here proclaim themselves to be the inheritors of an ancient and exalted tradition. And, in much the same manner as our own robed judges, they declare their willingness to assume the moral burden and civic responsibility which participation in the greater life of society entails.

As workmen, the artisans of the guild of stone and wood workers lead their quotidian lives in the bottega amidst sawdust and marble chips and the clanging of hammers and chisels. As creators of images, these same workmen give life to forms of power and beauty that continue to live in the heart of the community long after the workmen themselves have turned to dust and ash. If it is time for the workers of the *Arte* to clothe themselves in a new vision of their worth and purpose, then let the world now witness them midwifing the birth of angels through the humble doorways of their bottegas.

* * *

We know that certain early Renaissance artists looked back to Roman statues as a source of inspiration, and that they took some of their models from the ancient works of art that were being recovered during these early decades of the *Quattrocento*. Less well known is the curious fact that, while drawing on these classical influences, artists like Nanni, Donatello, and Masaccio simultaneously chose to make their figures resemble contemporary Florentines. While scholars may disagree as to which contemporary figure is represented by which painted or sculpted face, no one disputes the fact that these artists used contemporary models quite often.

This deliberate juxtaposition of ancient Roman prototypes with contemporary Florentine faces bridges the great distance between ancient world and contemporary life. It brings the saints of yore as close to us as our own neighbors, and it marries the virtues of the ancestors to the souls of men today. It insists that the timelessness of heroic and saintly lives ought to be represented in the lived texture of one's own particular time.

The way in which Nanni tells the story of the Quattro Santi also serves his effort to marry the sacred world of the saints with the mundane world of men. Nanni has chosen to show the patron saints of the guild in their suffering human aspect, awaiting death, rather than in the exaltation of their transcendent state. While we honor them as saints, we see them in their distress and in their heroism as mortal men. We are reminded that the saints were mere men after all. And, that through their spiritual strength, they have become something more than ordinary men.

* * *

There's a final aspect to Nanni's *Quattro Santi Coronati* that only comes into view when we situate the image within the context of the millennial battles over idolatry. Unlike Judaism and Islam, Christianity permitted the artistic representation of divinity and reverence towards images within certain defined parameters. Yet, we need to remember that the iconoclastic impulse, while dormant at times, was never long absent. From the Early Church Fathers to the Bonfires of the Vanities to the Council of Nicaea to the Reformation, the charge of idolatry, like that of heresy, remained a powerful and dangerous weapon in the hands of religious zealots.

It's possible that the guild may have anticipated a conservative backlash emerging in response to the enlarged scope of sculptural activities in the new Florence. Or they may have simply wanted a powerful apotropaic image to ward off what was feared. Be that as it may, there is a real sense in which the four martyred sculptors who stand as sentinels upon the walls of Orsanmichele were invoked and actually served as the guild's Guardian Saints, protecting the guild members from an evil fate.

We can think of Nanni's image as a sort of insurance policy for the sculptors' guild. When we consider its themes, we realize that it brings into the open the deepest fear of the artist in Christian culture, a hidden dread that is the precise inverse of what the image extols, namely, that sculptors will be seen as idolaters by the ecclesiastical authorities. Indeed the traditional selection of the *Quattro Santi Coronati* by the guild as their patron saints, martyred by the pagans for their refusal to make sacrilegious images, can itself be seen as a first line of defense against all such accusations and a preemptive bid for the high moral ground. And by commissioning such a complex and eloquent work, in which they star as defenders of the faith, the guild appropriated for themselves a mantle of moral legitimacy, and they stole the thunder of any opponent who might have wished to conflate their activities with idolatry.

In closing, let us imagine the artisans of the *Arte* having the final word:

> *"Lest anyone, ever, consider leveling a charge of idolatry against this guild, let it be known to all that the guild's spiritual ancestors, the Saints of our Faith, sacrificed their lives rather than use their talents for sacrilegious purposes. In remembering them we affirm our faith in the beliefs for which they were martyred. And, let it be noted, that we carry out this exercise in religious and civic instruction through the practice of our art, which, as it happens, consists in the making of marvelous sculpted images of the living, the illustrious dead, and the inhabitants of the celestial realms. Amen."*

Donatello's *St. George:* MAN AND SUPERMAN

When we read the Bible or look at all into Western religious history, we find constant references to the struggle against idolatry. Today we can only wonder what all the fuss might have been about. Can people ever have been so foolish as to think that a piece of wood or a stone carving was actually a living being? Did they really need the Biblical prophets and the Church Fathers to point out to them that these artifacts might have eyes, but couldn't see? As seems only reasonable, the battle against idolatry was won. In fact, the victory was so complete that it requires considerable effort on our part today to begin to understand what the battle might really have been about.

The crucial element in this story which has largely dropped out of view has to do with a long-standing tradition of animating statues. A block of stone carved to resemble a particular god may have been, at times, no more than a simple block of stone. But at other times, however, the ancients apparently believed that the spirit of the god could be invited to enter into the statue—if the statue were made in the proper way and if the invitation were ritually presented in the appropriate manner.

There is reason to believe that the enduring fascination of certain masterpieces of the Renaissance derives, at least in part, from the efforts of 15th century Florentine artists to bring life to their statues. In particular, I think that Donatello's statues reveal themselves most fully when they are contemplated against this background. But before we look at Donatello's sorcery in more detail, we will need to take a brief tour through the strange and forgotten world of wonder-working statues.

* * *

First of all, it's worth recalling that the notion that created artifacts might occasionally behave like living beings was part and parcel of common Christian belief. Recorded testimonies of the Christian faithful are filled with accounts of statues and paintings that speak, that bleed, that work miracles. In this context St. Francis' experience of being addressed by an image of the crucified Christ would have been considered unusual and miraculous, but hardly incredible.

Theological dogma notwithstanding, images were typically venerated by petitioners as if ensouled; chroniclers regularly spoke of the wonder-working Madonnas as persons; defilers of sacred images were subjected to punishments no less severe than those they might have received for inflicting comparable injuries upon living persons.

When contracts were signed or affairs of state discussed in medieval council chambers, these activities were typically carried out beneath the watchful gaze of sacred figures who were ritually invoked for blessing and guidance, as well as to guarantee oaths sworn before them. We must assume that, at times, the presence of these sacred personages was strongly experienced through their artistic representations by those present. The painted cover of a Sienese accounting ledger shows us a gathering of civic leaders standing before a painting of the Madonna where the figure of the Madonna actually leans out of the painting toward them.[21]

Common as this experience seems to have been, it was at the same time entirely unpredictable. The spirit would blow where it listeth: a hitherto humble figure of the Madonna in a parish church might suddenly become imbued with salvific powers and become an object of veneration and cult following. The animated image was cherished as a miraculous gift from a

---

21   Cf. the *biccherna* panel by Andrea di Niccolò (1483) which shows the Madonna leaning out of a painting as the keys to the city of Siena are offered to her.

source far beyond all human agency.

Compared to this passive acceptance of divine influx, the Renaissance impulse can best be compared to Prometheus' bold effort to steal fire from the gods. What was remarkable about the creative experimentation of artists like Nanni di Banco, Masaccio, and Donatello was the degree to which they *consciously* strove to create numinous figures, to deliberately produce a new generation of potent, animated images.

* * *

The impulse for this practice came primarily from classical rather than from Christian sources. From Greek myth and legend came the stories of Prometheus' skill at breathing life into his clay statues; of Daedelus' ability to create automata, mechanical marvels which seemed to have a life of their own; of Pygmalion, whose skill as a sculptor gave life to the woman of his dreams.

R.B. Onians in *The Origins of European Thought* discusses the ancient Roman belief in the nod (*numen*) of statues; the numinous statue of the god was, thus, a nodding statue, expressing its will to the petitioner.[22] In the Middle Ages St. Augustine in *The City of God* condemned the practice of animating statues, arguing that those who would thus speak with higher intelligences unwittingly invited demons who came to inhabit the statues so that they may be worshipped. Opposing Augustine's point of view were certain writers in the Neoplatonic tradition like Proclus and Iamblicus who extolled the benefits of the practice and provided instructions for its accomplishment.

And, even the most cursory survey of the classical tradition of wonder-working statues needs to acknowledge the potential influence of that great Roman magician, Virgil, more commonly known to modern readers as the author of the *Aeneid*. The tale of Virgil's transformation from writer to magician is recounted by J. Webster Spargo in his *Virgil the Necromancer: Studies in the Virgilian Legends*.[23] Beginning in the second half of the twelfth century, sto-

---

22 R.B. Onians, *The Origins of European Thought* (Cambridge: Cambridge Univ. Press, 1991), pp. 140-143

23 J. Webster Spargo, *Virgil the Necromancer: Studies in the Virgilian Legends* (Cambridge: Harvard Univ. Press, 1934)

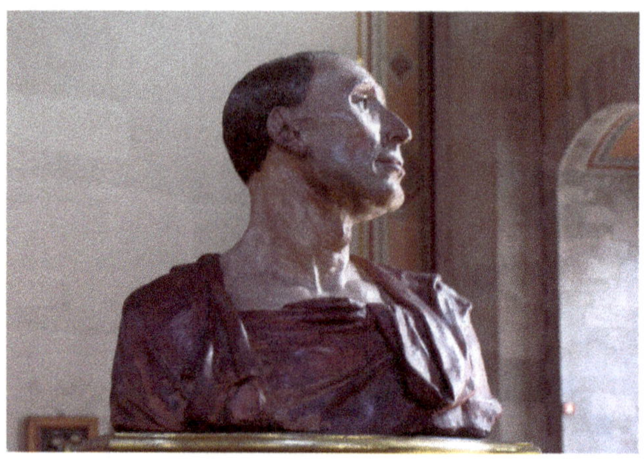

Fig. 8: Donatello, *Niccolo da Uzzano*, right profile.
Bargello Museum, Florence.

ries about Virgil's abilities to create talismanic objects, to animate statues, and to perform other acts of magic are apparently invented out of thin air.[24]

It seems that Virgil the magician had the ability to give life and intelligence to statues and that he had made several of these and placed them upon the roof of the Roman Senate. Each figure represented one of the provinces of Rome and stood with a bell in hand. "Whenever a power plotted against the power of Imperial Rome, the image of that province struck its bell."[25] And the army would soon be on its way.

In the early fourteenth century these tales of Virgil the animator, imported initially from abroad, begin to appear with increasing frequency on Italian soil.[26] Whether or not Donatello knew specifically of this legend, or of any of the other kindred tales from medieval legend or classical myth, no one knows. But it would seem reasonable to assume that, in some form or other, he must have been familiar with the tradition of magical animation of statues.

Apart from what we see with our own eyes when we look at Donatello's work, we have some anecdotal information provided by Vasari that bears witness to Donatello's interest in trying to animate his statues. With regard to the

---

24 The embarrassing lack of any precedent whatsoever for this group of legends led Comparetti, the last major researcher before Spargo, to make vague references to a certain "literary tradition" through which these stories were transmitted. After a thorough search, however, Spargo tersely concluded: "I have been unable to find one fact in what Comparetti calls the literary tradition of Virgil which leads in any way to this group of legends devoted to Virgil's magical powers." (Ibid., p. 304).

25 Ibid., pp. 117-118. The story itself (known as *Salvatio Romae*) apparently dates from the eight century but was first connected with Virgil by Alexander Neckam in *De naturis rerum* (c.1190). Fast forward for students of coincidence: in the main piazza of modern-day Orvieto, a rooftop statue strikes a bell every hour on top of a building which houses the Hotel Virgilio.

26 Ibid., p. 306.

figure of the proph-
et known today as *Il
Zuccone* ("Pumpkin-
head"), Vasari tells
us that "while he was
working on this statue
he would look at it and
keep muttering: 'Speak,
damn you, speak!'"[27]
And in his remarks
about the *St. George*
Vasari writes: "Life it-
self seems to be stirring
vigorously within the

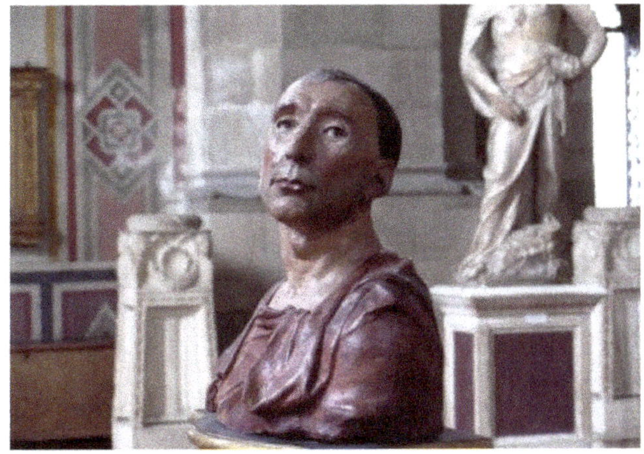

Fig. 9: Donatello, *Niccolo da Uzzano*, left profile.
Bargello Museum, Florence.

stone. And to be sure no modern statues have the vivacity produced by nature and art, through the hand of Donatello, in this marble."[28]

After five hundred years we stand in front of Donatello's figures and still feel the
same way. What is it that gives them this feeling of animated presence?

* * *

What is uniformly striking about the numerous figures that Donatello created during his long life is the degree to which they seem psychologically
inhabited. They have a vital presence and intensity that has not been seen
in previous sculpture. St. Mark wears his toga with greater embodiment
than any figure before him. The prophets quiver with indignation, distress,
anguished interiority, no two alike. Donatello's figures are uniquely characterized in their singular individuality, in their bearing, their facial expressions,
their homeliness or beauty.

Quite remarkable in many of Donatello's sculptures is the extent to which
their faces, like our own, lack bilateral symmetry. Stand before the bust of
Niccolò da Uzzano and walk around it slowly. His right profile shows us a

---

27 Giorgio Vasari, *Lives of the Artists*, trans. G. Bull (London: Penguin Books, 1988) in 2 vols., vol. 1, p. 178.

28 Ibid., p. 178.

man of strong-jawed determination and resolute strength. When we arrive to see the left side of his face, we find ourselves before a sensitive face that reveals a wistful, melancholy aspect of the inner man. Do the same with the figures of Jeremiah or Mary Magdalene or St. George, and you will see how their faces change and reveal different aspects of personality. As we look at them from various vantage points, we catch glimpses of the psychological depth of these complex souls.

To see in all this simply a greater degree of "realism" or a fascination with the styles of the past, is largely to miss the point. How different are Donatello's faces from those Roman portrait busts from which he is supposed to have derived his inspiration! Wandering through the corridors of the Uffizi and observing the busts of the noble Romans which line the walls, one is struck mostly by their utter banality. These are genuine faces, accurate as deathmasks, snapshots of the deceased for family albums. Wholly unlike the ideal forms of classical Greek statuary, the Roman figures are utterly realistic, human, merely human. As faces, they are as eminently forgettable as Donatello's are haunting.

The mystery of Donatello's figures is that they hover on the cusp between ideality and reality: they achieve the mystical marriage of heaven and earth, of the transcendent and the immanent. Donatello retains the prototype while humanly particularizing it to an unprecedented degree: his figures are both larger-than-life and realistic at the same time.[29] They retain their iconic power, their transcendent functions of blessing, judging, or protecting, but they are no longer merely symbolic representations of holy men. In Donatello's figures the archetypal realm has been coaxed into human form.

Critics have noted in looking at Nanni di Banco's *Four Crowned Saints* that the figures bring to mind simultaneously the portraiture of ancient Romans and of contemporary Florentines. We find a similar dynamic at play in much of Donatello's work. When we look at Donatello's prophets, for example, we gaze with certainty upon ancient, historical personages, yet we learn from

---

29 The statues are also literally larger than life size (many stand at around seven feet in height) especially in relation to Mediterranean body types. St. George stands 6' 8", St. Peter and St. Mark, 7' 9".

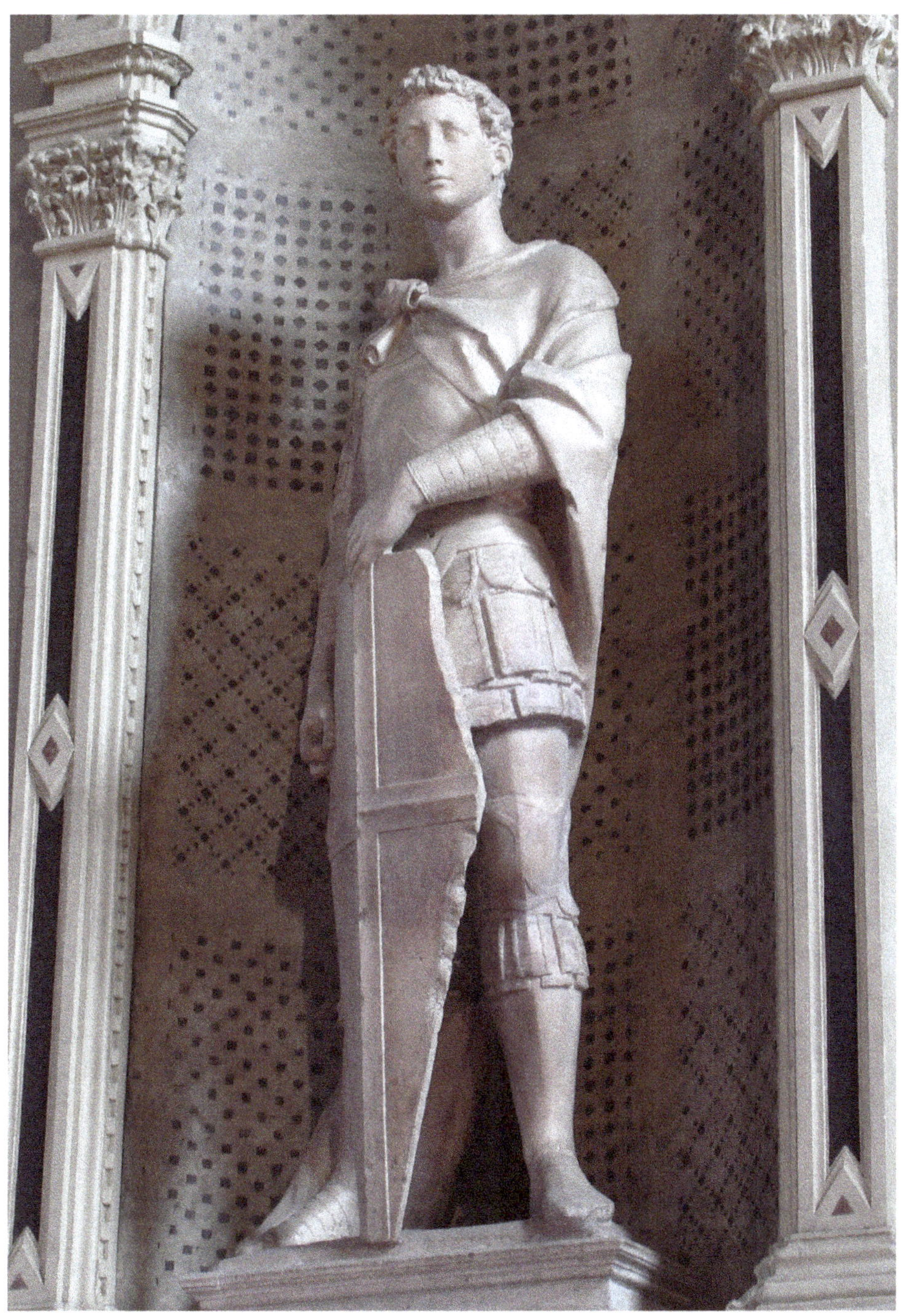

Fig. 10: Donatello, *St. George*. Bargello Museum, Florence.

Vasari's gossip that contemporary Florentines were probably the living models for the figures.[30] While this is surely an aspect of Donatello's strategy for bringing history to life, this achievement is not as simple as it might seem.

When we look at Victorian paintings of elegant ladies dressed variously as Greek goddesses, we have a distinct impression of a refined form of play-acting, of modern figures donning antique dress. Today we can hardly imagine a contemporary dressed like George Washington or Caesar except as a joke. But not so with Donatello. His figures of saints and prophets are compellingly ancient *and* modern. They incarnate the fusion of past and present in their very beings, and they become, through the potency of Donatello's imaginative alchemy, both timely and transhistorical. In Donatello's evident ability to create mythical beings who resemble our friends and neighbors, we find that he has straddled an abyss between reality and ideality which the medieval world had preserved for a thousand years.

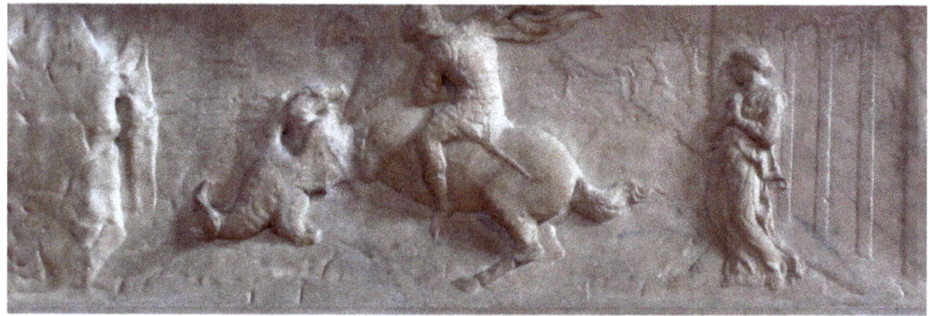

Fig. 11: Donatello, *St. George*, predella detail.
Bargello Museum, Florence.

Donatello's figures look out at the world which surrounds them, fully aware of its presence. And as they look out into our world, we see the response which it occasions reflected in their features. Each one is subject to a psychic state provoked "partly by what he perceives in the outer world, partly by his inner contemplation of himself" (Hartt).[31] As St. George gazes into the distance, his furrowed brow and tense carriage register his appropriate concern. It's dangerous out there, but he struggles to rise to the occasion. And when

---

30 Cf. Vasari, op. cit., p. 178 for the "real" identity of *il zuccone*, et al.

31 Frederick Hartt, "Art and Freedom in Quattrocento Florence," in L. F. Sandler, ed., *Essays in memory of Karl Lehmann* (New York, 1964), p. 120.

we consider that the prophets are looking out at the city from their perches on its public buildings, their expressions of passionate concern take on new meaning. With a degree of skill that seems almost to border on necromancy, Donatello has recalled these figures from their distant historical graves to bear witness to current events.

* * *

Throughout the Middle Ages St. George, the warrior saint, was revered in many parts of Europe all the way from England to Russia. The medieval representations of St. George typically show us a fearless knight, wholly Other, a hero who readily vanquishes the dragon by virtue of his irresistible might. His humanity is never in conflict with his function as an ideal type, because his personality is wholly subsumed by his archetypal function. In the predella below St. George's feet we catch a glimpse of the traditional representation of the warrior saint defending the fair maiden:

Yet to see Donatello's St. George merely as a brave warrior figure is to mistake it for its ancestors and to miss the tension in the image. Frederick Hartt describes this tension eloquently:

> The supreme warrior saint stands supporting his great shield and looking out on a hostile world with the supreme bravery of a man born a coward... [T]his is a reflective, gentle face, with delicate nose, pinched, nervous brows, sensuous mouth, even a weak chin. Yet with divine guidance he has put on the whole armor of the spirit and summons up all his inner forces to confront the enemy.[32]

Our St. George, then, is both man and superman at the same time. We may see an archetypal hero who has been given certain mortal traits, or, following Hartt, an ordinary man who has been inspired to become more than merely human. Either way, the figure hovers at the threshold.

Stop for a moment and think about our own superheroes today, those imaginary beings who embody our longing for superior powers and for

---

32 Hartt, op. cit., p. 125.

vigilant defense against the forces of evil. Pick any one of them and you will see how the archetype today is split, whereas Donatello was able to contain the tension in a single image. Superman, Batman, the Shadow, Zorro, the Lone Ranger, Spiderman, the entire Justice League of America—every last one of them has a super identity and a hidden civilian identity. Of course they each have a reason for keeping their special super powers secret—they need to protect their loved ones from possible harm, etc. But we are looking at the structure of the type, not listening to excuses. In every story we watch them deal with the logistical problems of shuffling between an ordinary citizen persona and a powerful alter ego, and the former is always as drab and uninteresting as the latter is super-magnificent.

We today cannot imagine Superman and Clark Kent as the same being. But Donatello did, and when we grasp that St. George is present before our eyes as both man and superman, we find ourselves again baffled by the power of the Renaissance imagination to hold together what for us has completely come asunder.

* * *

Let's look more closely at how the *St. George* does its magic.

While the face of St. George projects anxious concern about his task, his stature and bearing are brave: they show us the effort he has made to summon all his inner resources to face the enemy. Although his armor is surely necessary, on its own it is hardly sufficient. For without the presence of the virtue of Courage, the best equipped armed forces turn tail and run. We are, in fact, looking at a figure who does not simply *represent* courage, but who himself has *summoned* courage. Donatello's St. George inspires courage in the spectator by first incarnating it in himself; he is filled with that same virtuous energy which his figure would invoke in the soul of the viewer.

On the collective level, through the niche it occupies on the walls of Orsanmichele, Donatello's *St. George* also served to rally both the Armourers Guild and the greater community by inspiring them with a realization of their interdependence. The predella where St. George performs his daunting task of battling dragons is bordered on either side by the stemma of the Armourers Guild. While the daily work of smithing swords and shields may not be glamorous, it is indispensible. The *St. George* underlined the guild's critical contribution to the maintenance of a sovereign and free Republic: they provide free men the means to fight for and defend their liberty. The niche thus invited the guild's members to take pride in their own work, and it proclaimed the dignity and worth of the guild's labors for all to see. It reminds us, even today, that without the perception of common cause in the Republic, and of each social group's essential contribution and interdependence, the polis readily disintegrates into factions and special interest groups.

The image thus exercises its talismanic function in protecting both the individual and the community by evoking the requisite energies in the individual, the guild and the community and aligning these with the common good. No longer content to rely blindly on the salvific grace of a sacred icon, Donatello has fathomed the source of the image's power and dynamically directed the psychological energies that it constellates. In a single masterful stroke, the figure of St. George has been plucked off the gold mosaic ceiling of the medieval world and invited to inform the human soul.

* * *

The effort to enliven images in ways that would stir and inspire our souls is one of most passionate pursuits of early Renaissance art. From the great invocations of the Madonna to the pantheon of gods and saints in Donatello's *oeuvre*, to Masaccio's poignant renderings of fervor and suffering, to Piero's Resurrected Christ and Botticelli's Venus, we repeatedly find ourselves in the presence of powerful ensouled images who move us and enliven us in mysterious ways by the power of their own animation.

When we look ahead to the following century with its fierce iconoclastic reaction to these artistic developments, we have to ask how the love of images and the energies they invoke could be so troubling for so many.

Idolatry! Abomination! Heathen filth! The words still sound so nasty, even centuries after the battle was won. In place of an art that would invite the soul to experience and know itself, the sacred images were pressed into service to illustrate religious teaching. And those who would animate images were silenced by those who would enforce obedience to dogma and abstractions.

The Brancacci Chapel:
MANY HANDS AT WORK

THE INTEGRITY OF THE IMAGE

Spend an afternoon at any of the major shrines of Renaissance art and listen to the patter of the art guides. You'll hear the same narrow range of comments about art and artist time and again, those soundbites which each group leader deems essential to share with his flock. In the Brancacci Chapel you'll hear about Masaccio's bold new approach to representing bodies in space, their mass and weightiness, the novelty of a uniform source of lighting, and how the architecture reveals the influence of Alberti or Michelozzo. But, above all, no one fails to inform their group of the fact that this project was actually a collective venture, and not the work of a single hand.

Everyone from humble tour escorts to distinguished art historians apparently feels morally obligated to inform all comers that the entire fresco cycle is not, in fact, the sole work of Masaccio. We learn that certain portions were done contemporaneously by Masolino while others were completed late in the century by Filippino Lippi. Though the fact of multiple artists' participation cannot be contested, there is remarkably little consensus among experts as to the precise nature and extent of the collaborations. Even worse, no known documents have been found which might provide definitive dates and attributions for any of the frescoes.[33] Yet it is part of the ritual of commentary on this series for critics to express their considered judgments as

---

33 Bruce Cole, *Masaccio and the Art of Early Renaissance Florence* (Bloomington & London: Indiana Univ. Press, 1980), p. 148.

to which frescoes are pure Masaccio, which show signs of joint work, which faces and legs were done by whom, and whether or not there was an outline left by Masaccio which Filippino completed or whether he made it up out of whole cloth. Even in the popular Scala series publication clearly intended for amateurs and sold to tourists at the booth outside the Brancacci Chapel, Ornella Casazza (who directed the recent restoration of the frescoes) does not fail to discuss a single image without presenting a summary of the history of critical disagreements over attribution.[34]

We might reasonably ask: What value is there in such information for the non-specialist, for the visitor who seeks to appreciate the power and meaning of the images that compose this fresco cycle? What is the impact of such an approach on our ability to engage the images themselves in a meaningful way?

If we are armed with this knowledge of multiple artists' participation before a first visit, we are tempted to spend our time trying to figure out who did what where. If, on the other hand, we approached the Chapel naively and experienced an overall unity to the work, we are taken aback when we realize that we have been inadvertently deceived. Suitably humbled and chastened, we now look with suspicion at the apparent unity of the frescoes and realize that, if not for the art historians' deconstructions, we might have been, God forbid, deceived as to who painted which face in which scene. The point is that this methodical dismemberment of the work through speculation over attributions distracts us from what really matters, and it obstructs our ability to encounter the images in a meaningful way.

I would urge those who seek to imaginatively engage with the frescoes in the Brancacci Chapel to discard the notion that we are looking at some sort of pastiche of multiple artists' work. Notwithstanding the fact of many hands at work, we need not follow the path of deconstruction by artist's hand. Our alternative is to recognize that a major work can be received as idea and inspiration by numerous individuals over a considerable period of time. Collaborative works like cathedral facades or mosaic ceilings, even when executed

---

34 Ornella Casazza, *Masaccio e la Cappella Brancacci* (Florence: SCALA, 1990)

asynchronously, often display a palpable sense of continuity, as if each hand that added to the cumulative work did so by entering into profound empathy with the endeavor and becoming, in turn, a vehicle for its realization.

Our alternative approach will invite the viewer to focus on the unity of the work and to recognize both synchronous and asynchronous collaboration toward that end. Rather than attempt to analyze the fresco cycle in terms of the many hands at work, we will assume that there is a coherence to the structure of its imagery and see where that leads us.

In the course of our inquiry we will look successively at three major themes: Money, the Mission of the Church, and the Body—and the relationships represented between them in the Chapel frescoes.

MONEY

Of the many remarkable things about the fresco cycle in the Brancacci Chapel of Santa Maria del Carmine, one of the most unusual is its open and explicit concern with money. The scene on the upper left wall, known as *The Tribute Money*, is one of the most famous images from the first half

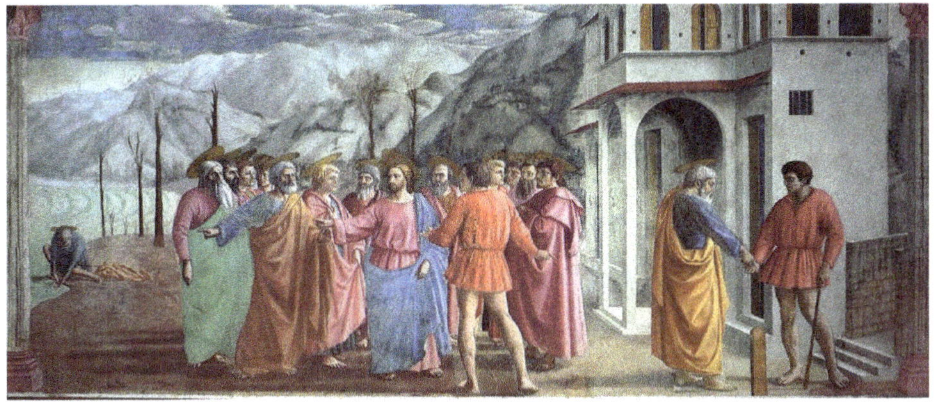

Fig. 12: Masaccio et al., *The Tribute Money*.
Brancacci Chapel, Church of Santa Maria del Carmine, Florence.

of the fifteenth century, and it has received the lion's share of attention from all commentators. Here we see Jesus gathered with the disciples outside the town of Capernaum in a scene based upon Matthew 17:24-27. The Biblical story tells us that Peter has been approached by the local tax collector and is seeking Jesus for his advice.

Jesus directs Peter to the lake and tells him that he will find a coin in the mouth of the fish he catches with which to pay the tax collector. On the left we see Peter squatting as he removes the coin from the fish's mouth; on the right we see him paying the coin to the tax collector.

Certain elements of the composition are enigmatic. Bruce Cole has noted that:

> ..in the *Tribute Money*, all the action occurs within a single moment and in a convincing, contiguous atmosphere. There is no disjuncture in time or space. In fact, so seamless is the combination of events that it takes the spectator several minutes to realize that St. Peter appears three times and the tax collector twice. By the time Masaccio began the *Tribute Money* the use of simultaneous narrative was no longer popular. We do not know why he utilized this old-fashioned form of narrative in a fresco of such sophisticated spatial and temporal setting.[35]

We might add that the scenic structuring of the image does not even follow the chronological sequence of events (which moves from the disciples in the center over to squatting Peter on the left and then back over to Peter and the taxman on the right). Although we don't know what Masaccio had in mind, let's assume that the image's enigmatic structure is deliberate. And let's try to interpret it in the context of the thematic concerns of the fresco cycle.

By combining three different moments of the story in this particular way, the image suggests that they are portions of a single reality. This temporal juxtaposition enables Masaccio to show the band of disciples standing poised between the acts of getting and spending. At the same time, the disciples are shown as standing at the threshold between the wilderness and the city, between God's created world and mankind's. Their situation reminds us that it is only through what we draw from the former that we participate in the

---

35 Bruce Cole, *Masaccio and the Art of Early Renaissance Florence* (Bloomington & London: Univ. of Indiana, 1980), p. 161.

latter, that all human society subsists upon the milk we take from cattle, the eggs we steal from chickens, and the fish we catch. Through their actions as well as their physical positioning, we are shown that those who would do the work of building the Kingdom of Heaven here on this earth must mediate between these two realms.

Indeed, how many of today's organizations that do the noble work of feeding the poor and healing the sick get their money by telephoning people at home during dinner, or by wining and dining potential donors in the hope of pulling from them a precious silver coin? Peter's ungainly posture as he pulls open the jaws of the fish reminds us that the work we might need to do for money, however lofty the ultimate purposes, may itself be neither noble nor particularly gracious. How down-to-earth is this squatting, fishing Peter, how different from the regal, key-toting figure we find so often elsewhere!

Indeed, the *Tribute Money* shows Jesus and the disciples dealing directly with the problem of where to get money to pay the bills. The prominence in placement and treatment given to this minor episode in Matthew (17:24-27) is unprecedented and extraordinary. We could have been shown Christ's entrance into Jerusalem, or the soldiers coming to Gethsemene to arrest him, or any number of more familiar and dramatically significant episodes in which Peter might have appeared playing a supporting role. Instead we see him with the disciples gathered together in solemnity and utter seriousness to deal with the issue of paying the taxman. We see that this group of men with haloes who stand before us were no more free of such concerns than are we ourselves. And the implication is clearly that such matters, which were worthy of their most earnest consideration, are no less worthy of our own. On the earth plane, rent is due on the first of the month, same as it ever was.

* * *

Many of those who have commented on the meaning of this image and the other related frescoes have tried to situate them within contemporary Florentine social realities. Frederick Hartt, for example, suggested that the theme of Peter and the fish has to do with a new form of income taxation then being introduced in Florence, the so-called *Catasto*. Florence's coffers were depleted by years of constant warfare in the struggle to retain its independence, and "in 1427 the Signoria adopted the *Catasto*, the first attempt at an equitable form of taxation in modern history, and in some respects the ancestor of modern income and personal property tax systems—complete with declarations, exemptions and deductions."[36] From this vantage point the monumental representation of the apostles concerned with finding tax money reflects "the earnestness and excitement of the Florentines themselves, confronted with the awesome task of finding the means to preserve their Republic and its threatened liberties..."[37]

Lauro Martines, in his superb study of art and society in Renaissance Italy, generally takes a more skeptical view of the civic idealism of the period than Hartt. Yet, with respect to the *Tribute Money* Martines proposes that:

> The fresco is a sermon on paying to the state what is the state's; it may also be suggesting that the Church should make contributions to government to help defend the community. In making such an unusual commission, the patron of the chapel, Felice Brancacci, a respected political figure, was evidently moved by a strong sense of civic feeling... As the scenes hauntingly suggest, Florence had a large number of paupers and unemployed people, known as "the wretched" (*miserabili*) in the famous Florentine tax census of 1426-1427.[38]

These were certainly the concerns of the day, and they must have been on the minds of the artists, patrons, and parishioners during the years when the frescoes were being conceived and executed. But the danger of such a sociological reading is that it would reduce art to propaganda, the image to an illustration in the service of concrete social objectives. While this fairly describes advertisements and campaign posters, it does not do justice to major works of art. After six centuries these images still move us because they partake of something that transcends the ephemerality of current events and

---

36 Frederick Hartt, "Art and Freedom in Quattrocento Florence" in *Essays in Honor of Karl Lehmann*, ed. by L.F. Sandler (New York, 1964), p. 128.

37 Ibid., p. 129.

38 Lauro Martines, *Power and Imagination: City States in Renaissance Italy* (New York: Random House, 1980), p. 255.

     THE BRANCACCI CHAPEL: MANY HANDS AT WORK

passing concerns. Social history *per se* is the realm of the merely contingent, whereas the archetypal dimensions of great works of art remain, like myths, eternally true.

To explore the social themes in these paintings without violating the integrity of the images, we need to proceed from their timeless aspect to their contemporary details. We need to shift our center of gravity from Florentine social reality to the imaginal reality of the fresco cycle, and to look at the former through the frames of reference which the latter provides. Rather than presenting the apostles as stand-ins for excited Florentines, the images actually invite us to contemplate the activities of Jesus and the founders of the early Church as they walk the streets of a city that looks much like fifteenth century Florence. If the Brancacci frescoes can tell us something significant about Florentine life in the early *Quattrocento*, it is because they tell us something about life in all cities, about the rich and the poor, about the things of Heaven and the things of the Earth, and about the potential role of an enlightened Church in civic life.

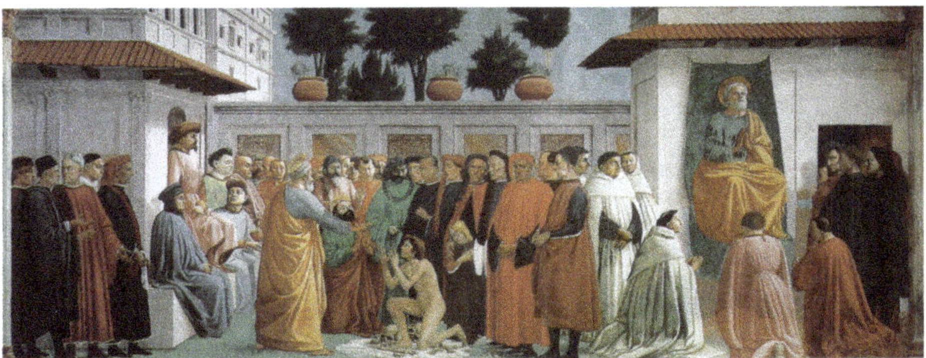

Fig. 13: Masaccio et al., *The Raising of Theophilus*. Brancacci Chapel.

THE MISSION OF THE CHURCH

Although representations of Peter appear occasionally in Florentine art, there is apparently no other treatment of the legend of Peter which is of comparable complexity.[39] How can we account for the decision to elaborate the iconography of Peter in the Brancacci Chapel to such an unprecedented degree?

---

39 Bruce Cole, *Massacio*, p. 156.

I believe that through the figure of Peter and the stories about him we are being invited to consider the proper role of the Church itself. In the chapter immediately preceding the incident depicted in the *Tribute Money*, Jesus turns to Peter and declares: "I say also unto thee, That thou art Peter and upon this rock I will build my church" (Matthew 16:18). If we consider Peter in his role as *Petra*, the rock upon which the church is built, then, stories about this man who was charged to establish the earthly foundations of the Church are, by the principle of metaphorical identity, also stories about the Church's ministry or mission.

Directly below the *Tribute Money*, in the right-hand portion of *The Raising of Theophilus*, we find St. Peter enthroned. Here Peter is presented in his "official" or institutional capacity, although the majority of the scenes clearly show him *ex cathedra*.

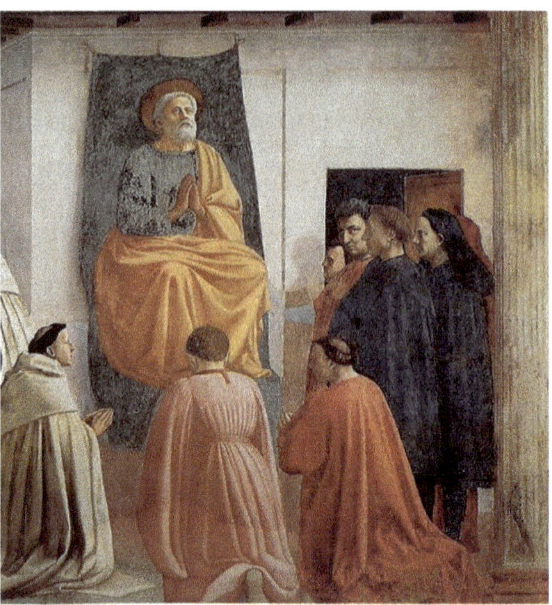

Fig. 14: Masaccio et al., *The Raising of Theophilus*, detail. Brancacci Chapel.

Peter's throne is remarkable in its simplicity, as is this rendering of what is, in fact, the essence of a church service. It is not Peter who is being revered in this image. Where two or more are gathered, he leads them in prayer. The exercise of his priestly function as an intermediary between man and God is here radically demystified: his mediating function is not based on Divine certification and licensing, but on the ardor of faith with which he prays.

Just to the right of Peter praying, there in the corner, stand four figures traditionally identified (left to right) as Masolino, Masaccio, Alberti and Brunelleschi. By their presence here, these architects of the early Renaissance vision surely declare that this is the Church to which they belong—and to which they would invite their viewers.

Now, isn't it curious that in the midst of this complex and extended exposition of the life and works of Peter, *the one thing we don't see anywhere is a key.* Perhaps because it concerns an absence, rather than a presence, no one seems to mention this. But since this is the one symbol invariably associated with St. Peter, we are forced to ask: Where are the Keys to the Kingdom?

When he is depicted as the Keeper of the Keys, Peter is imagined as a sort of custodian or gatekeeper. No one can get into heaven unless he opens the gate. The distinguished scholar of esoteric religions, Henry Corbin, assures us that this notion of the "power of the keys", the

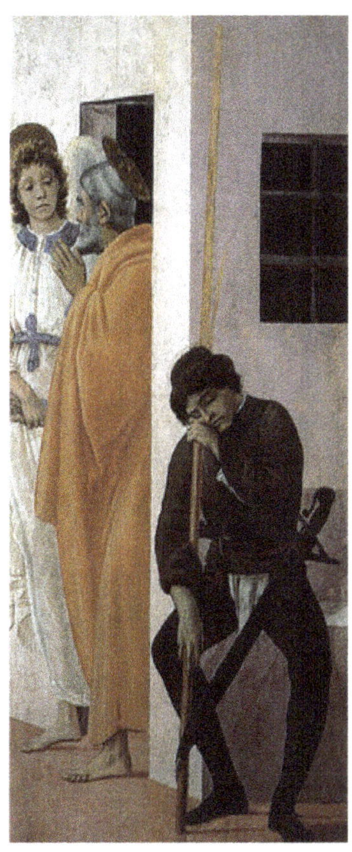

Fig. 15: Masaccio et al.,
St. Peter Leaving Prison.
Brancacci Chapel.

potestas clavium, is a corrupted literalization of the spiritual teaching implied in the story. "This is because the *key* of the kingdom is the Holy Spirit, which is granted to all believers, and the key is *eo ipso* given to all who possess the faith typified by the Apostle Peter. Thus the words addressed to Peter

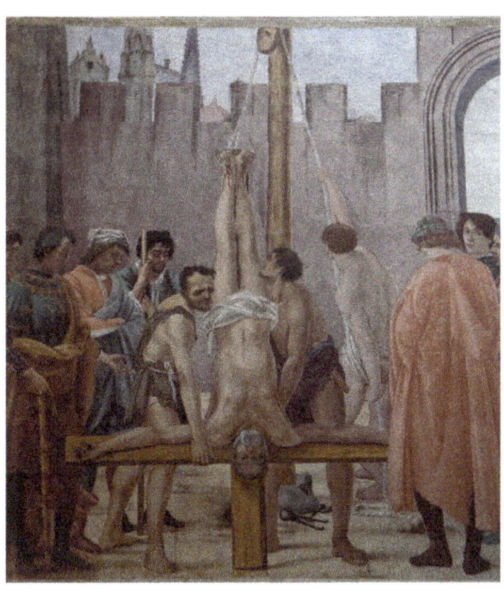

Fig. 16: Masaccio et al.,
Crucifixion of St. Peter.
Brancacci Chapel.

are addressed in his person to all who have such a faith, since every believer, through his faith, *is* Peter...It does not mean that certain men have the power to admit other men "into Heaven" or to exclude them from it."[40]

If Peter had previously been captive of the false popular notion of his role, the Brancacci Chapel frescoes would correct this distortion by depicting him in his true calling. They would, like the Angel, put the jailer to sleep and release Peter from his confinement to do his work.

Also conspicuously absent from the fresco cycle are any images of the Church as an imposing physical structure. In fact, the only time we see the grandiosity of church architecture is in the scene in which Peter is turned upside down and crucified by Imperial power. Can it be merely coincidental that where we find Peter turned on his head we see the outlines of the massive cathedrals that were to become the symbols of Christian power in a later age?

* * *

Now let's look at the frescoes on the central wall in the Brancacci Chapel situated behind the (former) place of the altar. On this wall there are four smaller frescoes, two above and two below. As we observe these four images, we may pose the question: How do Peter's acts shown here realize the mission with which he was charged?

The two upper images from left to right are *St. Peter Preaching* and *St. Peter Baptizing*, and the two lower images are, also left to right, *St. Peter Healing with His Shadow* and *St. Peter Distributing Alms*. In these images we see the mission of Peter, as Church, in four exemplary acts: *Preaching*: scattering the seed to the multitudes; *Baptizing*: initiating those into the mysteries who tremble at the water's edge; *Healing*: restoring bodily health and easing physical suffering; *Alms giving*: distributing charity to the wretched of the earth, helping those who are incapable of meeting their own basic needs. In place of the traditional static symbols of the Evangelists or the zodiacal tetramorphs, these four images of enactment provide a dramatic new background to this early Renaissance altar.

Like the altar itself which links heaven and earth, the imagery and place-

---

40 Henry Corbin, *Temple and Contemplation* (London: KPI Limited, 1986), pp. 256-257.

ment of the frescoes behind it echo the central theme of the proper relations between the things of heaven and the things of earth. The two upper

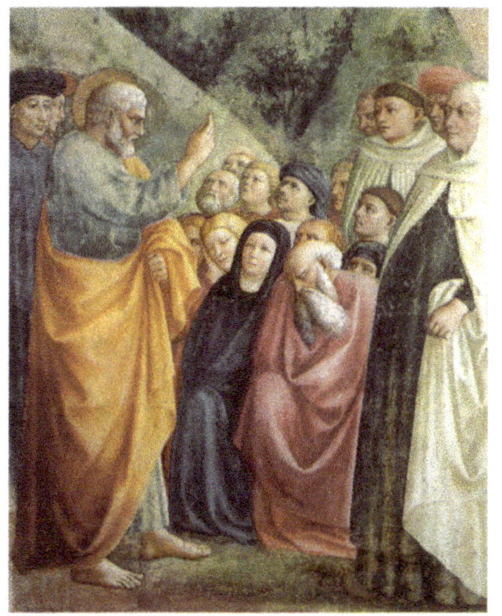

Fig. 17: Masaccio et al.,
St. Peter Preachng. Brancacci Chapel.

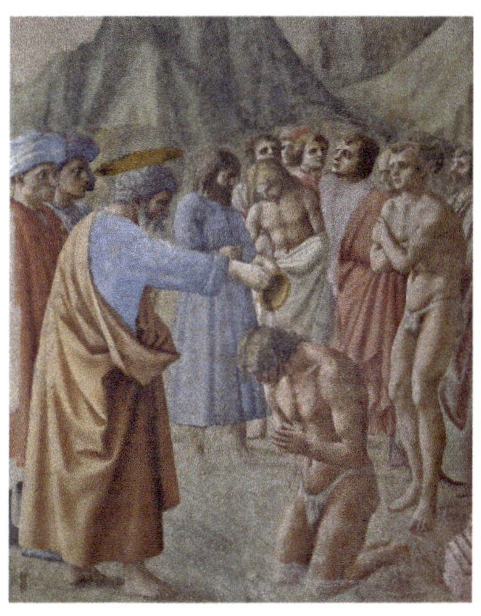

Fig. 18: Masaccio et al.,
St. Peter Baptizing. Brancacci Chapel.

paintings concern "higher" things, spiritual matters, and they are set against a background of the elemental world. The two lower paintings are about the needs of earthly life in community. They are set in the urban world, and they

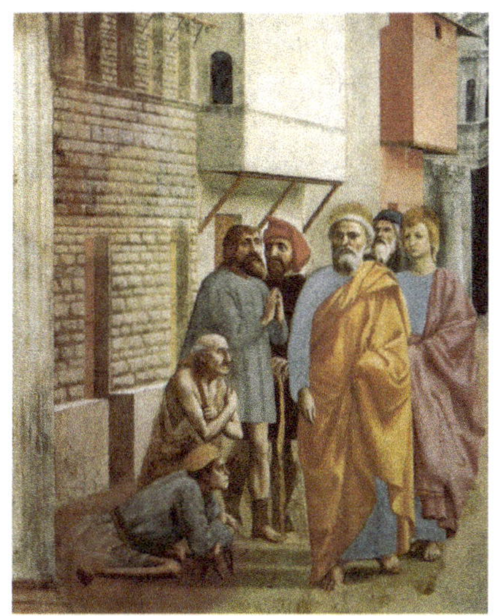

Fig. 19: Masaccio et al.,
St. Peter Healing. Brancacci Chapel.

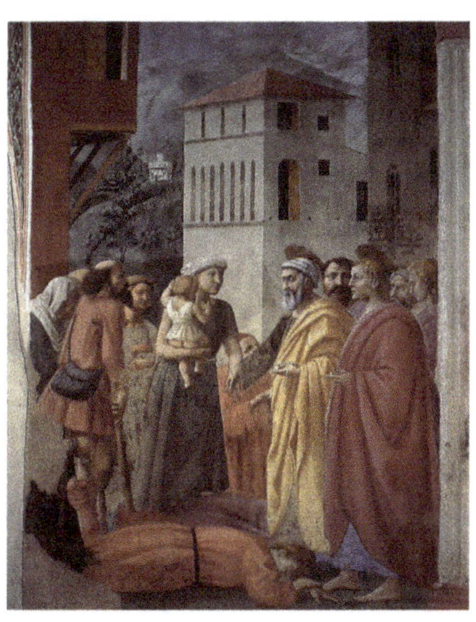

Fig. 20: Masaccio et al.,
St. Peter Distributing Alms. Brancacci Chapel.

show us the desperation of the infirm, the lame, the elderly, the people of the streets, those who beg for spare change, the folks with no health insurance and no insulation from the hard edge of suffering.

If the "higher" work is to lead souls to truth and salvation, the "lower" work is simply to alleviate bodily wretchedness and misery, to minister to essential earthly needs. And where is there a more uncompromising and poignant look at how the other half lives than here? Some have suggested that Peter occupies himself with holy thoughts as he makes his rounds in distributing alms. But perhaps he simply averts his eyes from shame and distress at the misery he sees.

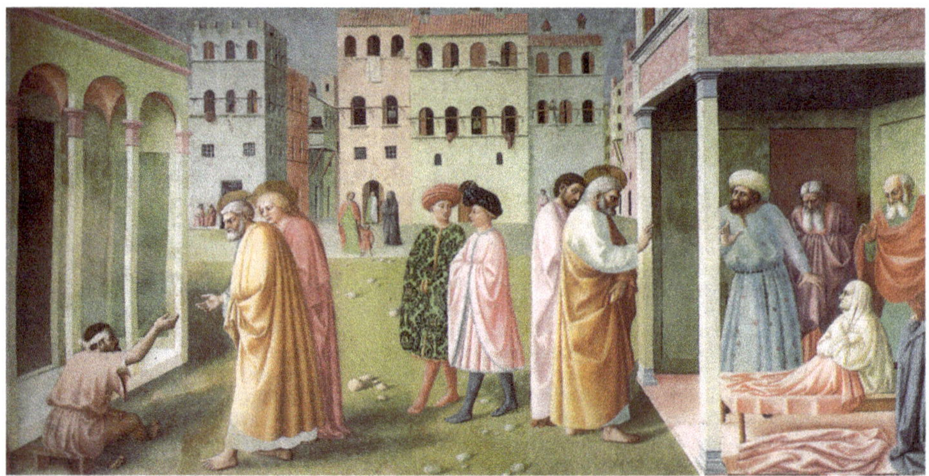

Fig. 21: Masaccio et al., *The Raising of Tabitha*. Brancacci Chapel.

The fresco cycle portrays the pathos of the poor, but it also shows us the lifestyles and psychology of the wealthy with equally unflinching honesty. Throughout the various frescoes we see the barefoot apostles and the poor who walk on the earth, contrasted with the shod and stockinged feet of those who merely walk over it. We see the difference in the *Baptism* between the agitated, animated faces of those who await baptism, and the two well-dressed figures who stand behind Peter and observe the proceedings with stiff, dispassionate looks.

The same contrast between facial expressions is revealed when we compare the gathered disciples in the *Tribute Money* with the oligarchs assembled in the fresco beneath them. When we observe the disciples, we see men who live from their hearts, whose hopes and fears clearly are written in their facial expressions and in their movements. Beneath them, in the privileged position of the front row, are the gathered dignitaries whose faces show only a world-weary sophistication.[41] Another day, another miracle. Will there never be an end to these official functions? Judging from their blasé faces one would think that the resurrection of Theophilus' son from a pile of dry bones were an everyday occurrence.

In the large fresco on the right wall, *The Healing of the Lame Man and the Raising of Tabitha* a pair of dandies strolls through the barrio. Their hats and stockings are color coordinated, and they wear the latest fashionable wraps. Consider how firmly Peter's feet are planted on the earth while the dandies seem to float slightly above it. They are stylishly attired from head to toe; only their faces are exposed and they tell us precious little. As Peter heals the lame and raises the dead, they exhibit a remarkable capacity to remain self-absorbed and oblivious to the miracles which surround them on either side.

In one scene after another we see that while the wretched suffer in their way, the rich, who have hardened their hearts to suffering, have become blind, numb, and emotionally dead. Their privilege and insulation has its costs; it prevents them from noticing and responding to all that is miraculous in their midst. Worse yet, it is disturbing to note how much the faces of those blandly observing the resurrection of Theophilus' son resemble the faces of those in the entourage of the Emperor who orders Peter to be crucified.

We may assume that in early fifteenth century Florence there were some who responded wholeheartedly to the appeals to aid the Republic and who, in an act of faith, pledged their lives and fortunes. Some Florentines must have been astonished at the sudden appearance of so many uncommonly talented painters, sculptors, and architects in their midst, doing ingenious things that

---

41 In anticipation of the possible objection that these faces were most likely rendered by Filippino Lippi, hence different from Massacio's above, we may respond that Filippino had the perceptiveness to notice the thematized differentiation of faces in several of the earlier frescoes by Masaccio and Masolino and chose to elaborate this element in his own work.

had simply never been done before. To some, the deliverance of the city, in 1402 and again in 1414, from prolonged siege through the serendipitous death of the enemy leader may have been taken as a sign of Divine intervention on behalf of their beloved city. Others, no doubt, during these same times devoted their attentions as always to the maintenance of their affairs, to the struggle to secure political advantages, and to the consolidation of their economic power, all the while waiting for things to get back to normal.

We can only imagine what it might have been like to live with open eyes and hearts in these heady early decades of the fifteenth century. Whether inspired by Dionysus or the Holy Ghost, the mad intoxication of the feeling of true community seems to sweep through civilizations occasionally only to pass on its way like a midsummer night's dream. But the chorus of appeals for a transformed Christianity which would serve as an instrument for the betterment of earthly life, and the vision of a community in which the things of heaven and the things of earth are creatively intertwined remain behind for us to contemplate on these walls to this day.

The Redemption of the Body

The two pairs of narrow frescoes which frame and border the rest of the fresco series depict Adam and Eve on the upper row, and Peter in jail on the lower row. Interestingly enough, although scenes in the larger frescoes progress temporally from left to right—from Christ and the disciples, to Peter's acts, to Peter's trial and crucifixion—the Adam and Eve images are chronologically reversed. We move from the Expulsion at the far left to the moment of innocence before the Fall at the far right. The paired images directly below these show Peter in jail beneath the fallen Adam and Eve, and Peter freed from jail beneath their innocent, naked bodies in the Garden of Eden.

The redemption of the body appears thematically several times in the various depictions of acts of healing and of raising the dead. Not coincidentally, Masaccio and company, as noted earlier, appear in the large fresco which shows the transformation of a pile of dry bones into living flesh. Surely this points to one of the greatest miracles which we are called to witness in the Brancacci Chapel: the vivification of serious, stately figures which artistic genius has brought to life upon a flat plaster wall! Flawless perspective, chiaroscuro, uniform lighting: a new suite of technical skills are used to create a religious miracle. The themes of raising the dead and the acts of physical healing are joined to the act of painting itself which here becomes a vehicle for the redemption and resurrection of the body, both in its naked splendor and in its simple, clothed dignity.

The figures we have been looking at reflect a new vision

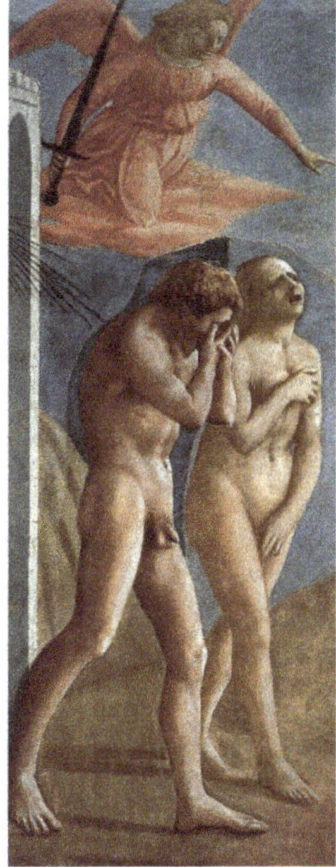

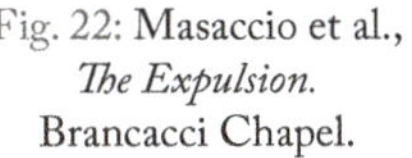

Fig. 22: Masaccio et al., *The Expulsion.* Brancacci Chapel.

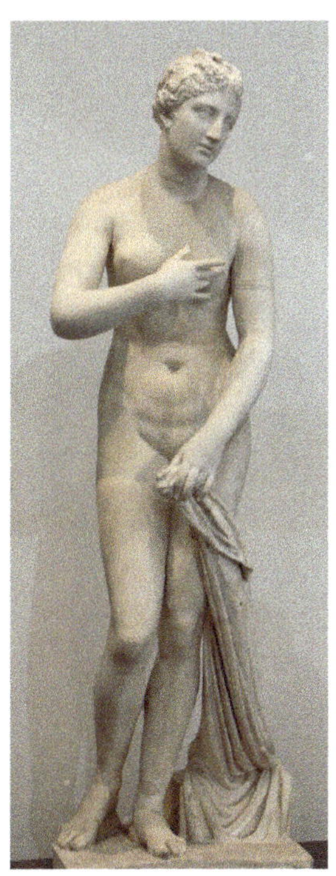

Fig. 23: *Venus Pudica.* Rome National Museum, Rome.

of the dignity of the body—as well as a new means of representing it pictorially. The sense of physical presence of the people in these frescoes is palpable to a degree never before realized. Bernard Berenson credited the pleasure he received from these frescoes above all to the substantial presence of these imaginal figures:

> Dust-bitten and ruined though his [Masaccio's] Brancacci Chapel frescoes now are, I never see them without the strongest stimulation of my tactile consciousness. I feel that I could touch every figure, that it would yield a definite resistance to my touch, that I would have to spend thus much effort to displace it, that I could walk around it... Then what strength to his young men, what gravity and power to his old! How quickly a race like this would possess itself of the earth, and brook no rivals but the forces of nature.[42]

---

42 Bernard Berenson, *The Italian Painters of the Renaissance* (New York: Meridian, 1958), pp. 80-81.

Though we needn't go so far as to see Berenson's *Übermenschen* in the scenes before us, his remarks clearly convey his visceral excitement over the tactile, bodily presence of the characters who inhabit the world of the Brancacci Chapel.

* * *

While, on the one hand, we find here a renewed celebration of the physical body, the counterpoint to this theme, the vision of the fallen body, is introduced through the extraordinary image of Adam and Eve's exile from Paradise. As the angel hovers overhead with sword drawn, Adam and Eve depart naked into the wilderness in a starkly rendered nightmare of shame.

Critics have noted that Eve's pose is based on a classical prototype known as the *Venus Pudica* or "modest Venus." This pose is probably most familiar to a modern audience from Botticelli's *Birth of Venus*, and shows the Goddess with her left hand covering her pubic region while her right hand partially covers her breasts. The pose occurs widely in classical statuary and would have been known to Masaccio either from Giovanni Pisano's Pisa pulpit figure of this type or perhaps directly from some of the Roman statuary which was then being recovered.

Much has been written about such borrowings from antiquity by Renaissance artists, but rarely do we get to hear a word about the *significance* of the borrowing. Mere cataloguing of artists' "quotations" takes us nowhere and serves only to distract us from the work at hand. It also implies that Renaissance artists were borrowing formulae either because they were not clever or energetic enough to invent their own, or that they used antique forms because they sought to please and conform to fashionable trends.

If we would do more than see Masaccio's use of a *Venus Pudica* formula for Eve as an example of popular infatuation with all things ancient, we need to consider why this particular antique figure was picked as a source rather than some other. How does Masaccio's choice of this ancient prototype deepen the meaning of this Renaissance image of the Expulsion?

We might begin by noting that the identification of this traditional image as a *Venus Pudica* or "Modest Venus" is somewhat of a misnomer. Aphrodite's stance is really an erotic invitation made by way of feigned modesty. Ginette Paris, in a remarkable study of Aphroditic consciousness in her book, *Pagan Meditations,* reminds us that the tension between revealing and concealing is part of the traditional iconography of Aphrodite. The times of day which were associated with the Goddess were dawn and dusk, those twilight times when we see suggestive contours rather than crisp outlines.[43] Paris tells us of "Aphrodite's attraction for veils which both cover and reveal"[44] and helps us recognize that the tension between covering and revealing in the *Venus Pudica* is the epiphanic image of Aphroditic erotic beauty.

When we turn from contemplating such an image of Aphrodite to look at Masaccio's Eve, it simply stops the breath. Masaccio has dared to imagine Eve as a fallen Aphrodite. Here there is no suggestion at all of calculated modesty, but rather an effort to cover herself while crying out in the ferocity of her pain. Eve, imagined as Aphrodite, the Goddess of love and physical beauty, surrenders her place in Eden in an agony of bodily shame.

* * *

In a cryptic passage in *The Marriage of Heaven and Hell*, William Blake tells us that at the end of time the world will be consumed in fire:

> For the cherub with his flaming sword is hereby commanded to leave his guard at the tree of life; and when he does, the whole creation will be consumed and appear infinite and holy, whereas it now appears finite & corrupt.

> This will come to pass by an improvement of sensual enjoyment.

> But first the notion that man has a body distinct from his soul is to be expunged...

We could think of the resurrection of the body as depicted in the Brancacci

---

43 Ginette Paris, *Pagan Meditations,* trans. G. Moore (Dallas: Spring Publications, 1986), p. 14.

44 Ibid. p. 45.

Chapel frescoes as an attempt to end fallen time, to end the age of the fallen body. Partly this is done by "an improvement of sensual enjoyment" to which we have seen Berenson bear witness. The figures we see in these frescoes are no longer symbolic representations of spiritual truths. We discern the state of their souls in the stance of their bodies and the look in their eyes. They move our souls through their bodies' simple gestures and challenge us to imagine a world which might have become ours had a different religious vision prevailed.

The fig leaves that covered the genitals of Adam and Eve for centuries until the recent restoration of the paintings are eloquent testimony to the failure of that bold vision of a bodily redeemed humanity to which the Renaissance imagination aspired.

GENTILE DA FABRIANO'S
Adoration of the Magi

The beauty of Gentile da Fabriano's *Adoration of the Magi* seduces even the most casual visitor to Florence's Uffizi Gallery. The splendor and majesty of this work stop us and lure us into its realms of hammered gold. The three Magi visiting the Christ child are lavishly clothed in rich and fanciful garments; the upright figure of the youngest Magus sways slightly in a graceful stance while the gleam of gold captures our eye in numerous places amidst the burst of other vibrant colors and patterns.

Gentile's *Adoration of the Magi* (1423) is typically identified by art historians as belonging to a stylistic tradition known as International Gothic which emerged from ecclesiastical and courtly circles.[45] Though this style of painting was longer lived in Siena and certain other locales, in Florence the International Gothic style was destined to be quickly superseded by that more realistic style pioneered by Donatello and Masaccio. Since it supposedly exemplifies a moribund style destined to become historically irrelevant, art historians have generally regarded *The Adoration of the Magi* as "unimportant" and have treated it, by and large, as just another pretty face.

In recent decades objections have been raised to this critical dismissal of Gentile's work, and efforts have been made to rescue him from the dustbin

---

45 Gardner's *Art Through the Ages*, for example, describes Gentile's painting as "the masterpiece of the International style" and informs us that "Gentile's purpose is to create a gorgeous surface" and that the picture "proclaims the sanctification of aristocracy in the presence of the Madonna and Child." Helen Gardner, *Art Through the Ages*, rev. by Horst de la Croix and Richard G. Tansey (New York: HBJ, 1986), Vol. II, p. 564.

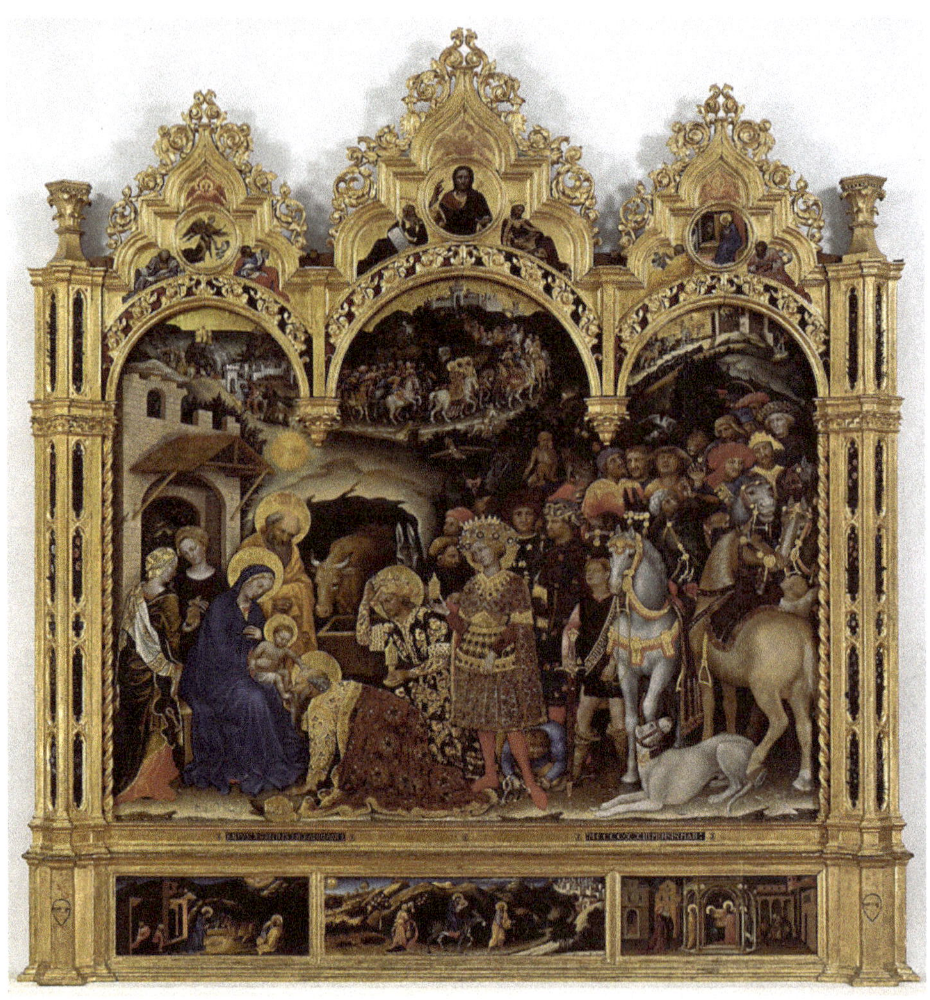

Fig. 24: Gentile da Fabriano, *Adoration of the Magi*. Uffizi Gallery, Florence.

of history. For example, Keith Christiansen, in his monograph on Gentile da Fabriano, notes several instances of Gentile's precocious experiments with lighting sources and cast shadows, and he argues that these pioneering elements probably influenced subsequent artists in their optical explorations.[46] Though he certainly rescues Gentile's opus from casual dismissal as a Gothic

---

46 Keith Christiansen, *Gentile da Fabriano* (Ithaca, NY: Cornell Univ. Press, 1982). From the innovative early use of shadows in Gentile's *St. Francis Receiving the Stigmata*, which Christiansen cites as marking "a new chapter in the history of Italian art"(p. 12), through the sophisticated compositional arrangements and natural detail of the later *Adoration* and its predellas, Christiansen adduces elements which support his central argument that Gentile pioneered a new notion of the relation between painting and experience (pp. 29-38).

irrelevancy, Keith Christiansen himself has little interest in the meaning of Gentile's work. He reserves his praise solely for those elements which show evidence of a new interest in nature and rational representation. While this approach may satisfy art historians who seek to document "firsts" among the emerging techniques of pictorial mastery, it does little to help us appreciate the artistic vision inherent in the paintings themselves. Gentile's interest in nature and optical phenomena is taken as evidence of his "modernity," and Christiansen even goes so far as to suggest that Gentile's work "firmly repudiates the notion that the value of art is its ability to symbolize sacred truths."[47] I respectfully disagree and will do my best to convince you that Gentile's "obsolete" medieval notions about the sacred purposes of art are the *raison d'être* of his masterpiece.

* * *

When we look more closely at *The Adoration of the Magi,* we notice that only certain portions of the painting that are rendered in what may be described as high Gothic style. These elements would certainly include the gold back-ground and the aristocratic figures of the Magi themselves. Meanwhile, the rest of the painting is filled with a variety of characters and events—some quite common and others truly ignoble—that are strikingly different in style from the central figures. The more one observes this image, the more one is struck by the wealth of anecdotal material and the astonishing details that would seem at first to have so little bearing on the central theme of the painting.

The painting reads as a narrative proceeding from top left to top right before bringing us to the central event in the foreground below. It is in the gable on the left that we first see the three Magi, tiny figures on a mountaintop surrounded by the brilliant sheen of gold, their upper bodies almost indis-tinguishable from the golden sky. From here they begin their descent into our world. We see their procession beneath the central gable approaching

---

47 Op. cit., p. 64. In Christiansen's reading of the situation, Gentile's interest in nature and optical phe-nomena is taken as evidence of his modernity and this is assumed, without evidence, to prove that Gentile had outgrown obsolete medieval notions about the sacred purposes of art.

Jerusalem where they will meet with Herod, and in the rightmost arch we see them about to enter the town of Bethlehem where they will ultimately present their gifts to the infant Christ.

On a literal level Gentile's depiction of the events simply follows the Biblical narrative in Matthew (2, 1-12). Yet there are many ways in which a story can be told, and we should consider how Gentile's particular way of crafting his image invites us to respond to this familiar tale. If we treat the Adoration of the Magi as an archetypal event, as one which occurs repeatedly in the world and timelessly in the soul, we can approach Gentile's treatment of his story as a meditation upon the significance of this theme. To appreciate the particularity of Gentile's vision, we first need to gain some familiarity with the traditional elements which characterize the iconography of this theme.

A Disturbance Among the Horses

Let's begin with one apparently inconsequential element which might easily escape the viewer's notice: the scuffling which takes place among the horses in the right foreground of the main scene. It could be dismissed simply as a fanciful element which Gentile introduces in a playful moment. Yet when one looks at other renderings of the same scene of the visit of the Magi in fourteenth and fifteenth century Italian painting, it is remarkable to notice how often there is a representation of discord among the horses or, sometimes, among the camels.[48]

This particular motif is a recurring element in the iconography of this image. We could account for it in the way that art historians often seem to do, as evidence of borrowings and "influence." But this really begs the question as to why certain innovative elements are retained and become standard refrains while others are discarded. Is it not, ultimately, the mythopoeic value of novel elements that accounts for their persistence, i.e., the degree to which they

---

48 Examples of this motif, both before and after Gentile, may be seen in the Adorations by Andrea di Vanni (Isaac Delgado Museum, New Orleans), Bartolo di Fredi (Pinacoteca Nazionale, Siena), Cenni di Francesco (S. Donato, Florence), Masaccio's predella of the Pisa polyptych (Dahlem Museum, Berlin), Giovanni di Paolo (National Gallery, Washington), and Botticelli (National Gallery, Washington).

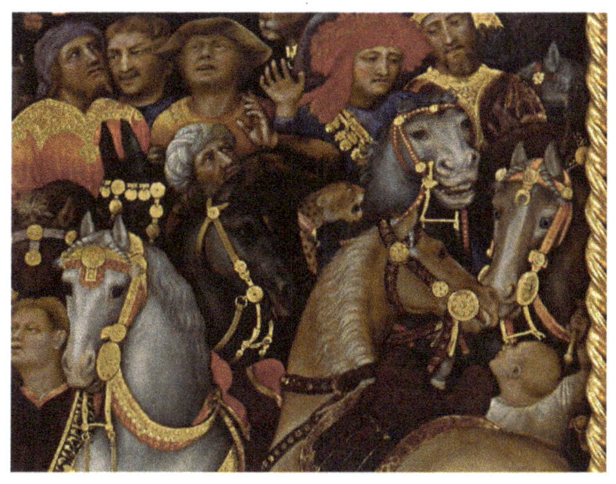

Fig. 25: Gentile da Fabriano, *Adoration of the Magi*, detail of the horses. Uffizi Gallery, Florence.

contribute meaningfully to the ongoing elaboration of a story?

So, to address this smaller matter, we need to broach the larger question: What is the meaning of the Magi's visit as an archetypal motif? It's worth noting that in the Gospel narrative the Magi are nowhere identified as kings; neither is it stated how many of them there are; nor is there any indication of their ages. Yet, by the time of the Renaissance, they would come to be represented regularly as three regal personages: a youth, a man of middle age, and a balding elder. There is no mention of their national origins, yet, in later treatments, especially in Northern Europe, they are frequently shown to be of different races, having come together from Africa, Europe, and Asia.[49]

The apocryphal elements which continue to accrete during the Middle Ages may be treated as clues that help us explore the significance with which the theme was gradually being invested. Now the most significant source of extensions and elaborations of the original stories of the Gospels prior to the late Middle Ages was the Hebrew Bible. In the search for prefigurations of Gospel events, the Old Testament was scanned carefully by the Church Fathers and later theologians for passages which foretold major subsequent events. Thus, for example, certain passages in the Old Testament (as well as in the writings of pagan authors like Virgil) were approached retrospectively as prophecies of the coming of Christ. Their details were cited to provide meta-historical validation of the truth and legitimacy of later New Testament events. Since the Magi's visit was an important acknowledgment of Christ's

---

49   Gertrude Schiller, *Iconography of Christian Art*, trans. by J. Seligman (Greenwich, CT: N.Y. Graphic Society, 1971), pp. 94ff.

special status, we can reasonably expect that it would have received its share of attention in the ongoing elaboration of Christian mythology.

The elaboration of the story of the Magi's visit was inspired by several Old Testament passages.   Isaiah had spoken of the coming of the light (60, 1), of the arrival of multitudes of camels and the bringing of gold and incense (60, 6), and of kings being drawn by the brightness of this rising light (60, 3). Meanwhile, Psalm 72 had prophesied the coming of a righteous judge to whom various kings would bring gifts of honor and that "all kings shall fall down before him: all nations shall serve him" (72, 10-11). During the course of the millennium the gift-bearing Magi of the New Testament slowly merged with the gift-bearing kings of the Old Testament as the Christian imagination wove these elements into a single story. Representations of the Magi's visit were thus gradually transformed into representations of the recognition and acknowledgment of Christ by all the powers that be: all ages of mankind from youth through age, all classes, all races from the far corners of the earth. The lavish pageantry of the long winding processions which accompany the Magi on their visit became popular in the late Middle Ages and was also inspired indirectly by Isaiah's multitude of camels.[50] It was frequently adopted by Renaissance artists because it worked so well to advance that greater story which attempted to show all creatures coming to pay homage and rejoicing in Christ's birth.

* * *

Why, then, this disturbance among the horses? Why the discordant note in the midst of such perfect harmony? To help us configure the subtle undercurrents which the Renaissance masters explored in their treatments of this theme, we need to take a brief detour into the mythologies of other cultures.

The Scandinavian myth of the death of Baldur tells of a contest which the gods hold in honor of that young, beautiful god beloved by all. All things on earth pledge their fealty to Baldur except for an insignificant shrub deep in the

---

50 Its more immediate source apparently derives from the *Meditationes* of Pseudo-Bonaventura. Cf. Schiller, *Iconography*, p. 111.

  Gentile da Fabriano's Adoration of the Magi

forest which is discovered by the evil Loki. During a day of exuberant festivity, tragedy darkly awaits its time. The gods in their sport hurl all manner of missiles and spears and arrows at Baldur, and all of these turn away from harming him—all except the mistletoe dart made by Loki which strikes him dead and plunges the world into mourning. How difficult it is to notice the darkness during these sublime moments!

In the classical Greek imagination, where each of the gods was associated with a particular time of day, a similar archetypal configuration was evoked by imagining Pan's moment of apotheosis to be high noon. At the moment when the Apollonic solar power was at its height, the goat-footed god—who also presided over the nightmare—would cast no shadow.[51]

The Taoists captured a similar insight in the Yin-Yang symbol where the dark center remains always present in the field of white and initiates the enantiadromic movement which continually transforms each aspect into its opposite.

Returning to the *Adoration of the Magi*, we may surmise that the disturbance among the horses serves as a reminder, even in the midst of this perfect moment, of the somber undercurrent which runs through our story, the dark spot in the noonday light. As in so many of the paintings of the Madonna and Child, where the blissful serenity of the scene is belied by the presence of a certain object which references the Crucifixion, the disturbance among the horses reminds us that even in this moment of peaceful celebration, the elements of disaster are biding their time.[52]

The horses will return to make a final appearance during the martyrdom of Jesus. In many scenes of the Crucifixion, where we are shown the powers

---

51 Cf.. James Hillman, "An Essay on Pan", in *Pan and the Nightmare* (New York: Spring Publications, 1972) pp. lvi-lvii.

52 A different strategy for sounding the note of discord seems to have been used in the tondo *Adoration* by Fra Filippo Lippi and Fra Angelico, today in the National Gallery in Washington, which depicts in the foreground of the painting a hideous looking dog whose back is turned upon the festivities. Also in the National Gallery one might note the small Nativity panel by Duccio which shows two rows of angels rejoicing in Christ's birth: one row looks down at the Holy Family, the other row gazes toward heaven--all except for a single angel that turns its head away. To the extent that Christ's birth recapitulates the original creation, this dark figure recalls the rebellion of Lucifer. In J.R. Tolkien's cosmogonic epic, *The Silmarillion*, the "spirit that denies" is the one who quite literally sounds the discordant note.

of darkness at their height, the horses are again powerfully present: wild-eyed beasts, sometimes frothing at the mouth, straining at their bits, pacing with restless agitation, infected by the madness abroad. The background disturbances of that earthly harmony which accompanies the visit of the Magi afford us no more than a glimpse of this forthcoming event, the merest shudder of breeze on a midsummer's day, yet surely it is this agitation among the horses which heralds the coming storm.

THE ADORATION OF THE MAGI

How do various other elements in Gentile's patterning of the image evoke and explore the deeper meanings of the Magi's visit? In Bernard Berenson's useful phrase, how does the image incarnate the idea it represents? And how does it invite us through its self-presentation to participate in that which it represents?

Although the identification of Jerusalem as a city upon the mountain is wholly traditional, the depiction of the Magi upon a mountaintop at the start of their journey is quite uncommon.[53] It is clear that the image of the mountaintop has been carefully emphasized in these gables. The mountaintop is familiar to Biblical readers as the place where Noah saw the rainbow after he was saved from the flood, where Moses spoke with God in the burning bush, where he later received the Ten Commandments, where the Binding of Isaac took place and the Temple of Solomon was built. Indeed, the mountaintop functions in Biblical typology as the *locus classicus* of interactions between God and man, of encounters between the divine and human realms. By representing this location in each of the painting's gables, Gentile invokes the relationship between the sacred and the mundane. The gables thus give us not only the narrative background to the central scene but also an *imaginal context* or topological background against which it may be contemplated.

The appearance of gold throughout the painting certainly adds to its splendor,

---

53 This last innovation dates also from the late medieval period, appearing in print for the first time in *The Golden Legend*. With the notable exception of the Limburgh brothers' *Trés Riches Heures*, few illustrators besides Gentile seem to have utilized the motif in their storytelling.

but there is more to it than mere opulent display. Gold is used throughout the painting in the thematic elaboration of the image, and the three gables which physically constitute the upper portion of the painting may be taken to represent the higher world, the ultimate source of gold. In the haloes and costumes of the sacred personages and in the gleam of the golden gifts which the Magi bring, we witness an event which results in the dispersion of gold from the upper reaches of sky to the world below. In a sense, Gentile da Fabriano's masterpiece may be seen as an exposition of the relations between the realm of gold and the lower domains in which we live.

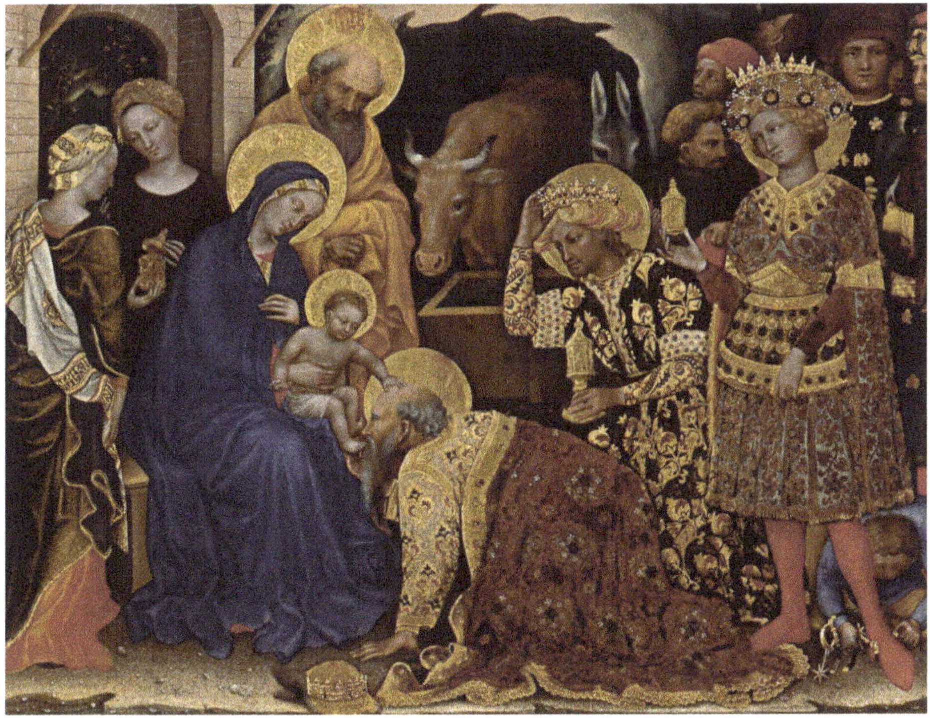

Fig. 26: Gentile da Fabriano, *Adoration of the Magi*, detail of The Three Magi. Uffizi Gallery, Florence.

Although Gentile was one of the earliest of Renaissance artists to explore the luminous subtleties of shadows (as in the Adoration scene in the predella below where the shepherds are illuminated by the angel's light), it is significant that the three Magi presenting their gifts cast no shadows. Although other figures in the painting are modeled in the round using chiaroscuro techniques, the Magi are presented in the flat, patterned manner that was traditionally used in altarpieces to represent sacred personages.

In the older sacred style the use of elaborate patterning and the absence of shadows served to create a pictorial image which remained on the surface of the picture plane. By contrast, the great technical revolution initiated by Brunelleschi and Donatello through the use of perspective construction and chiaroscuro was to situate figures *in* the picture as if seen *through* the picture plane. Although Gentile's use of perspective in this painting is not systematic or mathematically consistent, it is clear that he is able to utilize techniques which create the illusion of depth and physical substantiality when they serve his purposes. Since he is quite capable of rendering figures in both sacred and realistic modes, we may assume that the juxtaposition of styles in this image is deliberate and that it has thematic significance.[54]

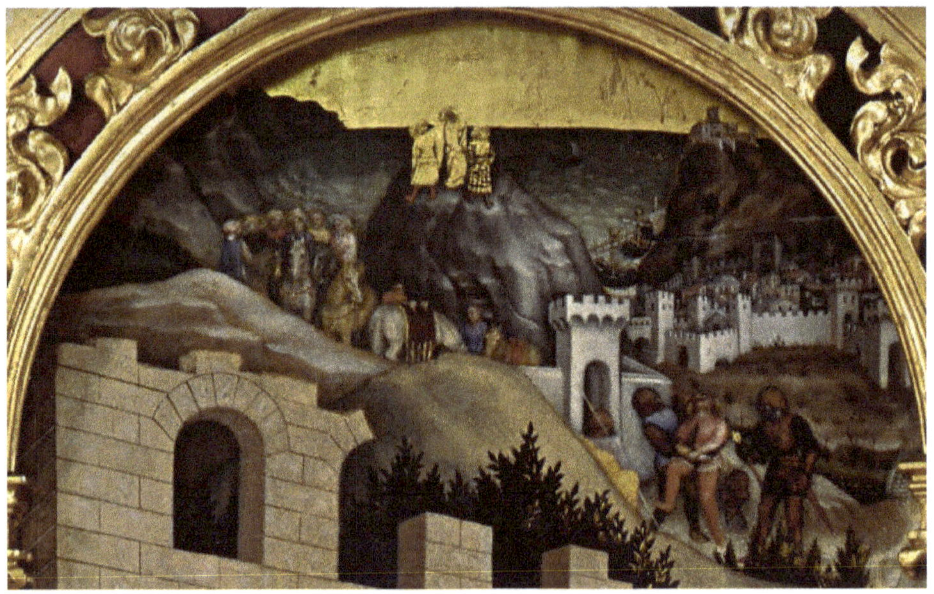

Fig. 27: Gentile da Fabriano, *Adoration of the Magi*, detail, left gable. Uffizi Gallery, Florence.

Using the sacred style to depict the figures of the Magi forces them to "float" on the surface of the picture plane while various other figures remain more

---

54 The common alternative, of course, is to split the image into its progressive and regressive elements, praising the former and lamenting the continued presence of the latter. So, for example, Frederick Hartt appreciates Gentile's subtle shadows and careful depiction of flora, but notes the continued presence of raised gold surfaces and landscapes that end with a golden sky, concluding wistfully that "with all this display of visual richness and this naturalism, basic archaisms remain." Frederick Hartt, *Italian Renaissance Art* (Englewood Cliffs: Prentice Hall, 1987) p. 181.

deeply embedded in the landscapes. This ingenious ploy enables Gentile to depict the three Magi as beings *who are in this world but not of it*. Indeed, the contrast between these otherworldly beings and the motley world of humanity is a core motif of the painting.

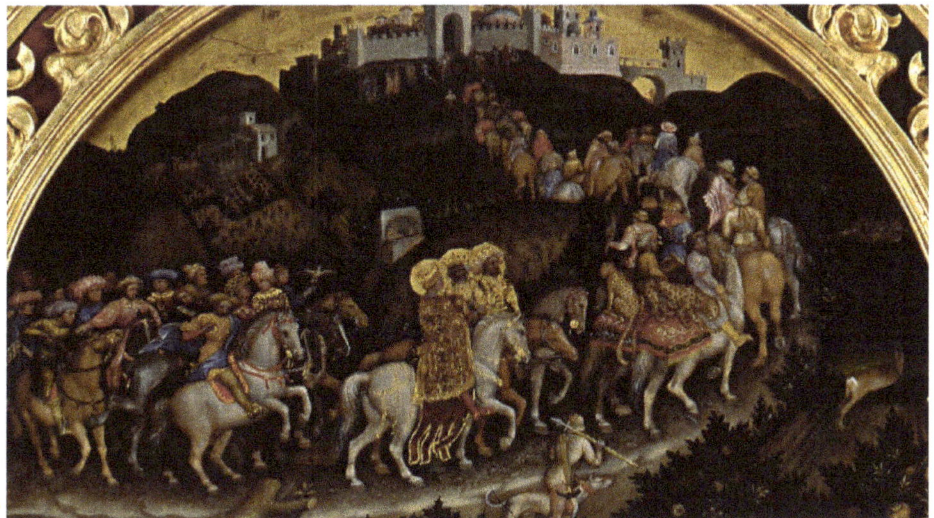

Fig. 28: Gentile da Fabriano, *Adoration of the Magi*, detail, central gable. Uffizi Gallery, Florence.

In the leftmost gable the Magi stand on the mountaintop looking at the star in the distance while in the right foreground below someone is being mugged. Look next at the procession in the central gable. In the bottom right corner a white-tailed deer flees while a leopard crouching on the back of a horse prepares to pursue it. A hunting dog in the bottom center has also caught sight of the fleeing deer, and we are left to imagine the sequel. Behind the Magi, a white horse rears up: an adjacent gray horse has just kicked the beige horse behind him directly in the chest and retribution appears immanent. Meanwhile, the three kings, set slightly apart from the crowd behind and before them, ride on, unperturbed.

In the central foreground image, in the entourage surrounding the Magi and the Holy Family, we see the faces of the common people, their mirth and frivolity, the raw vitality of their gestures and expressions. And we find an odd and entirely implausible profusion of animal life: monkeys, greyhounds, leopards, camels, hawks swooping in mid-air. Here we are in the world of

10,000 things, as the Buddhists call it, in the midst of the pandemonium of worldly life. Struggling horses, copulating birds, grinning peasants, jostling crowds, bursting pomegranates, jabbering, chained monkeys. And in the center of this flurry of earthly activity, we find the solemn, still figures of the Magi, crowned with gold, prostrating themselves before a baby born in a manger.

The journey of the Magi is an arc of descent, one which passes through the world while beginning and ending on the mountaintops, in the land of gold. Note how the haloed figures in the foreground form a semi-circle from Joseph in the upper left to the youngest Magus standing on the right. This semi-circular formal pattern, configured by the main actors in the foreground, recapitulates the movement of descent and return which is the journey that the Magi undertake, and it is homologous with the theme of the painting itself. This is, of course, also the formal structure of Christ's own journey, and lest we forget, the three roundels over the gables depict the Annunciation—the moment of descent into incarnation—and the resurrected Christ. Finally, in the predella below, we find the scene of the flight into Egypt placed, non-chronologically, between the Nativity and the Presentation in the Temple. This forms yet another descending arc, represented physically in the central predella image by the curvature of the road and typologically by the placement of a journey of exile and danger between two panels representing the benign moments of adoration and recognition.

The dramatic moment which Gentile has chosen to emphasize at the nadir of the arc in the central scene is, appropriately enough, the act of the eldest Magus kneeling and kissing the foot of the child, a gesture of the utmost humility. The actions of the three Magi are choreographed to form three phases of a single descending movement: the youngest king stands erect, his crown still in place; the middle king commences to kneel as he begins to remove his crown; the eldest stoops low, his crown beside him as the Christ child blesses his bald pate. The Magi deign to pay homage to the golden haloed child who has appeared in a small village, born in a barn amidst the animals. That which is noblest and most regal prostrates itself before that which is most lowly, most helpless. This act of humility is the gesture which brings heaven into relation with the things of this earth. The high makes itself low and sublimity descends to earth—thus the marriage of heaven and earth is consummated.

In his commentary on the 42nd hexagram of the *I Ching*, "Increase", Richard Wilhelm wrote: "A sacrifice of the higher element that produces an increase of the lower is called an out-and-out increase: it indicates the spirit that alone has the power to help the world. Sacrifice on the part of those above for the increase of those below fills the people with a sense of joy and gratitude that is extremely valuable for the flowering of the commonwealth... This time resembles that of the marriage of heaven and earth, when the earth partakes of the creative power of heaven..."[55] Through another wise man from the East there has come to us also the tradition which reveres the figure of the Boddhisattva as the enlightened being who foregoes his own final exodus so as to continue working for the deliverance of other beings.

In our poignant and beautiful image of the early decades of the Florentine Renaissance, Gentile da Fabriano presents us with the Western version of what may be a universal dream of the illumined soul. Those who appear in every age and culture carrying gifts, bringing a vision of redemption, calling out "I have a dream!" to help the lowly and the wretched achieve human dignity, form a procession through the ages like the one we see in Gentile's image, descending from the mountaintop and bringing their vision into the community. One recent lineage moves directly from Martin Luther King back through Mohandas Gandhi to Leo Tolstoy. And, pulling the curtain back just a bit further, we might recall that the event which provoked the elderly Count Tolstoy to disturb the complacency of his fellow aristocrats in his twilight years was his careful reading of the Gospels. In this age of critical deconstruction of the privileged narratives of the Eurocentric canon and the Judeo-Christian tradition, it would behoove us to remember that the vision of social justice which inspires the critique itself originates from these very same Western traditions which are at times so vigorously scorned and so short-sightedly despised.

How interesting it is to recognize with our three modern Magi that, despite their very different life situations, each heard the other's call and undertook in his own way to surrender social privilege and make common cause with

---

55 *The I Ching*, trans. by Richard Wilhelm and Cary F. Baynes (Princeton: Princeton Univ. Press, 1967) p. 162.

the wretched of the earth. Curiouser still, we may note that the trio consists of a European, an Asian, and an African-American.

CONCLUSIONS

Gentile da Fabriano is one of the early Renaissance masters repeatedly mistreated and misprized by those whose vision of the Renaissance is constrained by a developmental paradigm. When the value of such a "transitional" artist is assessed, he is invariably considered in relation to his role—or lack thereof—in the development of those naturalistic techniques which are presumably the great achievement of Renaissance art. In analyzing his work we strive to identify and praise certain "progressive tendencies," and we separate these from those archaic and atavistic modes that have unfortunately persisted despite his partial modernity.

For many decades now modernity has fully accepted non-representational art. It is remarkable, therefore, that the dominant critical paradigm in approaching the work of early Renaissance artists still commends naturalistic technique and lament its lapses. We continue to judge the quality of artistic accomplishment based upon a given work's station on our road map of the evolution of technique. In the aftermath of a century of artists like Matisse, Klimt, Kandinsky and Redon, one may reasonably ask why adherence or divergence from the historical road towards "realism" should continue to guide our judgments of the artistic quality and importance of various Renaissance works. What we ought to care about is whether and how the techniques utilized in any given work serve to realize the vision implicit in that work. As Giordano Bruno expressed it some four hundred years ago, "Poetry is not born of the rules... but the rules derive from the poetry. For that reason there are as many genres and species of true rules as there are true poets."[56]

If we assess *The Adoration of the Magi* by isolating progressive from regressive elements, Gothic from true Renaissance technique, we make it impossible from the outset to appreciate the extent to which Gentile's blend of styles is deliberate and highly creative. The interplay between the sacred and secular

---

56 Giordano Bruno, *The Heroic Frenzies*, trans. P.E. Memmo, Jr. (Chapel Hill: University of North Carolina Press, 1966) p. 83.

styles that he utilizes works brilliantly in enabling Gentile to create his timeless meditation on the relation of the realms of gold and the secular world.

Although Gentile's style differs significantly from Donatello's or Masaccio's
or Piero della Francesca's, I believe he is no less driven than they by the central passion of his age: the search for a vital relationship between the things
of heaven and those of earth, and the dream of using art as the bridge between the worlds. In his inspired exploration of this theme, Gentile invites
us to contemplate the vast panorama of the natural world and the turmoil of
earthly life while reminding us of the enduring presence of a sacred axis in
the human soul which links us with the land of gold. And, in imagining the
deepest meaning of the Magi's gifts, Gentile, through his masterpiece, has
surely added one to their number.

DAVID'S PENIS

There is a Jewish joke about a visitor who comes to a shtetl, a little Jewish village, somewhere in Poland. As he walks through the narrow streets, he notices that many of the shops have an object hanging above their entrances which clearly identifies the type of activity that is carried out in the shop. He sees a hanging shoe, and inside he observes several shoemakers at work. He passes a clock over a doorway and notices the watchmakers busily making repairs. Then he passes a storefront and sees an old umbrella hanging there. He looks inside and sees an elderly gentleman dressed like a Rabbi reading quietly at his desk. Puzzled, he steps inside.

"Good day to you, sir. May I ask what kind of work you do?"

"Certainly, I perform circumcisions. I'm a moyl."

"Then why is it that you have an umbrella hanging outside?"

"And what do you propose that I should hang out there?"

* * *

In addition to being one of the most admired and visited works of art in the world, Michelangelo's David is also the most famous instance in a distinguished lineage of Davids that spans the prior century. Visitors are occasionally puzzled as they contemplate the statue to discover that the Jewish shepherd boy has not been circumcised. Scholars have offered various explanations, but to truly grasp the significance of David's penis we need to look at a couple of earlier Davids within the context of Florentine history and culture over the course of the preceding century.[57]

Here is a brief recapitulation drawn from the earlier essay in this volume of what was happening in Florence in the year 1400; it's offered here so that you can appreciate the context in which the very first David appeared.

It was the worst of times, plain and simple. In 1348 the Black Plague carried off nearly half of the population; in succeeding decades, flood and drought led to major crop failures and widespread famine; an economic depression caused the ruination of many of Florence's international banking houses and many families were left destitute. Then in 1400, Giangaleazzo Visconti, the aggressive new ruler of Milan, assembled an army and started marching down the peninsula. He conquered one city-state after another, and as he approached, he demanded that Florence surrender.

The Florentines refused and instead decided to hold an open art competition for a new set of doors for their Baptistery while the enemy was camped outside the gates. The theme that was chosen for the sample submissions by contending artists was, significantly, the harrowing tale of the Sacrifice of Isaac. And, one fine morning, while the City Fathers were discussing the relative merits of the various works submitted to the competition, the Milanese leader suddenly dropped dead. Not a good omen. By the next day his mercenary army was dissolving like a late March snow. Florence was delivered.

This sequence of events enabled the Florentines to convince themselves beyond any reasonable doubt that art was a very powerful form of magic. So, one of the first things that they did after successfully resisting the Milanese assault was to commission a series of new statues to fill various empty niches on their cathedral, its bell-tower, and the nearby church of Orsanmichele. Among the earliest commissions was a statue of David the shepherd boy to be placed in a niche on the façade of the church. This work has survived the centuries, and it is Donatello's earliest known work.

---

57 For a recent summary of speculative explanations for the lack of circumcision, ranging from inattention to political correctness, see: Journal of the Royal Society of Medicine, 2002 Oct; 95(10): 514-515.

Donatello's figure of David stood astride the severed head of Goliath with a stance and expression that conveyed courage, resolution, and cool self-confidence. Someone who was no fool saw that this statue had a potent political message that would be lost up on a church façade and, so, had it moved right in front of City Hall. Thus was born the first David-as-symbol-of-the-city-of-Florence. As David had fearlessly challenged and overcome the might of Goliath, so had Florence withstood the aggressive onslaught of the Milanese giant from the north. The analogy was too good to be ignored for long.

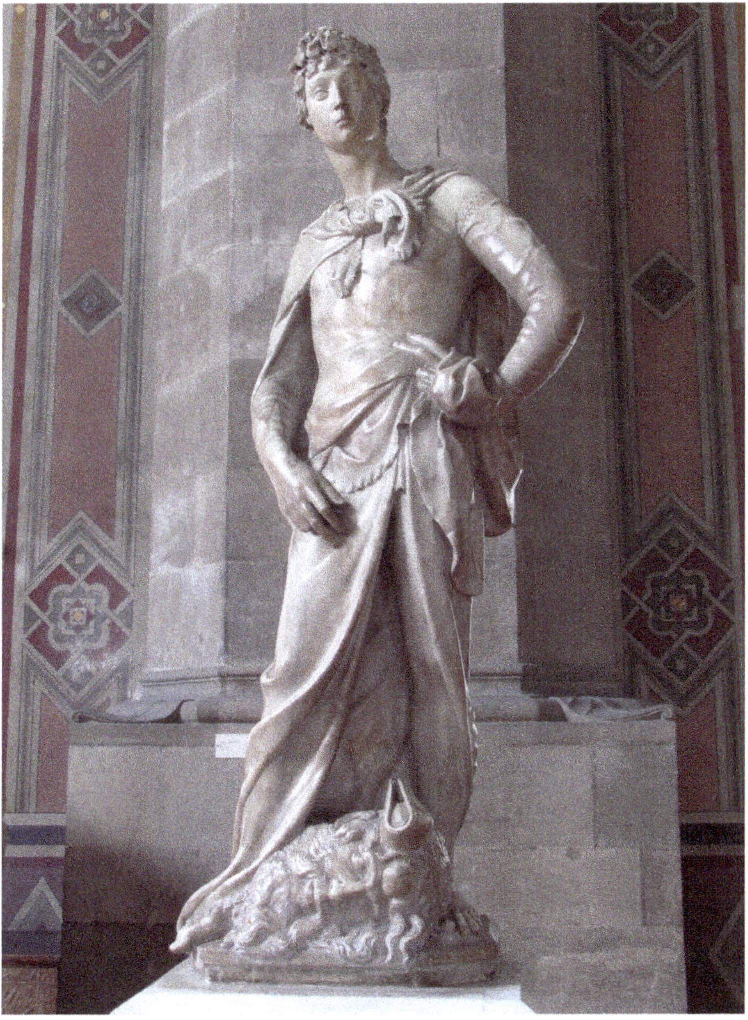

Fig. 29: Donatello, *David* (early). Bargello Museum, Florence.

There's a final detail here that may seem trivial but actually takes us right to the heart of the matter. The statue of David originally had a gold strap that ran from his right hand down and across to the pouch resting on Goliath's head where David's backup stone was ready in case the first one had missed. On the gold band was inscribed (in Fredrick Hartt's translation): "To those who strive bravely for their fatherland the gods will lend aid even against the most fearful foes."

Now here was a golden opportunity to coin the phrase, "God helps those who help themselves," almost three hundred years before Ben Franklin. Yet, rather than mentioning "God," what was chosen instead for David's gold band was a pagan reference to assistance from "the gods." Here's why:

At the dawn of the 15th century the cultural elite in Florence was actively engaged in recovering the riches of the Greco-Roman world that had been forgotten, lost and literally buried. After nearly a thousand years of dominance, Christian society no longer had a pagan opponent to be vanquished, disdained and despised. What happened next is similar to what took place some time after the Indian wars were decisively won in the New World: the younger generation took a second look and recognized that the "heathen savages" were Native Americans and had spiritual traditions and ways of living that were worthy of their interest and respect.

In Florence bright young men like Donatello and Brunelleschi traveled to Rome to marvel at the sophistication of the surviving architecture and the astonishing skill of the classical sculptors. Their literary counterparts meanwhile were busy recovering, translating and organizing the writings of the great Greek and Roman poets and philosophers. The recovery of the classical past became a cultural enterprise of the foremost importance.

The challenge looming on the horizon was how to integrate the existing Christian society's sense of itself with the sudden influx of the classical heritage. Although this attempted marriage was ultimately a failure, its creative efforts at fruitful union were responsible for some of the greatest works of Western art.

Donatello's David is one of the first images created in the new century that explicitly addresses this cultural tension. On the one hand he is clearly a hero stepping forth from the Judeo-Christian tradition. But the band across the front of him inscribed with a Roman proverb simultaneously invokes the classical tradition. He is clearly shown in this way to have a foot in both worlds, and we are to understand that having two legs to stand on can only make him stronger. As a stand-in for the Florentine Republic, he embodies the alchemical process of blending these two traditions that is the grand challenge of 15th century Florence.

* * *

Several decades later Donatello created another David. No one knows exactly when, but a reasonable guess is that it was done sometime around mid-century. This second David was recently cleaned and restored (2008/09), a procedure that took over a year to carry out. On our visits to the Bargello Museum in Florence, we would see him lying on his back, like a patient etherized upon a table, while women in white smocks went over every square centimeter of his torso.

This second David is an enigmatic creature. We know who he is from the stone that he holds in one hand, the sword that he holds in the other hand, and the severed head of Goliath that lies at his feet. After that we step into the realm of mystery. He has long, lovely hair that, since his cleaning and restoration, we now know was once brightly golden. He wears a bonnet decorated with flowers. Although he has male genitals, he has a decidedly feminine quality about him. No massive pectorals here. He has the soft protruding belly, budding breasts and rounded buttocks of an adolescent girl.

One strategy for explaining David's effeminate qualities is to speculate that Donatello might have been gay. But this is hardly a convincing proposal. Had Donatello done a series of statues of effeminate males over the course of his lifetime, this might tell us something about Donatello's proclivities. But since this David is very much a one-of-a-kind in the context of Donatello's hugely diverse work, speculating about Donatello's sex life doesn't really help us understand this figure's mysteries.

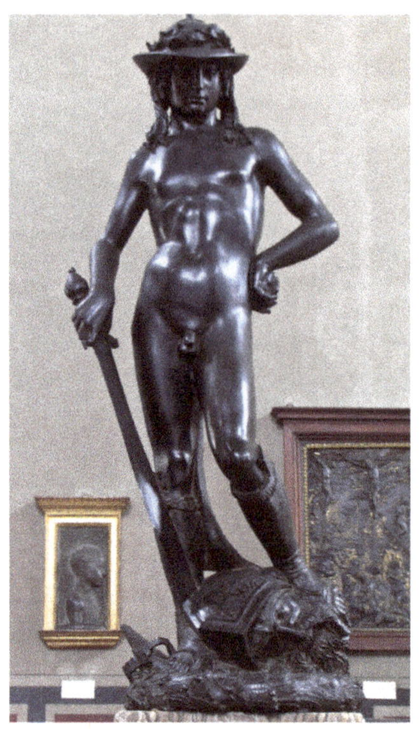

Fig. 30: Donatello, *David* (later, frontal view).
Bargello Museum, Florence.

I believe that a more fruitful approach is to recognize this figure of David as a hermaphrodite. In a sense it's obvious, but the sheer oddness of imagining David in this way has made it unthinkable. Yet, as soon as you unpack the term "hermaphrodite", it begins to make sense. The hermaphrodite in classical mythology was so named because he/she was the child of the Greek gods, Hermes and Aphrodite. So, this second David once again embodies the merger of the two traditions feeding the Florentine Renaissance: the Judeo-Christian and the Greco-Roman. Now, let's look at the implications of creating a figure that merges David, Aphrodite and Hermes.

* * *

Aphrodite, known to the Romans and to us more commonly as "Venus", was the goddess of erotic love, artifice and beauty. The metal associated with Aphrodite is gold, as in lovers' gifts of earrings and necklaces. Flowers, particularly as ornament and in the form of bouquets, are also part of Aphrodite's domain. The flowers in David's bonnet and the gold in his hair and boots, along with his graceful, fetching feminine attributes, establish his Aphroditic aspect.

Hermes, aka Mercury, is best known to most of us today from the Giambologna statue that was loosely appropriated as the logo for FTD, the instant floral delivery service. As the fleet-footed god with wings on his sandals, he moves between

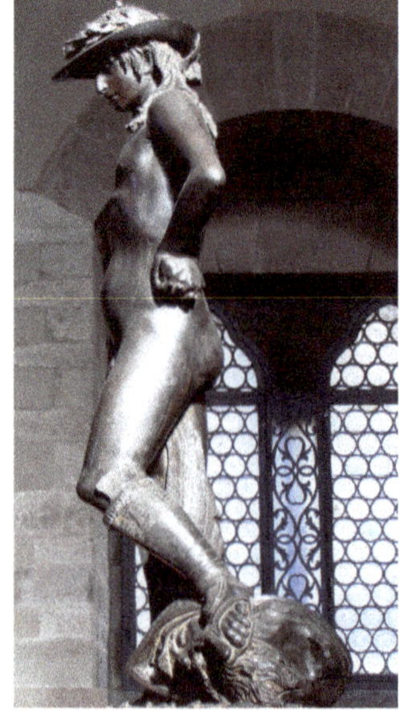

Fig. 31: Donatello, *David*
(later, side view).
Bargello Museum, Florence.

worlds faster than a mouse-click. If you look up Hermes in a dictionary of mythology, he'll most likely be identified as the messenger of the gods and the patron of travelers. But a more profound and encompassing way to think of him is as the god who facilitates communication between different realms.

For merchants traveling from one land to another, he was the god who might bring the blessings of fruitful commerce. But in addition to pragmatic, horizontal movement across the earth, Hermes also had a mystical, magical aspect: he constellated the possibility of vertical movement between the three worlds: the heavens, the earth and the underworld. In the Giambologna image, he's on his way from earth back to heaven, spiraling upward in a flash on a gust of wind. When heading in the opposite direction, he was known as Hermes psychopompos, the guide who led souls down to the underworld after death.

The Hermetic aspect our David figure is established partly by his sandals in association with the wing growing out of Goliath's helmet, and partly by the hat David wears. (Hermes, notably, is the only Greek god who wears a hat. You can see a similar derby on a Hermes statue in the upper-floor corridor of the Uffizi museum.) The stone that he holds in his hand reminds us that he is David. But the substitution of the sword for the sling turns the image subtly in the direction of Greek myth: the broad sword and the head at his feet also establish a resonance with the story of Hermes and the giant, Argus, whom Hermes decapitates. (If you are familiar with Botticelli's *Primavera*, have another look at the young man standing on the far left of the painting, then look at this David, and the Hermetic archetype common to both of them will become apparent.)

* * *

Now it's time to put it all together. Let's assume that Donatello's objective was once again to create a heroic self-image for Florence which merged the Judeo-Christian and classical traditions. This time around, the David figure is blended with two specific pagan deities, Aphrodite and Hermes. The final question we are left with is this: Of all the Greek gods, why these two?

If we posed this question to a Renaissance Humanist, here's how he might explain the choice of Aphrodite and Hermes: Of all the deities in the Greek pantheon, these were the two gods who nurtured the specific genius of Florence. Indeed, Florence's prestige among its fellow city-states on the Italian peninsula derived in no small part from its Aphroditic artistry, its capacity to create astonishing and unprecedented works of art that were the envy of its neighbors. Its monuments, palaces and public piazzas created a world of extraordinary beauty that millions today still travel around the world every year to enjoy. In Florence "the Goddess loves in stone, and fills the air around with beauty." That was how the English Romantic poet, Lord Byron, expressed it.[58]

The financial strength of Florence, meanwhile, was based on commercial banking implemented through a remarkable network of international offices. There was hardly a city in Europe where the major banking houses of Florence hadn't set up shop. Letters of credit and other financial instruments were developed to speed and secure the flow of capital. Commerce, travel, communication—these were some of the gifts that Hermes brought to Florentine endeavors.

Now in addition to these horizontal, earthbound gifts there were also certain mystical, Hermetic gifts that Florence received that were no less vital. Humor me for a moment as we take a historical digression, because I believe it's one that leads us right to the heart of the matter.

In 1437 a delegation from Byzantium arrived in Florence hoping to resolve doctrinal disputes with the Roman Church. More germanely, they were also desperately seeking help from the Christian West to resist the ever more ferocious assaults of their Muslim neighbors. For reasons about which one can only speculate, the Pope decided to withhold assistance. Perhaps he assured them that Islam was a religion of peace. In any case, within fifteen years, the walls of Byzantium were breached by the Turkish Sultan, Mohammed II. The Emperor and his family were slaughtered, the thousand-year-old city pillaged and destroyed, and the populace raped, murdered and enslaved.

---

58 Lord Byron, *Childe Harold's Pilgrimage*, stanza 49 of "Canto the Fourth."

As if in anticipation of the worst, the delegation in 1437 had brought with them their most sacred texts. These were consigned, not to the Pope, but to Cosimo di Medici, the de facto ruler of Florence. Among the texts was a collection of mystical writings known as the *Hermetica*. Cosimo was in the midst of having his resident philosopher, Marsilio Ficino, translate the dialogues of Plato, but work on that front stopped abruptly while Ficino took on the task of translating the *Hermetica*. What the Florentines believed they held in their hands were the most ancient, most sacred, and most profound teachings about the ultimate nature of things ever revealed to man!

Among the mystical teachings in the *Hermetica* there was one in particular that I believe sheds some additional light on Donatello's second David. Portions of these texts were concerned with the making of talismans and magical statues. The theory was complex and more than we can bite off here, but the goal was to create images that could capture certain desired qualities out of the ethers and then focus and amplify their power. If we consider our statue in this context, we can see him as a talismanic object that embodies the shared powers and energies of David the shepherd boy, the future King of Israel, along with the copious gifts of Aphrodite and Hermes thrown into the mix.

We are left wondering what Cosimo the Elder had in mind when he asked Donatello to create this second David. Did it further him somehow in his dreams of creating a dynasty, or in his quest to create the greatest city of the Renaissance? We only know for certain that it was intended for him as a private work for ritualized contemplation in his villa. This rest is silence.

* * *

In the first decade of the 16th century Michelangelo was invited to create his David out of an enormous block of marble that had been abandoned by an earlier sculptor and had been left lying out in the weather for twenty-five years. He was in his mid-twenties, and he worked on the David uninterruptedly for two years.

Michelangelo's David was originally supposed to be one of a series of statues mounted on the exterior of Florence's Cathedral. Just as with Donatello's first David, once it was completed, everyone could see that it belonged in front of Florence's City Hall. And there it stood for more than 300 years. Its physical placement confirmed its place in the tradition of Davidic statues

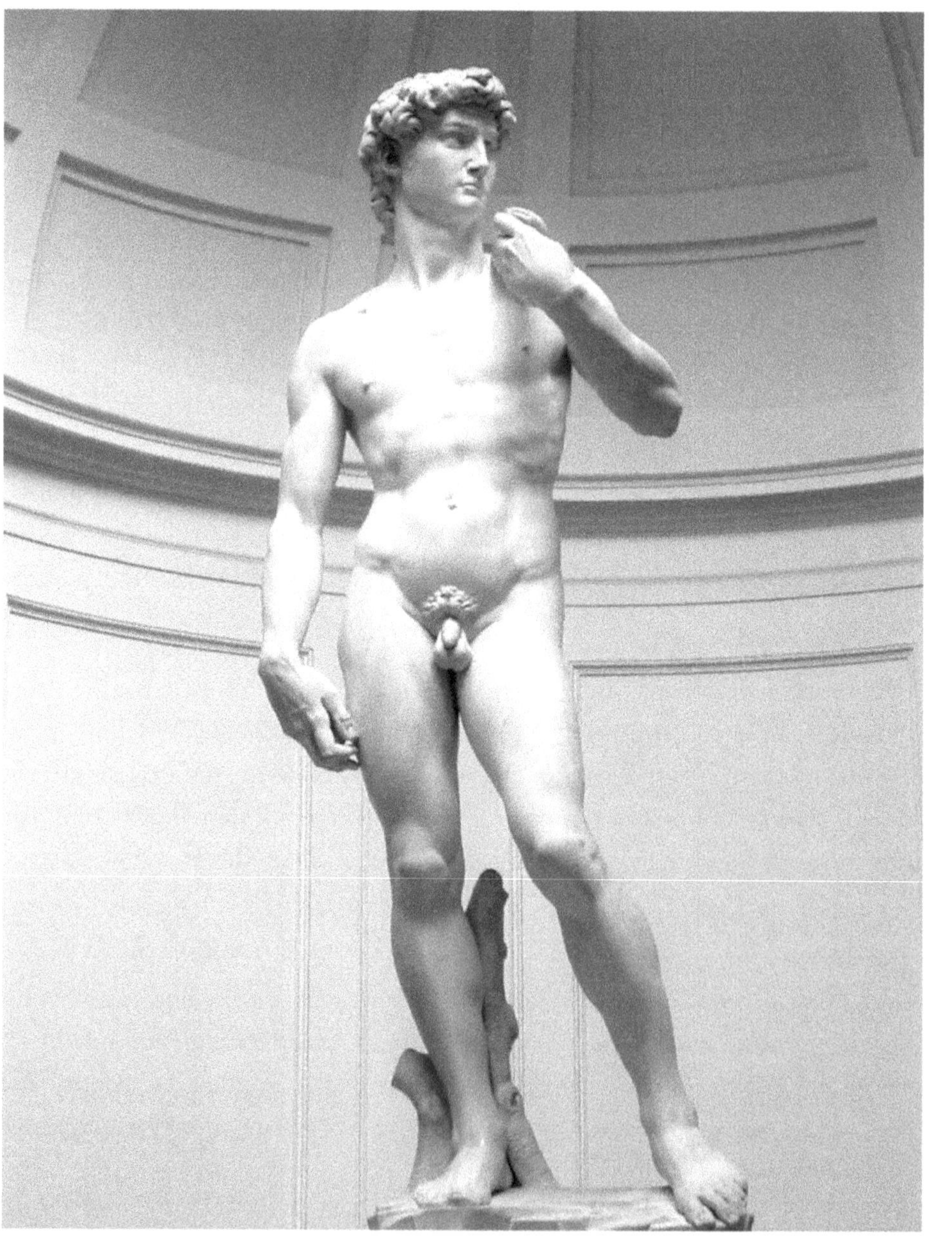

Fig. 32: Michelangelo, *David*. Accademia, Florence.

that embody and represent Florence, that proclaim its greatness.

Michelangelo's David carries forward the core themes of Donatello's earlier works—the fusion of the Judeo-Christian and Greco-Roman cultural streams into something greater than the sum of their parts. Michelangelo found his own unique approach to affirming this tradition. The Biblical half of the equation is clearly seen in the wary shepherd boy scanning the horizon, looking for trouble that will come all too soon. The pagan half of the equation is more subtly evoked. David stands in a position known as *contrapposto* where most of the figure's weight rests on one leg. This was a pose widely used in classical sculpture. He also stands naked and without shame, displaying bodily beauty and strength unselfconsciously, the way a Greek athlete might have done two thousand years earlier. And he is enormously tall and powerful, more than humanly so.

It's easy to see the shepherd boy, but when you step back and contemplate this work, you realize that this is only one half of the equation. Michelangelo's David is a fusion of a Biblical shepherd boy and an Olympian god. And, by the principal of synecdoche whereby a part represents the whole, as when a shoe over a doorway represents a shoe-repair shop, it's David's penis that stands for the vital legacy of the Greco-Roman world.

ANNUNCIATIONS

Until the middle of the eighteenth century, the Florentine calendar actually began with the Incarnation rather than the Birth of Christ.[59] Time was reckoned from the moment of the Annunciation, nine months before Christmas, on the twenty-fifth of March, and the New Year was ushered in amidst a profusion of lilies, the flower of the Virgin.

The Florentine decision to celebrate the beginning of the calendar year with the Annunciation was symbolically appropriate on multiple levels. It tied together the Virgin's conception of Christ with the renewal and flowering of the earth at springtime. And it tied the beginning of each calendar year to a new moment in cosmic time: the ancient Annunciation to Mary demarcated the birth of a new era, a new imagining of time, the one which determined our calendars and within whose millennia we still live. The particular Florentine reverence for the Annunciate and its emphatic celebration of the Annunciation made Florence an especially auspicious location for new beginnings.

The Renaissance is probably the era during which the Western fantasy of time changed most dramatically. It is the period when the study of the secular history of the West first became important, when belief in the greater wisdom and capacity of our ancestors was first challenged, when the Golden Age moved from a remote past into a future which could be attained through steady progress, when innovation in an ever-changing world became a fact

---

59 Mary McCarthy, *The Stones of Florence* (New York: HBJ, 1959), pp. 18-19

of life, when men first began to care about being remembered by name by unborn generations.

Here in Florence the repeated announcements of a new birth proclaimed the opening of that narrow gate through which the rough beast of the modern world would be born.

* * *

When we first encounter the art of the early Italian Renaissance, its subject matter seems so sharply constricted by religious convention, especially when compared with the vast range of topics that have occupied artists in more recent times. Everywhere we look we find the same themes: Nativities, Crucifixions, and Madonnas with Bambinos. And what is more familiar than those Annunciations which were commissioned for every church, monastery, and chapel? An Angel delivers the News, and the Virgin receives it. What could be simpler? Yet, the closer we look at the imagery of these *Quattrocento* Annunciations, the more difficult it becomes to generalize about even this most common of Christian themes. Under careful scrutiny these familiar Annunciations reveal no less remarkable a range of variations than do the colors of roses, the sounds of spoken English, or the flavors of Italian regional cuisine.

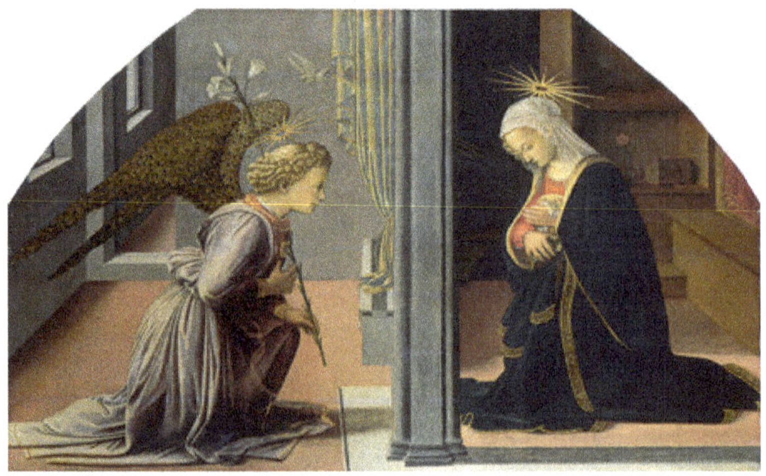

Fig. 33: Fra Filippo Lippi, *Annunciation*. National Gallery of Art, Washington, D.C.

Although the Renaissance artist worked with the inherited conventions of medieval religious traditions, he actively imagined them in new directions. Indeed, it is one of the hallmarks of the Renaissance imagination that so very little was ever simply accepted and merely repeated. Rather, traditions and sources were appropriated and then richly elaborated into a multitude of new forms. If for the medieval theologian the encounter of Gabriel and the Virgin had been an unequivocal cause for celebration, for the Italian Renaissance artist it was an event replete with nuance and ambiguity.

Because all Annunciation paintings are about the actual or attempted meeting of the human and the Divine, they typically have a dividing line to demarcate these realms, a threshold which clearly delimits and separates the Angel's space from Mary's. This separation is accomplished by various means: often a pillar or column stands between Gabriel and the Virgin; sometimes both figures are situated in different panels, as on the doors of diptyches; or, the distance of a courtyard comes between them; or, they are separated by furnishings or architectural elements. In every case the challenge of crossing of the threshold is always the reason for the Angel's visit. But the manner in which this threshold was approached and crossed became a subject of speculative inquiry, and we find Renaissance artists exploring the myriad of different ways in which the encounter between the Angel and Mary might have taken place.

* * *

Annunciation scenes are most commonly situated in an inner courtyard or garden, or a private chamber. Before we can appreciate the symbolic resonance of these different domestic settings, we need to consider the differences in the typical design of homes then and now. Bruce Cole informs us that: "Unlike our American contemporary houses surrounded by lawns... Renaissance homes, in general, turned inward, the walls enclosing a central courtyard that often supported an open loggia. This arrangement is an ancient one and affords the inhabitants light, air, and a safe protected place to enjoy the outdoors."[60]

---

60 Bruce Cole, *Italian Art:* 1250--1550 (New York: Harper & Row, 1987), p. 2.

Particularly in Florence the stone *palazzo* presented a formidable exterior that often gave little indication of its interior delights. As Mary McCarthy noted in *The Stones of Florence:* "Many Florentine palaces today are quite comfortable inside and possess pleasant gardens, but outside they bristle like fortresses or dungeons, and, to the passing tourist, their thick walls and bossy surfaces seem to repel the very notion of hospitality."[61] To deliteralize the architecture of such a home, we may consider a house symbolically as a structure within which we dwell. If the rough stone exterior suggests a defensive facade presented to the external world, then, as we move away from it, we come closer toward what the theologians of the period referred to as "the inner garden of the soul." The meeting with the Angel always takes place in a private, intimate interior where the Virgin is alone and far from worldly distractions.

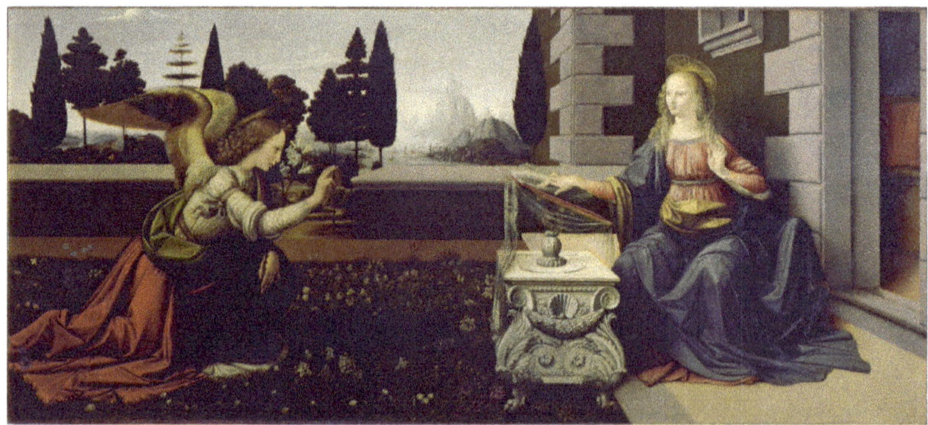

Fig. 34: Leonardo da Vinci, *Annunciation*. Uffizi Gallery, Florence.

Sometimes the Angel comes in glory as a Divine messenger; occasionally, he comes with simple, firm politeness to make an important announcement; or we may see him approaching awkwardly and tentatively as if embarrassed by these intimate matters; often, a deep humility and empathic tenderness seems to restrain him while the Divine Will inexorably impels him; sometimes he kneels and trembles before the sheer physicality of the Virgin; at times he beseeches the Virgin with his imploring gaze in the hope of obtain-

---

61 McCarthy, op. cit., p. 5.

ing her not-at-all-certain consent.

Meanwhile, across the threshold, the Madonna receives the influx of Divinity, often depicted as rays issuing from the parted beak of the Dove, or as the Angel's stream of golden words. We find certain Marys who hear the News with radiant gladness; some acknowledge their fate with humble gestures indicating acquiescence to the will of God; others turn away slightly with gestures of alarm or surprise appropriate to virginal modesty; some listen to the News as might a queen who receives periodic reports from an ambassador about recent events abroad; still others seem distressed or even somewhat dismayed by the sudden turn of events.

Particularly worth noting is an apocryphal variant of the Bible story which for some reason seems to return to prominence in Renaissance imaginings of the Annunciation. In the apocryphal *Protoevangelium of James* Mary has been sent home from the temple by the priests with purple and scarlet wool to spin. "One day as she was fetching water from the well she heard the voice of an angel hailing her as one blessed among women. Without having seen the angel, she hurried home and went on spinning."[62] In the Eastern Church this tale gave rise to occasional representations of the Annunciation as a 'serial' event. One scene

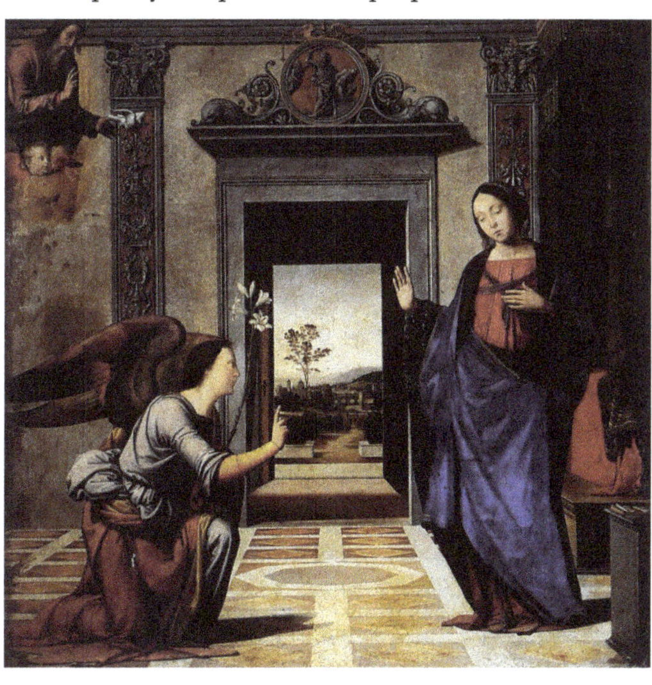

Fig. 35: Fra Bartolomeo, *Annuciation*. Duomo, Volterra.

---

62 Gertrude Schiller, *Iconography in Christian Art*, trans. by J. Seligman (Greenwich, CT: N.Y. Graphic Society, 1971), vol. 1, p. 34.

portrayed the Angel appearing to Mary who fails to notice him; a second showed his return in discouragement to his heavenly companions; and a final one depicted the Angel's return and his success in obtaining the Virgin's compliance.[63] The implications which may be teased out of the story are that Mary has struggled with her uncertainty before surrendering in humility, that at first she was not able even to see the Angel, that she had no faith in the validity of the initial encounter.[64] The serialized rendering of the event implied that the Annunciation is a process, and not a simple event. And it invited the Renaissance artist to wonder about the different stages of the process, what they implied, and how they might be represented.

The survival of this early apocryphal tradition seems evident in the sermons of popular preachers in the fifteenth century. Michael Baxandall brings to light the text of a sermon by Fra Roberto Caracciolo, a popular itinerant preacher of the period, in which he carefully distinguishes five phases to the process of the Angelic Colloquy: Disquiet, Reflection, Inquiry, Submission, and Merit.[65] These five conditions or states attributable to Mary recapitulate the Annunciate's initial response to the news, her inner struggle, and her final acquiescence. Baxandall suggests that many of the Annunciations which we see in fifteenth century painting directly reference one or another of these "states along the way." Though one might easily quibble with Baxandall's assignments of particular pictures to specific categories, the realization that such detailed distinctions existed in the theological commentaries of the period upon the Annunciation is an important one. It alerts us to the fact that we can expect to find no less subtlety among the visionary *Quattrocento* artists who also contemplated the same mystery.

With these initial remarks about the genre spread behind us as a backdrop, let us turn now to look at some of the different ways in which the Annunciation was imagined by one of the greatest of fifteenth century Florentine artists.

---

63 Ibid., p. 33.

64 Images of the infant Christ holding a yarn-winder directly reference this tradition.

65 Michael Baxandall, *Painting and Experience in Fifteenth Century Italy* (Oxford: Oxford University Press, 1988), pp. 49-56.

     ANNUNCIATIONS

Fra Angelico: THREE STAGES OF ANNUNCIATION

F*ra*, the short form of fratello, means brother in Italian. It was the name given to those who took vows and entered one of the monastic orders, thereby becoming a brother in Christ along with their fellow friars. Born around 1400, the man who began life as 'Guido di Pietro' took the name 'Fra Giovanni' (Brother Giovanni) when he joined the Dominican Order. He has, however, become known to posterity as 'Fra Angelico' following his description by a Dominican writer as "the angelic painter." In looking at his Annunciations, we shall see that he was well-named and was truly a brother to the angels. In Italy the honorific Beato (Blessed) has traditionally been added to his name and he was, in fact, beatified by the Church in 1983.[66]

The sophistication of Fra Angelico's images is often missed, largely due to the fact that commentators have long treated him as a simple, pious soul. Bernard Berenson, who was so often insightful in his comments on all sorts of matters, seems to have been largely incapable of appreciating Fra Angelico's particular genius, and he did much to set the modern agenda for the misreading of his work. In his enormously influential essays on the Florentine painters, written just before the turn of the 20th century, Berenson dismissed Fra Angelico with damning praise in a terse characterization that has continued to echo throughout subsequent treatments of the painter's work. To Berenson, although Fra Angelico's technique was progressive in certain respects, he remained mired in the naive religious fantasies of the Middle

---

66   Frederick Hartt, *Italian Renaissance Art* (Englewood Cliffs: Prentice Hall, 1987), p. 206.

Ages. "Simple though he was as a person", his sincerity and painterly skill touches us. Though he lacked any feeling for the "spiritually significant"(!), the "flower-like grace" and "childlike simplicity" of his work charms us into accepting "a world where real people are standing, sitting, and kneeling we know not, and care not, on what." In short, "He was the typical painter of the transition from Medieval to Renaissance."[67] And so, still today, one finds Fra Angelico included in that second-tier category of the "transitional painters", those odd ducks who hybridized progressive, modern technique with antiquated medieval superstition. And, as is the case with Gentile da Fabriano, those today who would affirm Fra Angelico's importance as a Renaissance painter always stress his technical and compositional skills while apologizing for his subject matter.

To see Fra Angelico in a different light we must first disabuse ourselves of the notion that there was something naive or childlike about the spiritual traditions of the late medieval world. Rather than projecting our naiveté upon the soul of such an artist, it would behoove us to recognize we have grown almost wholly ignorant of the spiritual realities that were the province of artistic visionaries like Fra Angelico. Hopefully, the subtlety and sophistication of his psychological explorations of spiritual life will become apparent as we look more closely at the work of this "simple soul."

* * *

Apart from its modest appearances on small reliquary panels, painted chests, and in manuscripts, the theme of the Annunciation appears three times in Fra Angelico's major surviving works: first in an altarpiece created for the church of S. Domenico in Cortona (c. 1432), and then, twice, in the frescoes painted at the Dominican monastery of San Marco in Florence (1441 and, c. 1450) where Fra Angelico resided.[68]

The Cortona altarpiece is breathtakingly beautiful, and here we have no doubts about the iconographic identification of theme: the image belongs

---

67 Bernard Berenson, *The Italian Painters of the Renaissance* (New York: Meridian, 1958), pp.77-78.

68 I am following the chronologies and attributions proposed by John Pope-Hennessy in his *Fra Angelico* (Florence: SCALA, 1981).

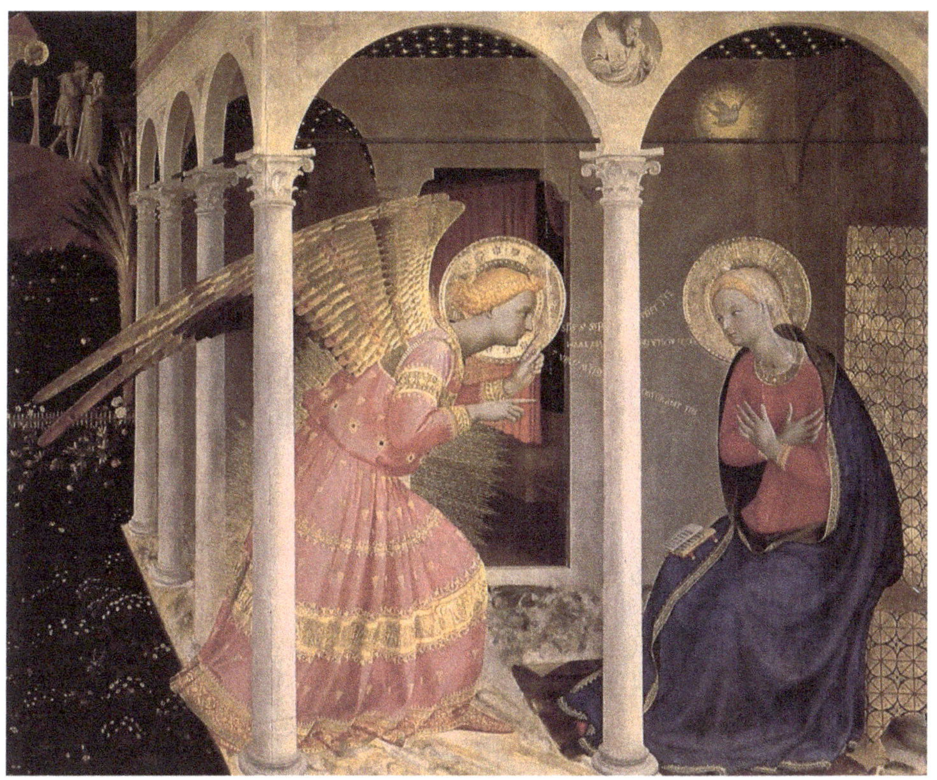

Fig. 36: Fra Angelico, *Annunciation*. Diocesan Museum, Cortona.

unambiguously to the genre of Annunciation. But, when we turn to look at the San Marco frescoes, we are less sure. We search in vain for any sign of the Dove or of those beams of light that reach Mary from the Angel or directly from the hand of God. In the absence of these traditional symbols of the miraculous transmission of spirit, we may wonder if we are justified in reading these frescoes as Annunciation images. I believe that we are, but with the caveat that we shouldn't mistake them for celebratory, epiphanic images. They belong, rather, to the early phase of the event, that stage of "disquiet" or doubt which derives from the apocryphal strand of the tradition that we glanced at earlier.

It will be helpful before proceeding further to discard the notion that the differences between Fra Angelico's several treatments of this event reflect the artist's progressive search for the most effective composition, i.e., his experiments in "trying to get it right." The Cortona painting, certainly the most glorious of his Annunciations and one of Fra Angelico's greatest works, is the earliest of the trio. That should be sufficient to discourage us from searching for a pattern of progressive development in this set of images. Rather than looking for signs of the artist's painterly "evolution," let's look directly at the images to see what they might tell us about their *raison d'être*.

Let's begin by orienting ourselves in relation to the physical placement and functions of the three images. I will be referring to them as the Cortona, the Cell and the Corridor *Annunciations*.

As noted above, the Cortona panel was originally painted as an altarpiece. Because the altar is the sacred hearth of the church—the place of ritual communion between heaven and earth—a church's resources were often spent most liberally on securing a work of high quality for the altar. The Annunciation was an ever-popular and appropriate theme for altarpieces, since it portrayed one of the most dramatic instances of communion between heaven and earth. Though we will soon look at the Cortona *Annunciation* in greater detail, for the moment I'd just like to note that its imagery is perfectly suited to its location and ritual function.

But, what about the San Marco images? What sense can we make here of the inter-relationship between physical placement, ritual uses, and the specific qualities of the images?

> Those who know the frescoes in the cells upstairs only from photographs miss their essential character. In relation to the rooms on whose walls they are painted, most of the scenes (and all of those associable with Angelico) are relatively large in scale. In each case the scene is placed on the window wall opposite the entrance to the cell, and the wall thus contains two apertures, one opening on the physical and the other on the spiritual world. Dominating their austere surroundings, they were designed as aids to meditation, not as decoration, and were intended to secure for the mysteries they described a place in the forefront of the friar's mind by keeping them constantly before his eyes. In this respect they form a spiritual exercise. The cursory examination of the frescoes which we make as we walk from cell to cell today is the exact opposite

of the use for which they were designed.[69]

So speaks that most unmystical of art historians, John Pope-Hennessy, in this lucid and insightful passage. Then, having shown us the royal road by means of which to approach the uses of art at San Marco, he proceeds to ignore this fact almost entirely as he comments upon the particular images. It is not that Pope-Hennessy's readings are cursory, only that they concern themselves almost entirely with typical art historical problems of dating and attribution while entirely ignoring the spiritual dimension of the paintings before our eyes. Nevertheless, following Pope-Hennessy's lead, we will consider the frescoes in the context of some sort of spiritual exercise, and see if the images themselves can show us what sort of spiritual exercise might be involved.

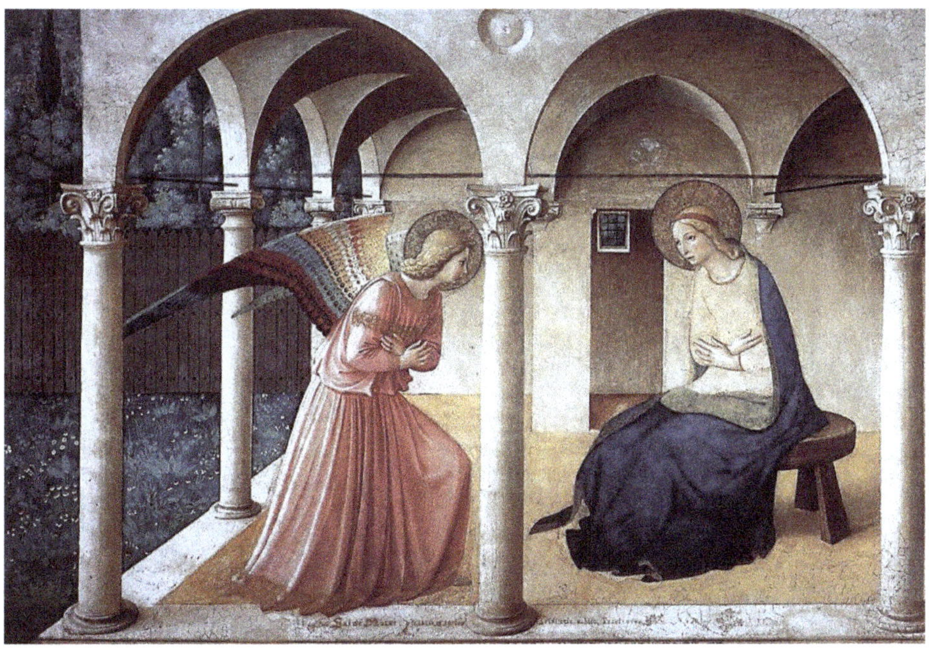

Fig. 37: Fra Angelico, *Annunciation* (corridor). San Marco Monastery, Florence.

The Corridor *Annunciation* at San Marco shows Mary seated on a plain wooden stool looking toward the Angel before her. The inscription at the bottom of the painting reads: "As you venerate, while passing before it, this

---

69 Ibid., pp. 39–41.

figure of the intact Virgin, beware lest you forget to say a Hail Mary."[70] The fresco confronts us at the top of the stairs as you climb to the upper floor and provides instructions for a proper salutation. This much has remained unchanged from the days when the friars would ascend from their communal space on the ground floor where they socialized with others to their private cells on the upper floor where they kept silence.

In the monastic setting of San Marco, we should consider that this daily act of physical climbing may also have been imbued with spiritual significance. Climbing, as metaphor, is a recurring image of spiritual questing in a thousand stories, and, in particular, it is prominent in the one story known by every Tuscan: Dante's *Divine Comedy*. I'd like to pause here and spend some time with Dante because I believe that he will be helpful not only in addressing the particulars of the images, but, also, in orienting us to the religious universe within which such images had their place and upon which they ultimately depend for simple intelligibility.

THE CORNICE OF PRIDE

We may recall that once Dante and Virgil leave Hell, they begin the ascent of the mountain of Purgatory. Here they pass bands of pilgrims who circle at each level until they are ready to climb to the next. The episode which is relevant to our purposes occurs in Canto X when our pilgrims arrive at the Cornice of Pride, that level where penitents expiate their earthly sins of vanity, arrogance, and over-reaching ambition. On the way in, Dante notices three elaborate carvings etched into the marble walls of the mountain pass, drawn directly by the hand of God. Dante struggles to find words to convey their extraordinarily lifelike qualities: the figures seem almost capable of movement, and he can very nearly hear the sounds of instruments and smell the fragrance of the incense burning.[71]

Each of the three images on the wall, drawn respectively from Christian, He-

---

70 Frederick Hartt's translation of the Latin, op. cit., p. 211.

71 I have used Allen Mandelbaum's translation of Dante's *Divine Comedy* (New York: Bantam, 1983) in 3 vols. Ref. is to Canto X: 28-93.

brew, and pagan sources, depicts an act of exemplary humility. The classical image shows the Emperor Trajan on his way to battle descending from his charger to address the pressing needs of an elderly widow. The Old Testament image represents King David dancing with joyful abandon when the Ark of the Covenant is recovered and brought into Jerusalem, while Saul's daughter scornfully watches his unseemly behavior. And the New Testament image depicts Mary receiving the news from the Angel and submitting to the will of God in utmost humility.

In this remarkable sequence, Dante not only presents the vividly animated image as the ideal of art, but he also tells us that this is the kind of art which God himself has created to aid the soul on its journey. What an extraordinary invitation to painters and sculptors to attempt the creation of such art!—along with the religious sanction and rationale for so doing. When we consider the profusion of strategies among the artists of succeeding generations to enliven and animate their work, it seems clear that that the poet's challenge was not left unanswered.

We may assume that the Annunciation image, like the other images of humility created by God, has been provided for the pilgrim's edification as he or she progresses toward spiritual realization through the surrender of egoic pride. But there is some question as to how these images could be helpful. Because, as soon as Dante and Virgil pass this point, they come upon a group of penitents who dwell on this terrace, and they find them bent almost double under the weight of huge rocks which they carry upon their backs. The weight of the stones is proportionate to the size of their egos, and it keeps them walking with their heads bent to the ground.[72]

The pilgrims are thus physically incapable of seeing those images of exemplary humility which model the state of being which their souls are seeking. All they can see as they walk along is another series of images which have been carved into the pavement beneath their feet: images of the destruction and devastation caused by unmastered pride. They are shown Lucifer falling from heaven, the Titans crushed in their rebellion against the Gods, Nimrod

---

72 Ibid., Canto X: 112-139.

the builder standing in the confusion of the Tower of Babel, and so forth. The pilgrims contemplate these cautionary images, and recite their prayers as they proceed to circle round and round the terrace.

Now, the question arises: How does one ever move on from here? We know that no soul remains eternally ignorant, that all the penitents eventually find their way to the Light, but where is the path that leads us onward beyond the Cornice of Pride?[73]

Since Dante is speaking about a certain state of the soul, it may be helpful to consider the situations he describes from a more familiar contemporary vantage point, namely, the arena of psychotherapy, within which so much of our modern soul work is done.

In the infernal world all the people who Dante and Virgil meet are victims, people who had no choice, poor creatures who got sent to Hell by some mistake, and who remain as self-righteous, obsessed, and as blindly self-deceiving in death as they were in life. There is the lovely Francesca who remains more deeply enamored of her role as a soap-opera heroine than of her lover or her life; the great Farinata degli Uberti, who still lives entirely in his moments of battle glory and seems not to notice that he is dead; and the frightful Ugolino, whose every waking moment is devoted to slaking his insatiable desire for vengeance, gnawing on the skull of his enemy. Dante the poet depicts the entrapment of these creatures in their self-created hells, while Dante the pilgrim (and, by extension, the reader) is challenged to see through their stories, to avoid becoming complicit and "co-dependent" in their dramas, and to keep moving (as Virgil repeatedly urges him to do).

In Purgatory, on the other hand, in contemporary psychological idiom we might say that the pilgrims at this stage of their journey are comparable to those who have entered therapy. In this respect they differ entirely from the souls whom we have just met in Hell. In Purgatory we meet the people who have begun to take responsibility for their situations and who are willing to work on their problems.

---

73 In my reading of these Cantos I'm indebted to Professors John Tallmadge and Joe Meeker of The Union Institute for their thoughts about Dante's therapy of the imagination.

These are the troubled souls who have joined AA, or a Twelve-Step program, or gone to seek the assistance of a counselor. As every therapist will confirm, the problems that clients present—the ruts of lusts, greeds, and gluttonies-—are extremely tenacious and are very often accompanied by a sense of going in circles. Dante's Canto suggests that this repetitive circling is actually an integral part of the soul's journey through Purgatory—and, by implication, of the phenomenology of therapy, as well.

One of the tools of therapy which Dante's pilgrims use to full advantage is what we today call "negative re-enforcement." Bent down by the weight of the stones they carry, looking down continually at the images of the destructive effects of rampant arrogance and egotism, they work to restrain those impulses which could again lead them astray. But is there no end to this work of resisting negative behavior? It would seem that the images of humility which were placed at the entrance are representations of the desired state of consciousness which the pilgrims seek. Yet how are they ever to consider these positive images if they are constantly bent low focused on their problems? There is only one way: by closing their eyes, turning their attention away from the external images, and contemplating in the mind's eye those images of the state of being to which they aspire.

It is Virgil who initially sets Dante the task of looking down at the images of pride below his feet, and it is again Virgil who tells him when it is time to leave off. As he looks up, Dante beholds an angel approaching him who touches his forehead lightly with his wing and points the way to the next level.[74] Virgil's actions imply that there is an appropriate time for contemplating the negativity in which we have been enmeshed, as well as a point of diminishing returns. What is needed to move on past this stage of life—the stage of diligently struggling against our negative habits—is the realization that the soul can move us through the power of internal representations. The travails of Purgatory are ultimately labors in the service of vision, achieved through a therapy of the imagination.

The powerful, emblematic images of humility which would allow the soul

---

74 Ibid., Canto XII: 97-118.

to continue its journey were presumably visible to each pilgrim upon his or her entry to this plateau, before they were bent low with the burdens they carry. Such images are given by God, i.e., they are archetypally present in the imagination. What is required of our pilgrims now is, first, to realize that they already have knowledge of the state they seek, and, then, by recalling it internally, to allow the touch of the Angel's wing to open the inner eye.

THE CORRIDOR ANNUNCIATION

If we return now to Mary and the Angel waiting patiently in the corridor at the top of the stairs at San Marco, it should be clear that we are looking at a prelude to that state of illumined vision and communion with the Angel which we find represented in the Cortona *Annunciation*. Here we see Mary portrayed in that stage of the spiritual journey which we've been discussing as "purgatorial. If we read the image in these terms, then the obligatory greeting to Mary ("As you venerate, while passing before it, this figure of the intact Virgin, beware lest you forget to say a Hail Mary") honors her in her struggle, rather than in her ultimate realization.

William Hood has noted that here "for the only time in his [Angelico's] life he showed Mary dressed in the black and white habit that she had given to the Preachers as a sign of her favor."[75] Which is to say, she is represented as one of them. This suggests that Mary's depiction in this image serves to exemplify for the friar, as penitent, his own tribulations, to mirror for him the truth of his existential situation.

Apart from any evidence we may deduce from the image itself, we have information from another source which supports our reading of Mary as an exemplar of the pilgrim on his or her spiritual journey. Frederick Hartt informs us of the fact that the Dominican theologian, St. Antonine, actually spoke of the Virgin as a representative figure of the seeker:

> St. Antonine claims that the true penitent can identify himself with the
> Virgin, and that through creating "the garden of the soul" the Christ

---

75 William Hood, *Fra Angelico at San Marco* (New Haven & London: Yale Univ. Press, 1993), p. 272.

Child can be born again in our hearts. (Antonine derived this doctrine from the teaching of his great mentor and his predecessor as prior of San Domenico in Fiesole, Giovanni Dominici.)[76]

Antonine, who later became Archbishop of Florence, was one of the most important Florentine theologians of the century.[77] And since Fra Angelico came to San Marco from San Domenico where Antonine had been his mentor, we can be quite certain that he would have been familiar with this teaching.

In terms of St. Antonine's metaphor, I believe that the Corridor fresco shows us the Virgin before the Christ Child has been born in her heart. One might even surmise that the very prospect of such a thing fills her with misgiving. Once we surrender the preconception that this is another splendid celebration of the Annunciation by a simple painter of sweet pieties, we can begin to notice the telling details. In fact, it is difficult to look attentively at this fresco without feeling the distress present in the image.

Mary has the look of a startled fawn. She appears tentative, distraught, even a bit afraid. Her focus is ambiguous; what alone is certain is that she is not making eye contact with the angel. The angel, though showing restraint, looks directly at Mary's heart with importunity and searching intensity. Yet though she looks toward him, it's really not clear whether or not she actually sees him. There is no sign of recognition in her face, no acknowledgment of his presence. Compare this with the look exchanged between Mary and the Angel in the Cortona *Annunciation*. There, as in virtually all the other images of Annunciation which Fra Angelico painted—apart from the San Marco frescoes— the sense of communion, especially the direct eye contact, is clear and unmistakable.[78]

---

76 Hartt, op. cit., p. 220.

77 John Shearman in *Only Connect...: Art and the Spectator in the Italian Renaissance* (Princeton: Princeton Univ. Press, 1992) p. 72, describes St. Antonine as "the greatest and most practical Florentine theologian of the period."

78 Cf. the Missal no. 558 illustration, the Reliquary Panel Annunciation, and the Annunciata Silver Chest images. In the Missal illustration, where the Angel is above Mary's head, she looks upward sharply to gaze directly at the Angel.

We have already noted the absence of the Dove in both of the San Marco frescoes. Also significant is the absence of a small red flame on the Angel's forehead above his third eye. The Corridor fresco is the only one of Angelico's images of Annunciation in which the Angel has been depicted without this symbol of imaginative vision.

In the Cortona *Annunciation*, Mary sits upon a glorious throne draped in gold cloth; here she sits upon a hard wooden stool, not comfortably, but on its edge, on edge. In place of a spacious apartment with scarlet draperies open to the starry dome of heaven, Mary at San Marco has only a bare, shadowy cell. Here Fra Angelico uses architectural design to emphasize the cramped quality of Mary's quarters. Though he was certainly a skilled, early practitioner of perspective painting, Fra Angelico always subordinates mere perspective to his more important goal of representing psychological space, the state of the soul.

Like Alice in Wonderland who has eaten something that's made her larger, Mary has been cramped into this all-too-small space in the right half of the painting. Her halo, which is larger than the Angel's, extends even above the tops of the foliated capitals of the columns. And whereas the Angel is portrayed in the spaciousness of multiple archways in a receding arcade, Mary is shown right up against the wall, which has been deliberately brought forward. To further support the sense of claustrophobic containment, the small decorative garden fence of the Cortona *Annunciation* is here replaced by a high enclosure of tightly spaced pickets.

These contrasts serve to make Mary's constriction even more emphatic. How can someone her size possibly fit through that aperture in the wall which opens into her dark, small cell? The barred window in the image is very much like the windows one still sees today in the friars' cells at San Marco. Though the cells are of various sizes, none spacious by modern suburban standards, none are so tiny as that suggested in the image before us. Mary's cell is here presented as metaphor: the confined soul in its chrysalis state before it has found its wings and discovered that it can be king, or queen, in a nutshell.

By placing this image on the corridor wall at the top of the stairs for the friars to pass on their daily rounds, Fra Angelico may have been directly inspired by Dante's Tenth Canto of the *Purgatorio*. In any event, what is almost certain is that through the placement of this particular image in its specific location, he was defining San Marco as a type of Purgatory, a realm of seekers.

While only a few of the images in the San Marco series were created entirely by Angelico's own hand, all of the images were apparently part of a program designed by and carried out under his direction.[79] The forty-odd images in the cells and corridors both represent and facilitate the work of spiritual transformation. And it is apparent that they represent different stages of the work.

The Corridor fresco invokes the friar as novice at the beginning of his journey: ill at ease, wary of his surroundings, feeling confined by his cloistered life and his small cell, burdened by a halo larger than his Angel's, and urged to salute a painted image of the Holy Mother every time he goes up and down the stairs. We must assume that such a friar might, at some point, begin to see this image of Mary no longer merely as an object of reverence before whom he must humble himself, but, rather, as a mirror of his own situation, as the embodiment of the state his soul. Having once seen himself and recognized his reflection, he would have met the first challenge of the spiritual life—to begin the work from the place where we actually live.

THE CELL ANNUNCIATION

If we turn now in our explorations to the Cell fresco, I believe we will see that it presents us with a vision of Mary midway between novice and Annunciate. Here Mary's look of discomfort has been replaced by a more contained and contemplative gaze. She is praying, her focus turned gently inward, wearing the plainest of clothes in this simplest and barest of rooms. It is as if during this period of meditative work, everything non-essential has been removed.

---

79 "That the class of frescoes in the cells was ideated by Angelico and that Angelico himself supervised the decoration of the convent is not open to doubt...." Pope-Hennessy, op. cit., p. 29.

The angel, whose visionary flame now appears, stares directly at Mary's brow,
which is bathed in light. In all
the versions of the event which
Fra Angelico rendered, the Angel is always attentively present
and focused directly upon Mary,
whether acknowledged or not.
It's as if the Angel is always there
and has the patience to wait a
lifetime for his presence to be
noticed. In this sense the "appearance" of the Angel would really be no more, and no less, than
an awakening to his presence.

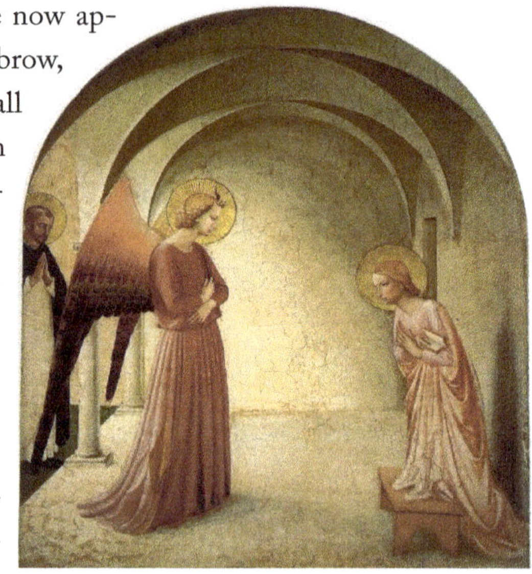

Fig. 38: Fra Angelico, *Annunciation* (cell).
San Marco Monastery, Florence.

One has the sense here that Mary is coming close to meeting the Angel, but
that it hasn't happened just yet. If we compare the haloes in our three images,
we can see that in the Corridor fresco, the haloes are a dull, flat ochre color
with Mary's being slightly darker and more brownish than the Angel's. In
the Cell fresco, the haloes are brighter and more yellowish. In the Angel's
halo we see rays sharply articulated, and we can see them also present in
Mary's halo, but not yet so clearly defined. Finally, in the Cortona *Annunciation*, both haloes have become luminous plates of bright, shining gold and
the beams of the Angel's aura radiate in all directions.

In the Cortona *Annunciation* we are invited in various ways to perceive the
event through the eye of the Angel. Here we enter a timeless visionary landscape where Isaiah projects animatedly from the spandrel, the Dove hovers
overhead, and Adam and Eve reenact their exile in the background while
Mary undertakes their redemption as she meets the Angel face to face. "The
palm tree at the end of the mind, Beyond the last thought" stands in the
garden.

The Angel's stream of golden words, like his hands, point upward and downward at the same time, affirming the relation between what is above and what

is below, and saying: "The Holy Spirit shall come upon thee, and the power of the highest shall overshadow thee." The upside-down placement of Mary's words is, at a practical level, a means of directing her acceptance speech to the Angel. But since we are far from the realm of practical exigencies in this land of gold, we might take it a step further. We could also read it as a hint of that inversion of perspective we experience when we move between worlds. Just as Dante realized upon entering into Purgatory that everything in Hell had been upside-down, we catch a glimpse in this inverted script of how our earthly reality might appear to Angelic eyes.

* * *

The approach to Fra Angelico's work which divides his "progressive" technique from his "archaic" subject matter fails us in another important way. It falsely implies that the two are separable and unrelated, and thus obscures the extent to which Fra Angelico's innovative modern techniques were deliberately and skillfully utilized to support the spiritual themes of his art.

Thanks to Fra Angelico's careful use of perspective construction, we are able to identify a vanishing point in each of the three Annunciations that we have examined. When we do so, astonishing as it may seem, we discover that the location of the vanishing point in each painting has thematic significance. In the Corridor *Annunciation* the vanishing point is the barred window of the tiny cell in the background. In the Cell *Annunciation* the vanishing point is in the space midway between Mary and the Angel. And in the Cortona *Annunciation* the vanishing point of the painting is the face of the Angel.

Now the vanishing point in perspective construction, as we know, necessarily defines a corresponding point of view for the spectator. The virtual space of the image can only be entered, without distortion, from a specific vantage point in the viewer's actual space. And, perceived metaphorically, this implied vantage point provides the viewer with an appropriate perspective upon the unfolding events. The different vanishing points in each of our three Annunciations posit the existence of three distinct viewers, each one seeing from a psychically distinct viewpoint, and each finding his or her own perspective mirrored in Mary's represented state of being.[80] How eloquently these shifts of point of view mirror the differing vantage points of the seeker's soul! Whereas the rules of perspective construction are unchanging, there is all the difference in the world between an Annunciation perceived from the transcendent perspective of the Angel and an Annunciation seen from the claustrophobic perspective of a confined soul.

* * *

In working with the conventional theme of the Annunciation, Renaissance artists like Fra Angelico try to reimagine the deepest meanings of the Angel's salutation to Mary. Their work is to take a literal event (an Angel told a young Jewish girl that she would become the mother of God) and to recast it in its essential import, to discern the undercurrents of psychological and spiritual significance which flow through the story. This act of "seeing through", as James Hillman has described it, cracks the shell of stories which have hardened into dogma, turns the opaque historicity of religious events into lived experience, and enables the soul to situate itself anew within tradition in meaningful ways.

---

80 The thematic use of perspective by Fra Angelico is not limited to his Annunciations. So, for example, the face of the enthroned Madonna serves as the vanishing point in the San Marco Altarpiece which amplifies her traditional role as mediatrix.

Fra Filippo Lippi:
THE MONK AND
THE MADONNA

Having explored several of Fra Angelico's Annunciation images, let's turn our attention now to the work of Fra Filippo Lippi, another great monastic painter who thrived in mid-century Florence. As different one from the other as day from night, these two artists may fairly be said to define the extreme limits of religious reverence and irreverence in 15th century Florentine painting.

Fra Angelico's work reveals a coherent conception of the Annunciation as a graduated process where the different images of the event that he depicted may be understood to represent phases of a spiritual unfolding. By contrast, Lippi's Annunciations dazzle us by the sheer richness and variety of their motif, and one looks in vain for a philosophical or theological framework into which they might neatly fit. The settings where the event takes place and the cast of supporting characters who appear on stage change repeatedly, as do the conceptions of the Madonna and the processes by which the divine impregnation is imagined to occur. Here the beams of light sent by God touch her shoulder, there they seem aimed at her heart, elsewhere they are directed toward her womb.[81] Indeed, among Lippi's surviving Annuncia-

---

81 In a fascinating look, in two parts, at Lippi's *Annunciation* in the National Gallery in London, Leo Steinberg and Samuel G. Edgerton discuss Lippi's possible references to Baconian visual theory in the manner in which impregnation is represented. Edgerton acknowledges that the aperture in Mary's tunic is oval and not circular as we might expect if Lippi were referencing the pupil of the eye. Edgerton argues, however, that to represent a round hole would have been "brazenly suggestive." The reader is left wondering why a circular shape would be considered a more explicit vaginal reference than an oval one. This argument apart, the articles are delightful displays of erudition, and Steinberg's contains a useful historical survey of theological approaches to the operational problem of how the conception of Christ was achieved. Leo Steinberg "How Shall This Be? Part I" in <u>Artibus et Historiae</u> vol. 8/16 (1987), pp. 25-44, Samuel Y. Edgerton, Jr. "How Shall This Be? Part II", pp. 45-53.

tions we find an extraordinary range of approaches to the contemplation and representation of this event, including to some of its more troubling aspects.

* * *

Unlike Fra Angelico, who took his vows willingly in his adult years, Filippo Lippi was constrained as an adolescent to enter monastic life. Whereas Angelico was drawn powerfully toward the sublimity of spiritual life, it is difficult to imagine anyone less temperamentally suited than Lippi for the religious discipline of monastic life. Fra Angelico's very name reflects an ongoing process of spiritual transmutation. He shed his given name (Guido di Pietro), along with his earthly attachments, when he took his vows and became Fra Giovanni. A fellow Dominican soon after dubbed him "Angelico" and his countrymen have referred to him as Beato Angelico (Blessed Angelico) since Renaissance times (even though his formal beatification occurred only in recent decades). In the years ahead, if an art-loving Cardinal from central Italy someday becomes Pope, there's an outside chance that Guido di Pietro may become known to posterity as Saint Angelico.

In sharpest contrast to this continuous process of nominative sublimation, Filippo Lippi simply became Fra Filippo Lippi when he took his vows—apparently a highly unusual circumstance. And although he left monastic life in his later years, he continued to sign himself as "Brother Filippo" to the end of his days. These details imply a certain fixity of character, a distinctive style of being oneself in relation to the institutions of religious life. And from this resolute tension between character and life circumstances there emerged a unique artistic vision.

If up to this point we have spoken hardly a word about the personal lives of the artists, the silence has not been due to a dogmatic belief that an artist's life must be ignored in a critical approach to his art. Rather, it's because we are precluded from exploring the interplay between the lives and the works of the artists in this period by our profound ignorance of the details of their lives. In the early decades of the *Quattrocento*, much painterly work was still unsigned. The painter remained, in his own eyes and in the eyes of his patrons, more of a skilled craftsman than a "creative artist" in our modern sense of the term. No one felt it was worth the effort to document the efforts of such men apart from receipts for labor and expenses. So, very little substantive information about the lives of the early Renaissance artists has come down to us. And, when we do reflect upon what we know about men like Brunelleschi, Donatello, or Fra Angelico, there is little reason to assume that they used their art as a vehicle for personal expression. John Shearman's comment about the eroticism of Donatello's later statue of *David* generalizes well: "If I thought that the bronze *David* told one something about Donatello's private life, I would say so even on a Sunday afternoon, but I think the opposite."[82]

Even in more fertile terrains than that offered by the early Renaissance, studying the artist's life to "explain" his work rarely leads the spectator into a deeper encounter with the paintings themselves. Instead, it usually tends to provide the viewer with handy clichés about the painter's madness or his homosexuality or his unhappy childhood. Armed with these catch phrases, the viewer can defend himself or herself from any active engagement with the work itself. In this respect much of the psycho-biographical writing about art has done little more to animate the viewer's experience of the image than would a Morellian analysis of earlobes.

Nevertheless, these caveats aside, the case of Fra Filippo Lippi presents an exception to the general rule, and to enter into the spirit of his art we need to pay attention to Filippo the man. Jeffrey Ruda, the foremost scholar today of Lippi's life and achievements and a sensitive reader of his work, has drawn attention to the remarkable fact that Fra Filippo has emerged as a colorful character in an age when only the ghostliest outlines of his peers have survived:

> A personality this strong would demand attention in any art-historical context. In the early Renaissance, where personal biography is seldom more than a shadow flickering through the dust of an archive, it can be intoxicating. The romantic stories would not have persisted if the art

---

82 John Shearman, *Only Connect...: Art and the Spectator in the Italian Renaissance* (Princeton: Princeton Univ. Press, 1992), p. 25.

had not made them seem plausible.[83]

Lippi the man somehow managed to leave behind enough of a trail to capture the fantasies of later generations. His imagined life has been memorialized in fiction, poetry, and painting, and his work marks the advent of a new level of interplay between the subjects of painting and the artist as a living personality.

When we look at his paintings, we become aware of his earthly personality in its relation to the sacred in a way that has no parallels in the earlier history of art. Late medieval and early Renaissance artists occasionally identify themselves by signing their names on the backs of paintings or upon their frames; or a prominent artist like Duccio might identify himself discretely in decorative script along a stair-step. But no one prior to Lippi draws attention to himself as deliberately within the fictive reality of the painting itself as does Lippi. He paints his own name on a tag that he adds to the base of the throne in the Tarquinia *Madonna and Child;* he carves it on an ax handle in the *Adoration in the Woods;* and he even makes daring cameo appearances in some of his formal genre paintings. Lippi's relation to his work and the play of his own perspective on the topics he renders are thus thematized: his signature presence exists as a dimension of the paintings themselves, actually and metaphorically. Since he *invites* us to think about him when we look at his paintings, it's only reasonable to turn to biography as our royal road for further exploration of Fra Filippo's work.

VASARI'S LIVES

The major source of information about the life of Fra Filippo Lippi, as for so many of the other Renaissance artists, is Giorgio Vasari's *Lives of The Artists,* first published in 1550.[84] Vasari's work is invaluable because it is often the primary and sometimes the sole source for basic knowledge about the great Renaissance artists and their works. Nevertheless, where modern scholars

---

83 Jeffrey Ruda, *Fra Filippo Lippi: Life and Work* (London: Phaidon, 1993) p. 10.

84 The edition I have used is Giorgio Vasari, *Lives of the Artists,* trans. G. Bull (London: Penguin Books, 1988) in 2 vols. The life of Fra Filippo Lippi is found in Vol.1, pp. 214-223.

have been able to find other sources of documentary information, Vasari's work has occasionally been shown to be either factually incorrect or misleading. Indeed, finding a factual error in one of Vasari's Lives has almost become a rite of passage for aspiring Renaissance art historians. Hence, in those areas where Vasari remains a sole source, scholars are both immensely grateful for the information he provides and bitterly resentful of the fact that we can't be absolutely certain of almost anything he says.

The present essay does not seek either to affirm or dispute the facts of Vasari's treatment of Lippi's life. Instead, we will approach Vasari from another perspective entirely: we will treat Vasari as a collector and transmitter of legends, a secular successor to the chroniclers of the lives of the saints. If we approach him not as a flawed historian, but, rather, as a faithful hagiographer to the artists, we may be able to perceive the value of his work in a new light.

The Lives of the Artists, then, may be seen as a secular sequel to that thirteenth century classic, *The Golden Legend*, which collected many of the apocryphal stories about saints and biblical characters that had made the rounds in the immediately preceding centuries. What the *Lives* really gives us, apart from its factual information about the Florentine art scene, are folktales about the great artists who lived in the previous century. Composed of an assortment of actual facts, half-truths, honest mistakes, and embellishments, Vasari preserves for us those stories which had sufficient vitality to persist in the public mind between the time of the artists' deaths and his own day. These fantasies about an artist's life and work which have passed into history certainly can not be confused with biographical facts. Yet, sometimes, key insights into the enduring value of an artist's legacy may be gleaned from the legends which have been preserved through the centuries. These tell us something about the projected values which the artist has constellated and carried for posterity.

*   *   *

The facts of Filippo Lippi's life given to us by Vasari which have been confirmed by other documentary sources may be briefly summarized as follows.[85]

---

85 The documentable facts of Lippi's biography are given in Ruda, op. cit., pp. 22-43.

Filippo was born the son of a butcher in a working class district of Florence. Later orphaned, he was subsequently enrolled as a friar in the Carmelite Convent. At some point he became romantically involved with a nun with whom he had a son, Filippino, who became a distinguished painter in his own right. In the later decades of his life he was one of the most highly regarded of all Tuscan painters. He was buried in Spoleto, in a church where he had painted extensive frescoes, within a marble tomb commissioned by Lorenzo de' Medici.

From additional sources, we know that he was probably fifteen when he took his vows; that the first documented works which show him in full command of his artistic skills date from the late 1430s; that after resolving a legal dispute during the course of which he was imprisoned and tortured, he withdrew from monastic life; that he probably received a dispensation from the Pope to marry and legally adopt his child, and that he died in 1469.

So much for the matters of record. It was not these simple facts, but the apocryphal anecdotes about Lippi's personality which Vasari provided that effectively launched the career of Filippo Lippi as legend. The Italian art historian, Gloria Fossi, a recent scholar of Lippi's work, notes that: "Vasari succeeded in creating a legend that is still difficult today to dispel (for example, there is even a Norwegian Rock group that has taken on the name of the sensuous monk)."[86]

One striking thing about Vasari's anecdotes is their thematic consistency. Vasari paints a picture of Lippi as an artist with a strongly passionate nature whose art plays a distinctive role in relation to his erotic life. We learn, for example, that sometimes Lippi turns to his art when his sexual desires are thwarted:

> It is said that Fra Filippo was so lustful that he would give anything to enjoy a woman he wanted if he thought he could have his way; and if he couldn't buy what he wanted, then he would cool his passion by painting her portrait and reasoning with himself.[87]

---

86 Gloria Fossi, *Filippo Lippi*, trans. by L. Pelletti (Florence: SCALA, 1989), p. 26.

87 Vasari, *Lives*, p. 216.

     FRA FILIPPO LIPPI: THE MONK AND THE MADONNA

While we often think of Freud in connection with the notion of sublimation, we might note that Vasari in the sixteenth century is telling us quite plainly how Lippi attempted to sublimate physical desire through his art. But this strategy was apparently not always successful. Once, Vasari confides, Cosimo de' Medici tried to lock up Filippo in an upper-story room so that he would concentrate exclusively on his painting. But tormented by his unsatisfied lusts, Filippo cut up the bedsheets and made himself a rope ladder to escape, and he spent several days carousing before he was located by his patron.[88] It seems that the restive Filippo was not constitutionally disposed toward continence nor toward the imposition of any externally mandated discipline. As a young monk, Vasari tells us, he was unwilling to do anything but draw. And so, eventually, the friars permitted him to specialize and develop his talent. His art, like his romantic life, seems rooted in a headstrong, instinctual nature.

What emerges consistently from all these apocryphal tales is the remarkable interchange and interplay of erotic and artistic energies. The most dramatic instance is recounted in Vasari's story about how Filippo met Lucrezia Buti, the nun who became his lover and then his wife.[89] Vasari claims that while Filippo was involved in painting an altarpiece for the nuns at Santa Margherita, he became enamored of a young nun whom he saw in the convent. In order to get closer to her, he somehow managed to persuade the Mother Superior to allow Lucrezia to pose as the model for the Madonna in the painting. Later that year, little Filippino was born.

Step back and think about this for just a moment in the context of the Renaissance impulse to take the sacred images and dramas of the medieval world and bring them down to earth: A wolfish monk in painterly garb invites a nun to portray the Mother of God so that he might become her lover! Was there ever a more brazen act of radical de-sublimation in the history of art?

---

88 This is the scene which caught Robert Browning's fancy and with which he begins his marvelous paean to Lippi's lust for life.

89 Ibid., p. 217-218.

Is it not the extraordinary richness of this interplay of the sacred and profane which lies at the heart of Lippi's legend and sustains its enduring vitality?

* * *

Now one of the reasons that artists continually fall in love with their models is that the model becomes the carrier of the artist's projected ideal; in Jung's terms, she becomes an *anima* figure. Before artists began to use actual living models, this obviously wasn't an issue. No one would ever suggest that the Byzantine icon painters had affairs with their models because it is obvious that there were never any sitters for their stylized portraits of the Madonna or the Saints. The medieval artist's love for the Madonna was always a sublimated love because it was imaginally conceived and imaginally consummated.

When we cross the threshold in the early *Quattrocento* into the use of physical models, the archetype now becomes constellated by the model; the living person becomes an *anima* carrier, the image in the artist's soul is now projected upon a living figure. And here, of course, the trouble begins. For now the artist must struggle to resist falling in love with the Queen of Heaven as she sits posed before his admiring gaze.

Although there is no independent corroboration of Vasari's tale, and even if it is all "merely" a fantasy, it is one which became firmly anchored in the facts of art and literary history through its contagious appeal. In her recent monograph of the artist's work, Gloria Fossi examined Lippi's *fortuna critica* through the centuries. She also surveyed the history of the darkly colorful character of Fra Filippo as it has continued to influence the artistic imagination through the years, fostered primarily by the account of the painter's life given in Vasari's *Lives*.[90] On the one hand, the tales of Fra Filippo inspired nineteenth century writers (Stendhal, Browning, D'Annunzio) and painters (Delaroche) to depict him as "the sensuous friar", a sort of Byronic hero in clerical garb who loved life's pleasures and who would not let moralistic rules obstruct his romantic passion. Moreover, in the cases of D'Annunzio and Delaroche we have artists whose own work was directly inspired by their

---

90 Fossi, op. cit., esp. pp. 24-33.

fantasies of Lippi's romance with his model. It's as if they themselves fell in love with the fantasy of the artist falling in love with his model. Though there may be no truth to any of it, we might notice, nonetheless, just how potent and persistent the fantasy itself is. And not just among his admirers.

For, conversely, on the basis of this same lifestyle, Lippi was scorned and castigated by those who were not amused by stories of sexual indiscretion, and who no doubt felt that they themselves might be guilty of encouraging that sort of thing if they said anything favorable about Fra Filippo Lippi's work. While the artists tended to celebrate Lippi's freedom from conventional restraints, the critics generally played the part of the elders sitting in judgment. Monographs of his work through the centuries invariably repeated all of Vasari's gossip about his private life, and Fossi identifies a particularly virulent strain of moralistic critique which ran through the studies of Rio (1861), Cavalcaselle (1864), and Supino (1902). And we ought not to assume that we are done with it. Still today, there remains something in Fra Filippo's legend that continues to provoke the critical confusion of art and life. Even such an urbane and sophisticated scholar as Frederick Hartt apparently could not resist a disparaging, moralistic comment: "The irresponsibility of Filippo's life corresponds, in a sense, to the undisciplined quality of his style."[91]

The persistence of such confusion of art and life on the part of both admirers and detractors invites the question as to whether there is not something special about Fra Filippo and his work that constellates this confusion. For just as Lippi transgresses the boundaries between sacred and the profane, he just as strongly violates the boundaries between art and life. For the historian seeking to establish the facts of Lippi's biography, it is most appropriate to attempt to unravel the respective threads of his life, his art, and his legend. But those seeking access to the spirit of his work would do well to recognize that the confusion of boundaries is itself an integral aspect of the phenomenology of Lippi's art.

When we contemplate the work of artists who insinuate their own personas into their creations, who deliberately transgress the boundaries between

---

91 Frederick Hartt, *History of Italian Renaissance Art* (New York: Harry N. Abrams, 1987), p. 215.

art and life, we need to honor the thematic relevancy of this confusion of boundaries and work with it, rather than simply struggling to segregate what the artist has so diligently confounded. While herself joining the chorus of recent scholars calling for an end to this sort of sentimental confusion of art and life, Gloria Fossi performs the invaluable service of documenting its history (though, of course, strictly for scholarly purposes and certainly not because of the reader's nor her own fascination with these issues.) Then, having given us the essential biographical information that we need to continue the tradition of speculating about Lippi's erotic life, she urges us to put all such thoughts aside![92]

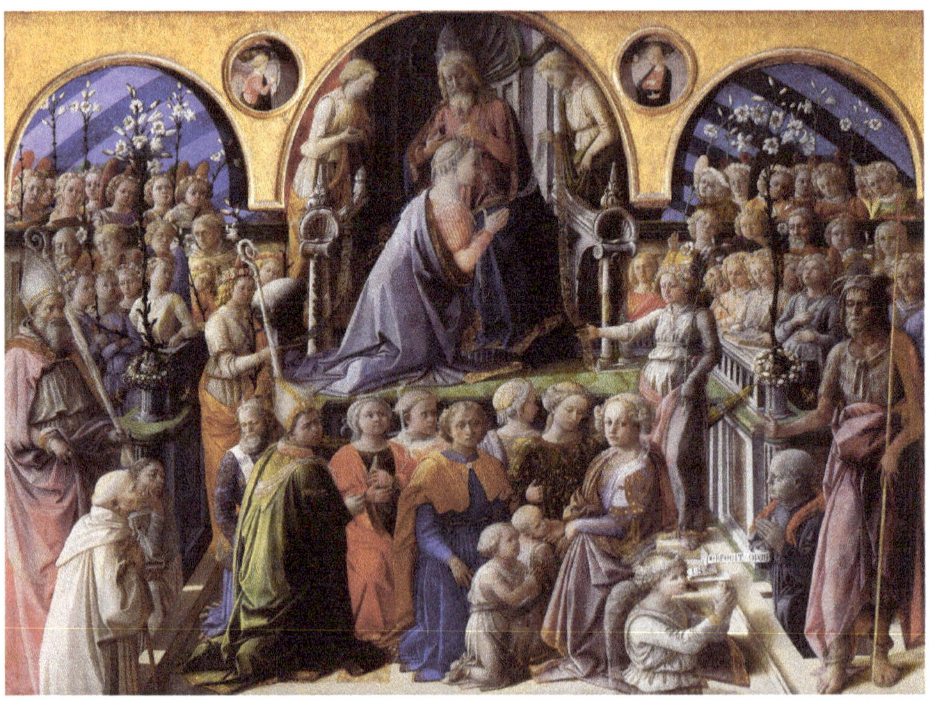

Fig. 39: Fra Filippo Lippi, *Coronation of the Virgin*. Uffizi Gallery, Florence.

Let me urge the reader, rather, to keep these thoughts in mind as we look more closely at the tensions between the sacred and the profane and at the

---

92 "Today's observer, too, thinks primarily of Lippi's love life and all too frequently examines the artist's gentle Madonnas in the hopes of discovering a message from the beautiful Lucrezia. Let us then recover and interpret with less sentimentality the extraordinary heritage that Fra Filippo's painting has left us." Fossi, op. cit., p. 28.

art/life boundary games that we find in Fra Filippo's work. Those who are not constitutionally disposed to see everything through the lens of piety may enjoy the ironic, the irreverent and the outrageous in a variety of works painted by this black sheep in the house of God.

* * *

In Lippi's *Coronation of the Virgin* the central event of the Coronation dominates the image through its enlarged size and top-center placement. The use of relatively larger size for the two main figures derives originally from the hieratic styles of representation of the Byzantine tradition where size reflected spiritual status. This "regression" to earlier conventions of sacred art is occasionally used in 15th century paintings to indicate mystical or holy modes of perception. In such instances, mathematically correct perspective may coexist with enlargements and distortions: the former denotes "normal" perception while the latter cues us to the presence of the miraculous.

The use of this convention appears to be perfectly appropriate in the treatment of the treatment of this sacred theme. However, if we watch carefully where our attention actually goes when we spend some time in front of the *Coronation of the Virgin*, we begin to notice some interesting things. Though it is ostensibly the *raison d'être* of the painting, the act of Coronation itself is only modestly capable of sustaining our interest. The Virgin's slight turn away from us removes the possibility of representing any expressiveness of character, and the act of Coronation itself seems almost perfunctory. If one looks, for example, at Fra Angelico's treatment of the same theme in his Uffizi *Coronation*, the act of placing the crown is solemn, ritualized, and supremely dignified; it results in an explosion of light. In Lippi's painting, Christ appears to be mostly concerned with the logistics of placing the crown carefully so that it doesn't fall off.

As we scan the faces of the assembled angelic hosts of heaven, there is nary a one which engages us with a look of beauty or intelligence or spiritual power. To anyone who has exchanged glances with the angels that inhabit the worlds depicted by Duccio, Giotto, Fra Angelico, or Piero della Francesca, the contrast is palpable. Lippi's angels are slightly sleepy kids with vague,

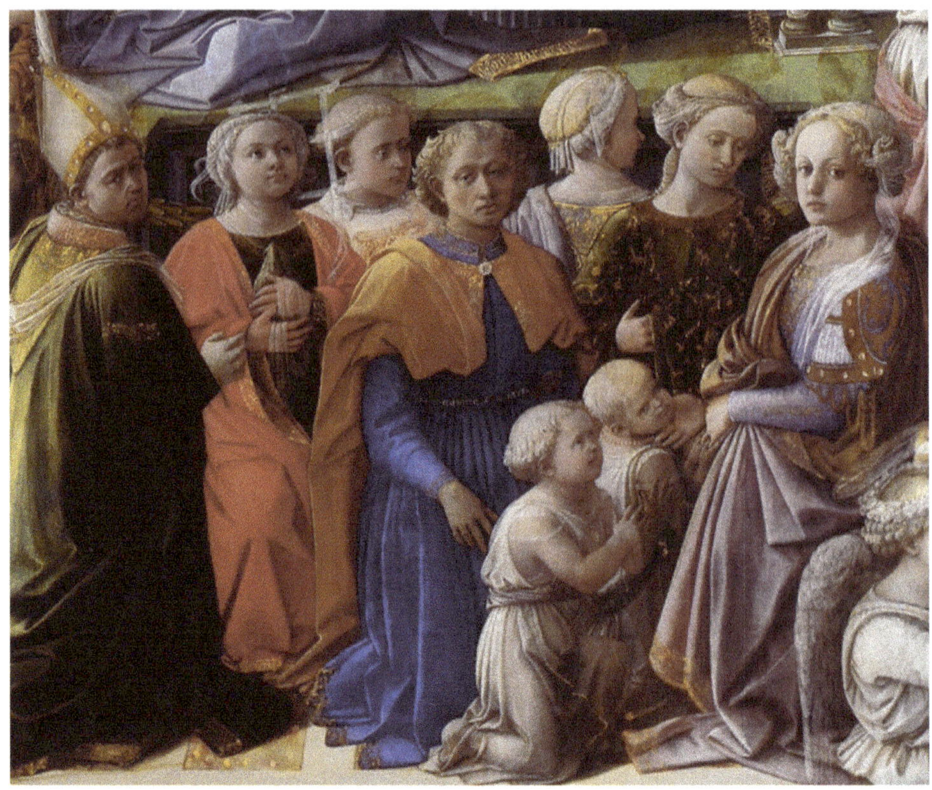

Fig. 40: Fra Filippo Lippi, *Coronation of the Virgin*, detail. Uffizi Gallery, Florence.

diffused looks. Not one of them is paying the slightest bit of attention to the Coronation. The most remarkable thing about them is their ordinariness.

What I believe anyone will discover, after a few moments in front of the painting, is that the group of figures which actually merits and captures our attention are those closest to us in the foreground. In particular, there is a beautifully coiffed, blonde-haired woman in the front right with two children. Once we notice her looking at us, it is hard to look at the picture without being drawn immediately to her face. What an interesting face she has! When we compare her poise and her strongly delineated character with that of any of the angels, we see the difference between a woman who has lived and the childish angelic faces of those who seem to have tasted so little of life.

If we look more closely at her children, it is intriguing to note the physical differences between the two. The child on the left has the same curly hair and refined features of his father, St. Eustace, who kneels behind him, while the child on the right doesn't resemble his father in the slightest. Yet it is the latter child whose face she holds and turns toward us; meanwhile the child with blond curls supplicates himself before her in an apparently futile bid for attention. Is there an implicit preference for the one over the other? Now doesn't the child whose face she presents to us resem-

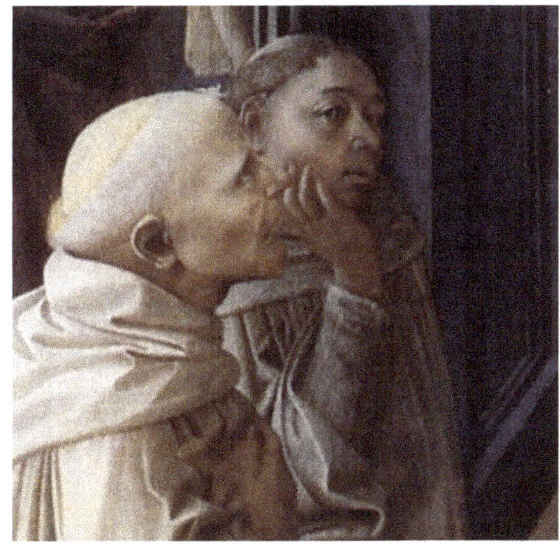

Fig. 41: Fra Filippo Lippi, *Coronation of the Virgin*, detail. Uffizi Gallery, Florence.

ble the kneeling figure on the left in the green robe wearing a bishop's miter? Remarkably, they have the same ears and same pudgy cheeks. It's interesting also that mother has tilted this child's face toward us at exactly the same angle of inclination as the face of the man he resembles. How curious it is that these two should be the ones who look out at us directly—and with her melancholy husband directly between them!

Look at the strange way the child (whose face she touches) has grabbed his mother's fingers. He holds the ring finger and pinky of her left hand in such a way as to make his own fingers look like two little pairs of horns. In Italian culture the symbol of the horns has an unmistakable and invariable meaning: it is used to identify the cuckolded husband. In case we still harbor any doubts, we might ask why St. Eustace, whom one hardly ever encounters in Florentine art, makes one of his rare appearances in this painting. Could it be because he is best known as the saint who had a vision of a stag in the wilderness with a gigantic pair of horns?

At some point we notice the figure of a monk in the left foreground with his head propped in his hand, looking directly at us. It's the artist himself making a cameo appearance, looking directly at us. His look says: "There's a

Coronation going on, a sacred event, and somehow you've gotten caught up in fantasizing about the love life of the proud beauty with the young children. *O, hypocrite lecteur, mon semblable mon frere"* *("You there, you hypocrite, my brother, my twin," as Charles Baudelaire put it.)*

* * *

In the film, *History of the World*, Mel Brooks, who cast himself as Louis XIV, gropes Marie Antoinette as she passes by, turns to the audience and says with a self-satisfied grin: "It's good to be the King!" And, almost as good, one must assume, to be the director. Brooks' lustful gesture accompanied by a turn to the audience may be seen as a profane parody of a longstanding theatrical convention that dates back at least to the religious drama of the fifteenth century.

Michael Baxandall informs us that fifteenth century theater typically included a character called the *festaiuolo* who would remain on stage and point out the significant events to the audience, a sort of professional sleeve-tugger.[93] Baxandall suggests that it is from the stage that this figure made his way into painting where we see him so often looking out at us and pointedly directing our attention toward a significant event or personage in the picture before us.[94]

Originally, then, this figure plays a religious, admonitory role, always drawing our attention to what is important and spiritually significant. But in comical, secular transformations of this genre, as in the example of Mel Brooks, we find the gesture performing quite the opposite function. Rather than exhorting his audience toward moral improvement, Brooks issues an invitation to the viewing public to acknowledge the existence of their "inferior" selves and to celebrate the needs and perceptions of this despised and concealed Other.

Filippo seems to me to be doing something quite similar, albeit centuries earlier. The manner in which he appears in the *The Coronation of the Virgin* carefully identifies him as the odd man out. For maximum contrast, he

---

93 Michael Baxandall, *Painting and Experience in Fifteenth Century Italy* (Oxford: Oxford Univ. Press, 1988), p. 72.

94 In Masaccio's *Trinità*, for example, it is Mary who performs this function.

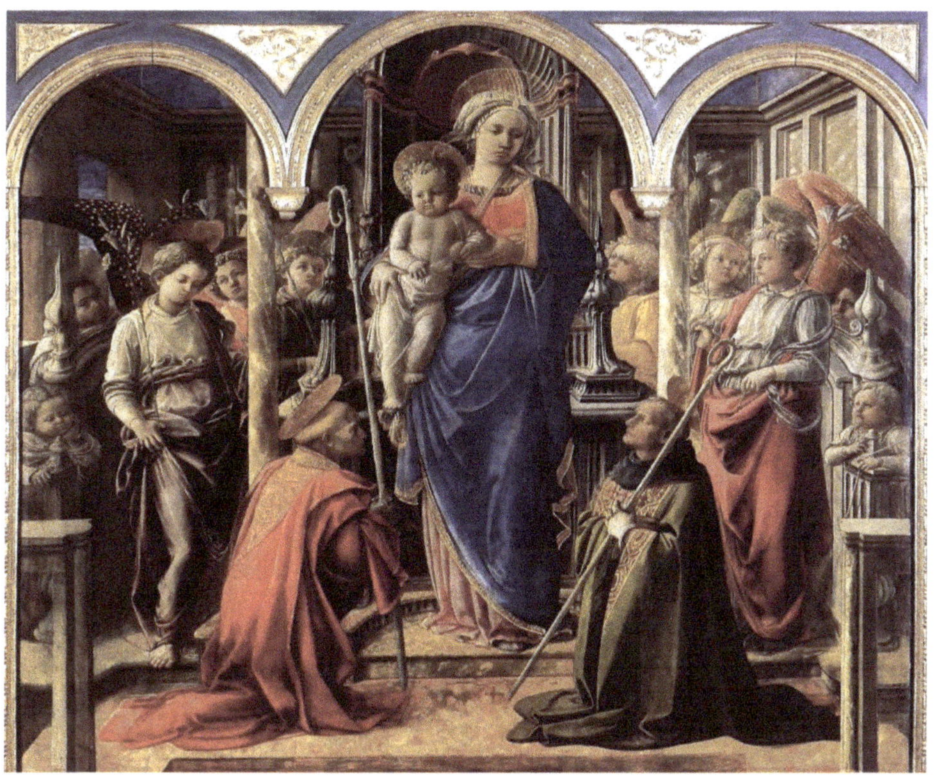

Fig. 42: Fra Filippo Lippi, *Barbadori Altarpiece*. Louvre Museum, Paris.

places himself right next to the reverent elder, the only figure who is actually gazing piously at the Coronation. The reverent elder is bathed in light while Filippo stands in shadow. He ignores the Coronation and looks right at the audience. At the same time, Job stares at Filippo with a challenging look that asks, "Who in the world let you in?" By stepping out of the framework of the fiction and observing us, Lippi invites us to see the situation from the vantage point of a peripheral figure, someone who doesn't share the dominant perspective of this august gathering. We can imagine him wondering whether anyone has noticed his irreverence, whether anyone is even amused by how ugly he has made the patron, kneeling on the steps over on the right, a gray midget who could be mistaken for a cement lawn ornament.

* * *

If we look for a while at the *Barbadori Altarpiece*, as we did with *The Corona-*

tion of the Virgin, we will find once again that there are cross-currents at play. What could be more conventional and non-controversial than an altarpiece featuring the Madonna and Child surrounded by saints and angels? Yet all is not as it may seem at first glance.

Have a look at Lippi's angels. Then, look at any painting by the *trecento* masters of Angels contemplating the Madonna and Child, and you will find that the Angels gaze with love and awe at the holy personages before them. Lippi's angels are bit-part actors stuffed into religious costumes: there is nothing holy about them, nothing even remotely reverent. Their heads are turned every which way; they look up, down, sideways, only not at that which is supposed to be the object of their wholehearted devotion. The angel on the front left raises the skirt of his robe just enough for us to see his bare foot, which is emphasized by the way its toes stick out over the edge of the platform. The child to the left of the angel, with his chin resting in his hand, seems to be fascinated by this bare foot above all other things. And just behind him we find Filippo with his chin resting on the banister, a figure without a halo or a touch of gold, peering out at us from the psychic as well as literal backstage.

However we might choose to interpret the expressions of the Madonna and Child expressions, we could hardly describe them as basking in the glow of the attention they are receiving. Rather they evince a wariness and resignation in the presence of—perhaps towards the presence of—all the figures surrounding them. They appear to be boxed in by the bishops before them, and we wonder if, having risen from her throne, Mary will be able to exit without tripping over Augustine's crosier. The Madonna and Child appear to star reluctantly in this drama, isolated in the midst of their entourage, and psychologically distant from each other.

To the extent that we can notice the dissonance in his paintings, we approach the angle of vision of that shadowy figure who lurks in the background. We are presented with a conflict between reverent and irreverent modes of perception, and we are invited, ultimately, to confront that tension within ourselves. We are challenged to discard rote, clichéed ways of responding to religious imagery, to see through mere formulae of sublimity. For Filippo Lippi, unlike Fra Angelico, the conventions of religion and religious art no longer seem to serve as adequate containers for the sacred aspects of experience.

* * *

In the San Lorenzo *Annunciation* Mary evinces neither a gracious, humble acceptance of her fate, nor even a pained modesty. Lippi depicts, instead, a young woman whose face shows shock and distress, whose arms and posture signal alarm while she gazes warily at the Angelic intruder suddenly present before her.

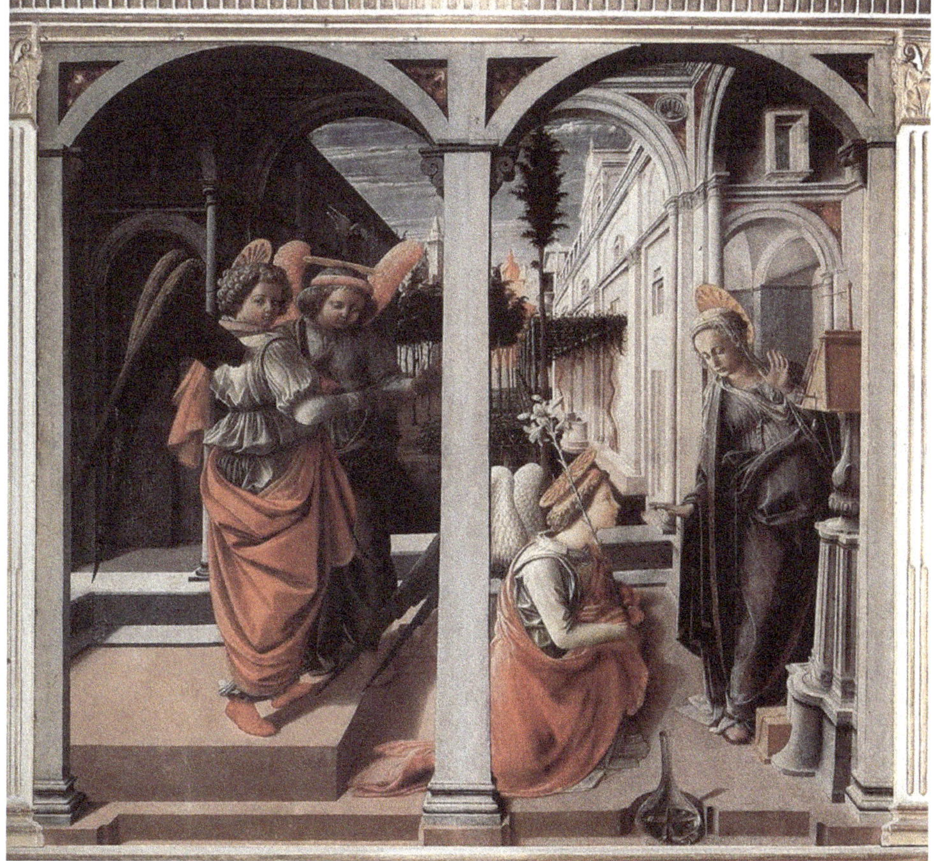

Fig. 43: Fra Filippo Lippi, *Annunciation.* Church of San Lorenzo, Florence.

Filippo Lippi is perhaps alone among his contemporaries in daring to explore the darker aspect of the drama of Annunciation. His Angels are shady characters; two of them stand in the darker, left half of the painting, grayish against the background of the darkened building, while Mary stands opposite them, illuminated against the background of the building's white sunlit walls. Even Gabriel's wings change dramatically from white to a dark grey as they pass behind the central pillar which functions as the threshold of liminality within the picture. There is no indication that Mary has any awareness of the other two Angels who remain in the shadows. Only Gabriel, who has crossed into her space, has engaged her attention while the others proceed to perform their mysterious offices beyond the range of her awareness.

In his broad survey of Italian Renaissance painting, Frederick Hartt informs us that the presence of these additional two Angels has still not been successfully explained.[95] In his recent work on Filippo Lippi, Jeffrey Ruda identifies several possible antecedents for Lippi's conception which show several angels at an Annunciation. Of these, the ones which involve groups or clusters of small angels do not seem to me to be closely related. But a band of three angels from an early Christian Annunciation mosaic at Santa Maria Maggiore in Rome is indeed quite similar with respect to the sense of concerted, joint action that we find in Lippi's image.[96] The existence of earlier images with three angels relieves Lippi's painting from the burden of uniqueness, but it still leaves us with the task of trying to understand the meaning of their presence in the San Lorenzo *Annunciation*.

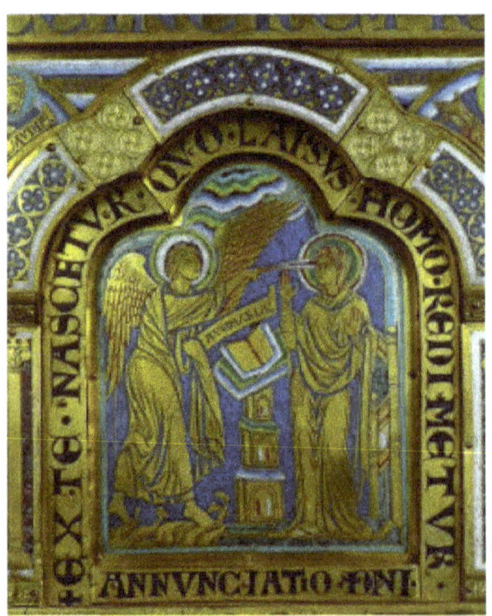

Fig. 44: Nicholas of Verdun, *Annunciation to Mary.*
Klosterneuburg Altarpiece,
Klosterneuburg Monastery, Austria.

Another image of a trio of angels which I stumbled upon may afford us a clue. In the Klosterneuburg Monastery near Vienna on the 12th century altarpiece by Nicholas of Verdun,, there are three rows of juxtaposed panels that run across the face of the altar. In the very first column we find represented

---

95 Frederick Hartt, *Italian Renaissance Art* (Englewood Cliffs: Prentice Hall, 1987) p. 216.

96 Jeffrey Ruda, *Fra Filippo Lippi: Life and Work* (London: Phaidon, 1993) pp. 121,123. The Santa Maria Maggiore mosaic is Pl. 70.

in descending order the Annunciation to Sarah, the Annunciation to Mary, and the Annunciation to Samson's mother (Judges 13:2-5).[97] By joining the New Testament type with its Old Testament antitypes, the images propose that the Annunciation to Mary is part of a family of Biblical stories all of which treat of a common theme: Divine intervention in the process of birth. In the Old Testament, we find a long line of childless couples from Samson's parents through Samuel's all the way back to Abraham and Sarah, all of whom are made fruitful through Divine intervention.

The Annunciation to Mary is typologically related to these Old Testament precursors even though it takes the story to a new level by presenting the Spirit of God as the sole agent of the pregnancy, rather than simply its enabler. But once we recognize in the type of the Annunciation the fulfillment of an Old Testament anti-type, we can readily find a place in imaginal history for Lippi's three Angels. They are successors to the three Angels who came to visit the first of the patriarchs and his wife on the plains of Mamre; when they left, the aged matriarch

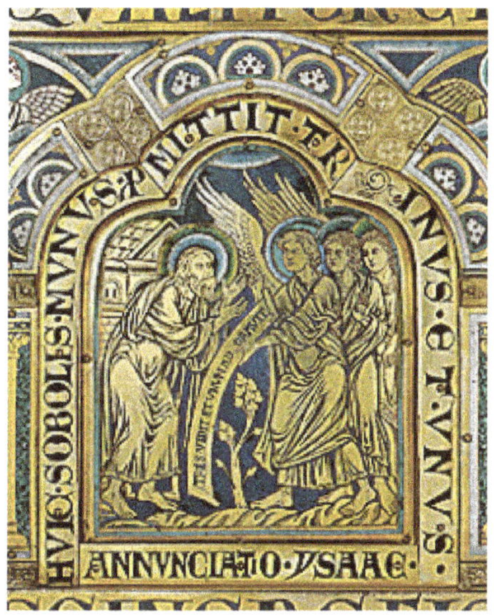

Fig. 45: Nicholas of Verdun, *Annunciation to Sarah.* Klosterneuburg Altarpiece.

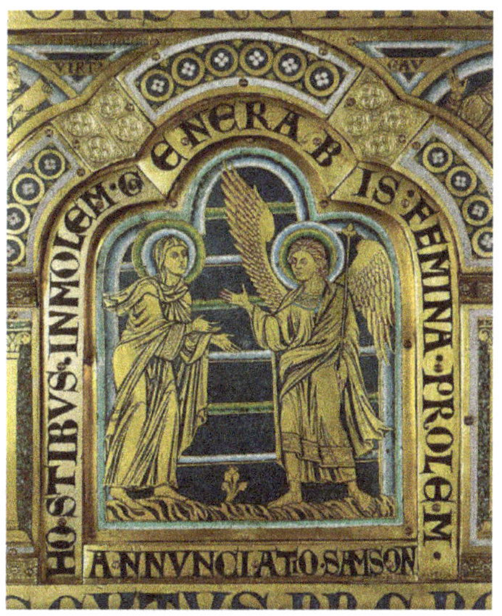

Fig. 46: Nicholas of Verdun, *Annunciation to the Mother of Samson.* Klosterneuburg Altarpiece.

---

97 Gertrude Schiller, *Iconography in Christian Art,* trans. by J. Seligman (Greenwich, CT: N.Y. Graphic Society, 1971), ref. p.41; illus. no. 85; attrib. to Nicolas of Verdun.

Sarah mysteriously became pregnant with Isaac. The history of the Jewish people flowed from this event in much the same way that Gabriel's visit to Mary marked the beginning of Christian history. The left and right panels of Lippi's painting thus function, respectively, as anti-type and type; and the movement from the shadowed panel with the accompanying Angels to the brightly lit panel where only Gabriel appears recapitulates the movement from the Old Testament story to the New.[98]

The more distant of these two Angels appears to be summoning the Holy Ghost in the form of the Dove; we see it, barely visible, over the head of the second Angel winging its way toward Mary from out of the deepest shadows. How different is this shadowy bird from all those representations of a luminous Dove released from God's own hand, trailing beams of glory! Here Lippi has brought us perilously close to the pagan story which parallels the Annunciation.

The tale of Leda and the Swan is that more ancient vision of the coupling of a bird with a woman which William Butler Yeats saw echoed in the Christian Annunciation. The offspring of the union of Leda and Zeus included the lovely Helen of Troy, whose face launched not only a thousand ships, but also the epics of the Iliad and the Odyssey which recount the whole story of the Trojan War and Ulysses' return. As the Annunciation initiated the Christian era, the union of Leda and Zeus, in the form of a swan, initiated the era of the Mycenaean Greeks. But whereas the Christian story has only a mild undercurrent of distress (i.e., Mary's departure "into the hill country with haste" presumably out of concern over how to explain her changed circumstances to Joseph), the pagan myth portrays the intervention of the Divine in human affairs quite plainly as a rape and impregnation.

Lippi explores more boldly than any of his contemporaries this shadow aspect of the Annunciation, perhaps of many annunciations: the element of violation. Look closely at the vessel in the right foreground of the painting that is set right between Gabriel and Mary. The vase is womb-like in form,

---

98 My thanks to Professor Susan McKillop of Sonoma State University for her suggestion of a typological reading of the light and dark panels.

and it hosts a phallic shape which rises from the bottom and extrudes above the surface of the water. Through the play of shapes Lippi alludes to the loss of virginity that this visit entails. Now look at the flower that Gabriel is holding; follow the line of its stem and you will see where it was just a moment before. Gabriel has not come to visit bearing a lily; he has entered the Virgin's inner chamber and plucked her flower.

*　*　*

Lippi's Angel has crossed the central threshold and moved almost entirely into Mary's space in a manner possibly unique in Renaissance images of the Annunciation. Is there another Gabriel anywhere in Renaissance art who looks at the Virgin so placidly, with such aplomb? His utter composure and apparent nonchalance presents the sharpest foil to Mary's agitation, and there is no sign on his part, nor on the part of his companions, of any discomfiture at her shock and distress. Fait accompli. And even if we are to assume that Mary has acceded to her destiny, we may fairly ask: What could she really know about the myriad paths of destiny tied to the fateful choice she had made?

Yeats asks the question about Leda: "Did she put on his knowledge with his power?" Could she foresee the tragic war, "The broken wall, the burning roof and tower…And Agamemnon dead." The answer is clear. We might equally ask of Mary, when she said "Yes," whether she had a chance to consider, for instance, that the disciples of her son would blame her own people for his murder, and would persecute and vilify their descendants for generations to come?

As we look at the image, we become aware eventually of yet another threshold, one which serves to separate two distinct realms. Before us is the world of the *Annunciation* defined by Brunelleschi's gold frame and by the adjacent pillars which border the open porticos. Through these doorways we may step up and enter into the life-size world before us; and through these same doorways we also notice an Angel looking into our world, directly at us. While this image of an Annunciation may exist in our world as a painting on a wall, we now find that we also exist within its frame of reference as a part of its own implicit order.

We may notice that the vessel from which the lily was plucked stands at the threshold between us and the image no less than it does between the Angel and Mary. The Angel who points toward Mary with his dark hand is the one who looks right at us, implicating our world and our gazing presence within the purview of the Annunciation. We observe him at his work even as we meet his gaze. Is the Angel's bold look not a challenge to us to lose our own innocence about these matters?

* * *

Lippi seeks the sacred in the human heart in the poignant dramas of religious actors seen in their human, all-too-human aspect. When he succeeds, his characters move us through their dignity and simple humanity. His Annunciates are maidens apprehensive about the role into which they have been suddenly cast; his Madonnas are brave young mothers struggling to meet their fate. In his Nativities, Fra Filippo's Joseph, like the painter himself, is an older father with a newborn infant, a balding greybeard with his head on his hand pondering the magnitude of the change which has just taken place in his life. The human burden of the spiritual life is everywhere evident.

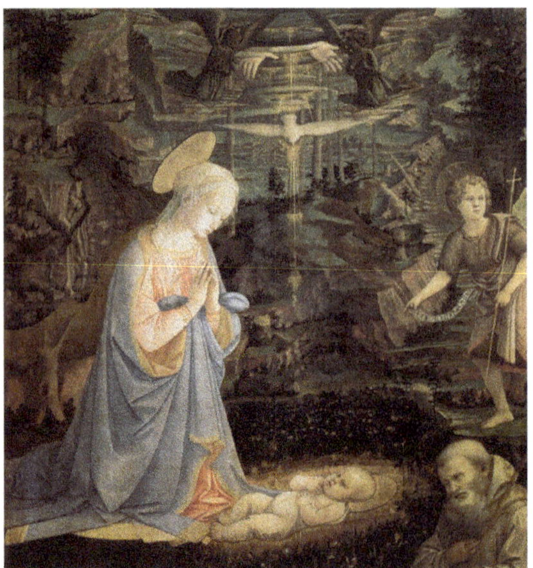

Fig. 47: Fra Filippo Lippi, *Adoration of the Child.*
Uffizi Gallery, Florence.

There are many Renaissance artists who show us the most profound rapport and affection between Madonna and Bambino in one painting after another. Yet the more you look at Filippo's images of mother and child, the more you realize how dysfunctional his mothers always are and how solitary and unloved are their infants. Through these paintings throughout the years, Filippo the orphan sings the poignant song of the motherless child.

It's not until after Filippo's own child is born in his later years that we find him painting images of babies receiving abundant love from adoring mothers. In fact, Filippo invents from scratch an entirely new genre during this period of his life called *The Adoration of the Child*. These are somewhat similar to Nativity scenes, but with a significant difference: they show the mother directly adoring the child. In these lyrical images of cuddly infants receiving their mother's direct attention (along with various saints and angels who come, as well, to pray for their well-being), we find images of the Christ Child which, for the first time in Renaissance painting, remind us of real infants. Gone are the wise, little-old-men babies of the Byzantine tradition, and in their stead we find cute little toddlers. We see them in their helplessness and neediness and their occasional bewilderment at the goings-on around them.

Lippi is perhaps the first artist to place his casual self-portraits into paintings of the gathered hosts of heaven. I suspect that he also the first artist to insinuate himself as a pudgy, homely babe into the arms of all those Madonnas who had no love to give him. In the Adorations, on the other hand, where fortune smiles and heaven sends down its glory, I'd be willing to wager that we are looking at portraits of the little Filippino.

* * *

Fra Filippo Lippi's work does not achieve the same heights of sublimity as Fra Angelico's, yet he approaches the sacred in a way that becomes more truly characteristic of the modern temperament. He transgresses the boundary of the painting's fictive world by reaching out and letting us know that he is there, and that he is looking out at us as we contemplate his work. He explores the tension between the sacred and the profane by presenting us with religious spectacles while gently reminding us of our all-too-human proclivities. Indeed, I think that much of the interest of Fra Filippo's work emerges from the vital tension between sacred and earthly realities which he certainly experienced and which he subtly portrayed. Of the many strategies which Renaissance artists explore to unite the world of the painting with the spectator's own lived world, Lippi's *modus operandi* is perhaps the most psychological in a modern sense.

Fra Filippo brings both simple, and not so simple, human needs and desires into the realm of the sacred, always carrying his earthly personality into his encounters with the religious universe. We might say that Lippi tries to bring us as close to heaven as he can get, but without leaving any of this earthly life behind.

Piero's
PREGNANT MADONNA

"Just like a prayer, I'll take you there."

~ Madonna

Questions surrounding the Madonna's pregnancy have always been somewhat awkward for theologians, and representations in art of Mary as a pregnant mother have been exceedingly rare. When treated at all, the fact of Mary's "delicate condition" was usually alluded to subtly and discreetly by representing a barely discernible rotundity beneath her robes. Although the fact of the Incarnation of Christ has been an essential element of Christian dogma, good taste and the transcendent "spirituality" of the whole affair have sharply discouraged any too vivid imaginings of the Madonna's tumescent belly.

The striking exception is Piero della Francesca's *Madonna del Parto* (c. 1460) which may be translated as the *Madonna of Birth* or *Pregnant Madonna*. The fleshliness and physicality of birth is strongly emphasized by Piero's decision to represent the Madonna, not slightly pregnant, but unmistakably late in her term. This Mary is *very* pregnant, and through her gestures and stance she conveys the full physical discomfort of her situation. Indeed, one is hard-pressed to find a less romanticized, less idealized image of the ponderousness of maternity with its garments that burst at the seams. There is great poignancy and humanity in Piero's evocation of the discomfort of pregnancy, the burden of child-bearing. Yet, at the same time, we meet the Madonna in

the company of angels. And through Mary's imposing stature and the formal solemnity of the entire presentation we remain wholly within the realm
of high religious drama.

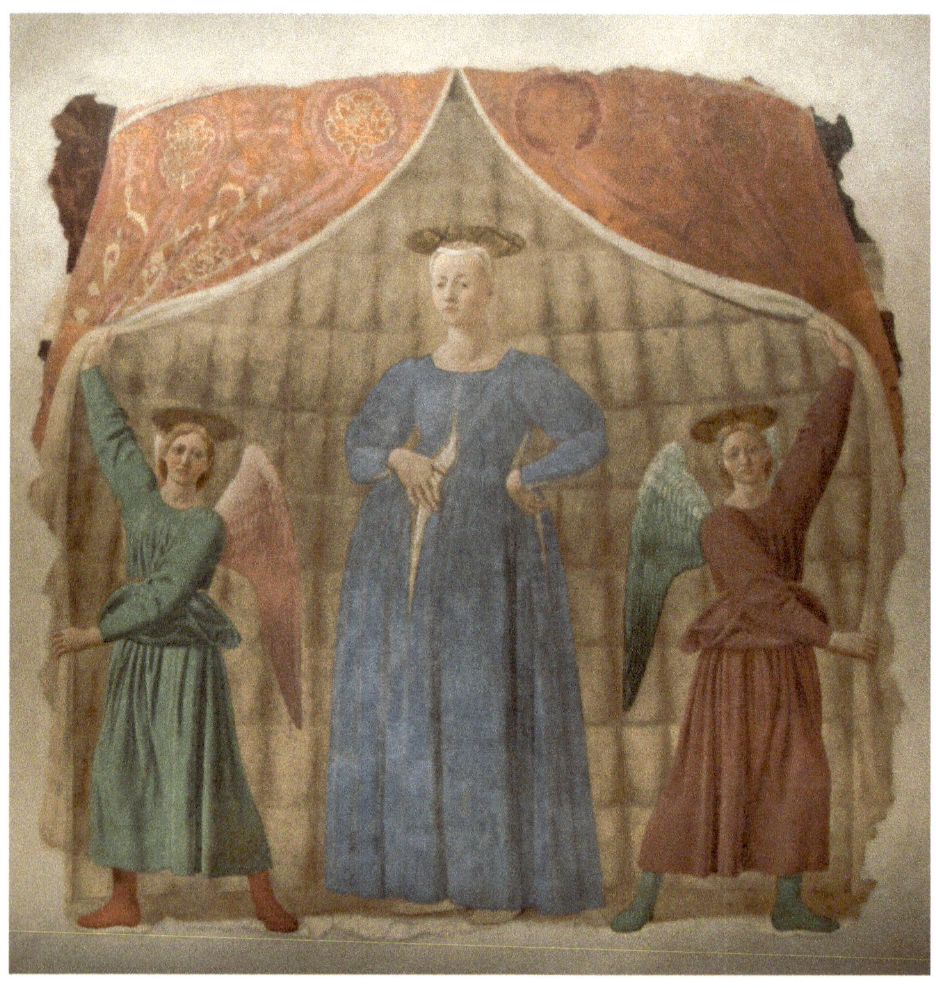

Fig. 48: Pierodella Francesca, *Madonna del Parto*. Museum of the Madonna del Parto, Monterchi.

HOW MUCH CLOTH DO WE NEED FOR THE MADONNA'S TENT?

The sense that heavenly things are degraded by bringing in vulgar, mundane
references to the daily world was as typical of medieval sensibilities as it is
characteristic of the modern temperament. Yet, during that period which
gave us the ideal of "the Renaissance man" we find the sacred and the profane

     PIERO'S PREGNANT MADONNA

juxtaposed in ways that sharply challenge modern prejudices. We know, for example, that Piero della Francesca was able to meditate profoundly upon sacred mysteries while yet not disdaining to write texts about business math and the commercial uses of the abacus. Indeed, the Florentine public that sustained and supported the extraordinary flowering of fifteenth century religious art was composed primarily of business people.

The art historian Michael Baxandall has pointed out the important fact that prior to the nineteenth century there was no standardization of weights and measures in Europe.[99] The traveling merchant needed to have basic skills in geometry and arithmetic so as to be able to calculate and gauge volumes and surface areas on the spot, from odd-sized barrels filled with wine to irregular mounds of grain to bolts of fabric. Many of the painters of this period came first through the secular schools where they learned these mercantile estimating skills and later turned them to profitable use in their painterly activities. Conversely, the business audience was equally able to bring its gauging skills to the act of contemplating a picture.

In researching the textbooks that were used to educate the Florentine mercantile class, Baxandall made a fascinating discovery about tents and pavilions like the one we see in Piero's image:

> ...almost every [school] handbook used a pavilion as an exercise in calculating surface areas; it was a convenient cone, or compound of cylinder and cone, or of cylinder and truncated cone, and one was asked to work out how much cloth would be needed to make the pavilion. When a painter like Piero used a pavilion in his painting, he was inviting his public to gauge. The beholder's precise and familiar assessment of the pavilion mediates between his own position in the everyday and the mystery of the Virgin's conception...[100]

Everyday commercial experience is invoked along with religious sentiment in a way which must strike the modern viewer as remarkably odd. For a brief

---

99 Michael Baxandall, *Painting and Experience in Fifteenth Century Italy* (Oxford, 1988) p. 86.
100 Ibid., p. 87.

moment the image invites us to stand in a space where the religious and secular spheres interpenetrate. Piero addresses the calculating mind and the spiritual imagination in the same breath and, by doing so, he invites the parts of ourselves which normally attend to such matters separately to be present to each other in the moment. Keeping these matters in mind, let's move on to explore other dimensions of this image.

CENTER STAGE BETWEEN THE CHERUBIM

One of the intriguing aspects of Piero's *Madonna del Parto* is the way it incorporates various well-established elements of iconography but employs them in novel ways. Let's look now at some of the specific references to tradition that echo within the universe of the image, beginning with the symmetrical angels who border the Madonna.

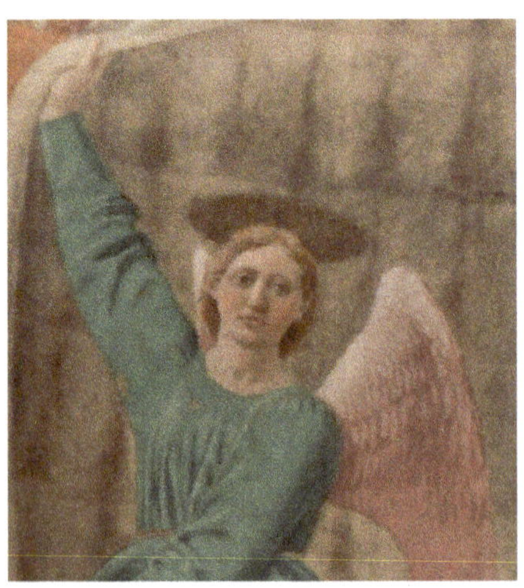

Fig. 49: Pierodella Francesca,
Madonna del Parto, detail, left angel.
Museum of the Madonna del Parto, Monterchi.

In the apocryphal legends about the cherubim who stand beside God's throne, one of them traditionally focuses his attention on earthly matters while the other is concerned only with divine and eternal things. Standing before Piero's life-size fresco you feel this strongly when you look directly as these two angelic figures. Though they are almost perfect mirror images of each other, they have a distinctly different "feel": one invites empathic relationship while the other remains inscrutable and aloof.[101]

Now during the Middle Ages the cherubim played an interesting role in certain esoteric meditative practices. One of the forms of meditation which

---

101 In support of this assertion I can only offer the following anecdotal evidence: in the course several years of working with this image with various groups, and asking them to assign roles to the two angels, 70-80% regularly identified the angel to our left as "more accessible" and his twin to the right as "more remote."

mystics pursued in seeking to experience union with the Godhead was to
imagine themselves in the Temple of
Solomon in the presence of the two
cherubim before the Ark of the Covenant, the Holy of Holies. The seeker would visualize in detail the twin
cherubim on either side of the Ark and,
ultimately, by meditating on the space
between them, he or she would seek a
gateway to direct experience of union
with God. In terms of this tradition,
in the sacred space between the angels,

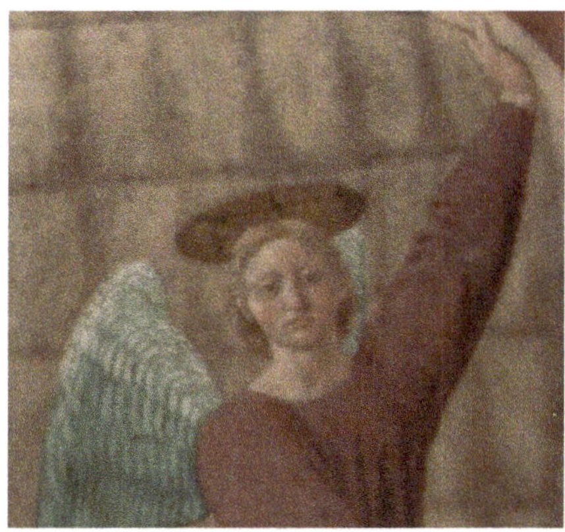

Fig. 50: Pierodella Francesca,
Madonna del Parto, detail, right angel.
Museum of the Madonna del Parto, Monterchi.

rather than placing a winged disk or an eye in a pyramid as a symbol of
the Godhead, Piero places the pregnant Virgin. The Madonna occupies the
place typologically of the Holy of Holies while fulfilling her traditional role
as Mediatrix, the bridge between heaven and earth.

As we contemplate the *Madonna del Parto*, we notice that she stands between
parted curtains, and we may wonder whether the curtains are being opened
or closed. The Madonna stands on the threshold between front and back
stage, and it's not at all clear whether she is emerging or withdrawing from
the stage. Or, perhaps, by holding open these curtains in this timeless space,
the angels invite us to contemplate a liminal moment on the very edge between revelation and concealment.

The parting of the curtains is a moment of crossing between the worlds. The
Italian word for birth, *parto,* which we hear echoed in the term *parturition,*
reminds us in a way that the English word doesn't that birth is a parting.
The parting of the curtains echoes the parting of Mary's dress and both are
homologous with that parting of lips and legs which accompanies birth, that
moment when the curtain between the worlds momentarily parts and souls
pass from one world to the other. Someone who was not, now is. Behold, I
show you a mystery, says Piero, with no words at all.

The Madonna as Containing Center

In Dante's *Divine Comedy* after the poet enters the celestial world, he asks about the different levels of Paradise and how people here may move closer to God. Dante's guide smiles at the question and explains that in heaven there is no need to move closer to God: God is everywhere and everyone here already lives and dwells within God. God's Being is the center which contains all.

The subtle and profound distinctions between earthly and celestial forms and conditions which occupied the attentions of our ancestors have nearly disappeared from view in the modern world. One of the contemporary figures who has done the most to reconstruct this perennial worldview and recover its imaginal landscapes was the French scholar of ancient Persian esotericism, Henri Corbin. In *Temple and Contemplation*, his study of relations between the earthly temple and its celestial archetype, Corbin explains:

> [T]he characteristic of spiritual forms is that their centre is both that which *is surrounded* and that which *surrounds*, that which *is contained* and that which *contains*, whereas in the case of material forms, the centre is purely and simply that which is *surrounded*.[102]

In trying to represent the discoveries made through their spiritual explorations, the Persian theosophers developed images and parables to express the inexpressible. One traditional tale informs us that in order to allow heaven and earth to communicate with each other "God then caused a pavilion to descend, a single tent from among the tents of Paradise."[103] The structure of the tent "is the structure of a spiritual form which contains its universe within itself."[104] And the supreme value of such a form is that, at least potentially, it "liberates him who contemplates it and meditates on it to a higher state of being, by opening up to him the new space which corresponds to such a state."[105]

---

102 Henri Corbin, *Temple and Contemplation*, trans. P. Sherrard (London, 1986) p. 214-15.

103 Ibid., p. 215.

104 Ibid., p. 220.

105 Ibid., p. 191.

The *Madonna del Parto* may be contemplated in precisely such a manner. To paraphrase the well-known Talmudic teaching, we may say that she who gives birth to a single soul gives birth to a whole world. And in this special case of divine incarnation, the inner sanctum contains the whole, the center of the sphere contains its circumference. In her finitude she holds the infinite: the Mother of God contains All That Is within her womb.

Within You and Without You: Death and the Mother

While we are certainly justified in seeing the *Madonna del Parto* as a meditation on the mysteries of birth, there is also another dimension in the image that points us toward a consideration of mortality. Indeed, death is implicated by two related observations, one regarding the painting's iconography, the other, its physical location.

The holy place between the cherubim that served as a traditional setting for mystical or ecstatic experience also figured in late medieval and Renaissance art as a sanctuary for the dead. As Philip Hendy points out: "On the walls of older churches all over Italy are to be found sculptured monuments with two Angels drawing aside curtains to reveal the recumbent effigy of the deceased."[106] How better to assure that the soul of the deceased would find its rest with God than to place it figuratively within this inner sanctum of the house of the Lord.

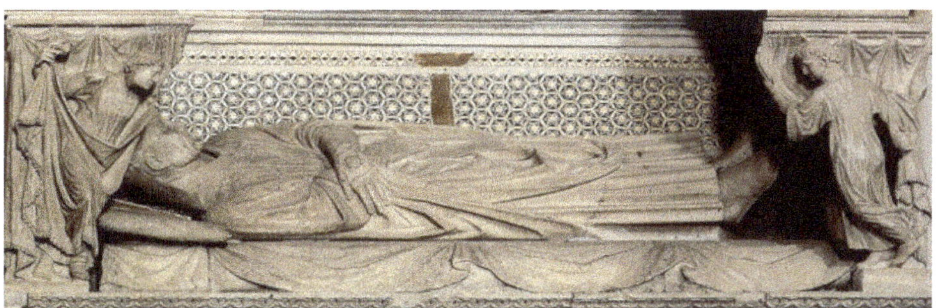

Fig. 51: Arnolfo di Cambio, *Tomb of Cardinal de Braye*, detail. Church of San Domenico, Orvieto.

---

106 Philip Hendy, *Piero della Francesco and the Early Renaissance* (New York, 1968) p. 112.

So, Piero's image invites us to ponder the nature of higher realms of being while at the same time reminding us thematically of the presence of mortality. Apart from all else it may be, the *Madonna del Parto* is also a funereal image. It is both an image of eternity contained in time, and a reminder of death.

Art historians believe that Piero's mother came originally from the tiny hamlet of Monterchi that was home also to the small church which housed the Madonna del Parto. Vasari claimed that Piero's mother died about 1460 (which would be consistent with the presumed dating of the painting), and it is reasonable to assume that she would have been buried in her home town as Italians typically continue to be to this day. These circumstances, in conjunction with the otherwise puzzling fact that Piero painted such a significant image in an otherwise insignificant village, allow us to presume with reasonable likelihood that the Madonna del Parto was created, at least in part, as a memorial to his deceased mother.

In this topos of funereal imagery, the deceased is figuratively imagined to be in that place between the curtains drawn by the cherubim, in the place of God. That imaginal space is here occupied by the pregnant Virgin, hence the deceased is now at one with the Madonna. Metaphorically, the deceased *is* that pregnant Madonna, and thus, Piero's homage to his mother is to memorialize her in death as the *Madonna del Parto*.

By virtue of the fact that Piero, her son, is the artist, the relation of son to mother is implicit in this funereal tribute. Piero's image invites us, on the one hand, to reflect on the relation of mother and unborn child while, at the same time, it serves as the tribute of a grown man to his departed mother. From being within her to being without her: this is every son's journey with his mother.

Piero's meditative image takes us on a journey that begins with trying to imagine ourselves in our mother's womb and ends by remembering our mother as we stand, alone, before her grave. We move from being conceived out of nothing and contained wholly within the mother to standing later in a world of our own, one in which our mother becomes, inexorably, no more

    PIERO'S PREGNANT MADONNA

than the memory of a presence. As she once circumscribed the being of that infant she carried in her womb, the artist who mourns her loss strives to contain her being in the fullness of a timeless image. Through this potent act of creative imagination he provides a place for her to live and to be held within the compass of the heart's affections. In the plenitude of this image Piero swallows death whole: birth and death become mirrors of each other no less than the cherubim who preside over their mysteries.

In the remarkable capaciousness of Piero della Francesca's vision, the extremes touch: heaven and earth, spirit and flesh, the sacred and the profane, all become architectural elements in an artistic vision sufficiently powerful to contain the tension between these polarities, to envision relationship between all that lies 'twixt heaven and earth. Such an image could only have been painted during the Italian Renaissance, when, for a brief period, the Western imagination sought actively to recognize the spiritual depths implicit in the dramas of daily life, to bridge the sacred and the profane, and to bring about the marriage of heaven and earth.

BOTTICELLI'S
Primavera

Although they languish today under greenish-tinted bulletproof glass, Botticelli's *Birth of Venus* and his *Primavera* still retain much of their magic. These are mysterious, dream-like images that invite interpretation, and there is certainly no shortage of fascinating and conflicting readings. While it's fun to speculate about their meanings, and totally appropriate, let's begin with what we know that can provide some orientation.

One of the first things worth noting about these two paintings is that they were among the first large-size paintings during the Renaissance to depict mythological subjects. Mythological themes were common on decorative platters and household furnishings, but, before Botticelli, painting on this scale was reserved for altarpieces with Christian themes. Simply by working on this scale Botticelli invites us to treat these images with a degree of seriousness not previously devoted to mythological themes.

Another remarkable fact about these two paintings is that they were intended for the edification of the adolescent nephew of Lorenzo de' Medici, ruler of Florence. We know something, even today, about teenage boys and pictures of beautiful naked women, so we can be fairly certain that he was not unhappy with this gift. But we also know that Lorenzo was the patron of the Florentine Platonic academy and that he and his cousin, Lorenzo di Pierfrancesco, probably had a more complex agenda in mind when they commissioned the work from Botticelli.

Botticelli was an integral part of this circle of poets and scholars and artists who were deeply committed to recovering the esoteric wisdom of the ancient pagan world and integrating it with contemporary Christian belief. One member of the group, Marsilio Ficino, even wrote a book called *Platonic Theology* in which he tried to show that Plato's mystical teachings about the soul were entirely compatible with Christian dogma. So, it's in this context of this intellectual milieu that we need to begin our explorations of the *Primavera* and the *Birth of Venus*.

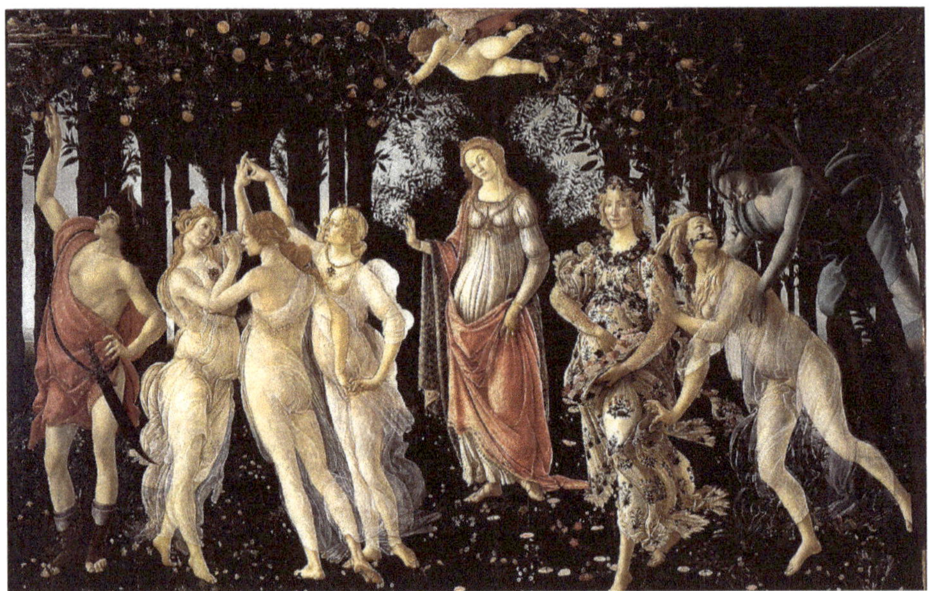
Fig. 52: Sandro Botticelli, *La Primavera*. Uffizi Gallery, Florence.

We'll start with the *Primavera* which was completed a few years before its companion piece. As we explore, we'll stay close to what we can actually observe without going too far afield into classical sources. First of all, if you step back and look at the movement within the image, you'll notice that things seem to move from right to left. Most of the figures in the painting are turned toward or facing our left; some are leaning that way; and blind-folded Cupid is aiming his arrow in that direction. So, the ways in which the figures are standing, looking and gesturing draw our attention across the canvas from right to left.

Notice next how our focus moves up and down as we move right to left. The winged blue figure descends from the heavens and bends the branches of the trees as he crashes through them. You can make out his blue wing in the upper right corner of the painting, which is, incidentally, the only area of the upper foliage that is barren of fruit.

From him we pass down to the nymph he has grasped; then, an upward diagonal carries our eye to the woman scattering flowers and on to the regal figure in the center of the painting. Her outstretched hand moves our attention down to the first of the dancing maidens; then we gaze up to the hand-bridge over the head of the middle dancer, down to the last and, finally, over to the young man who pulls our eyes upward as he pokes his wand into the clouds on the upper left.

The up-and-down dance that our eye performs as it moves across the painting perfectly mirrors the dance of the three maidens who raise and lower their joined hands as they circle. Isn't this an exquisite way of inviting us to join the festivities?

* * *

Let's look more closely at the figures in this dance as we make our way from right to left. The movement begins with the aerial creature who has come down from the heavens. He's blue— like the sky behind him, like our flesh in the cold of winter, like depression, like aching gonadal longing. His entrance on the scene seems is abrupt, unexpected, somewhat frightening, at least for the nymph who leans away from him as if trying to flee. Yet, whatever it is that transpires between them brings forth a stream of flowers from her mouth.

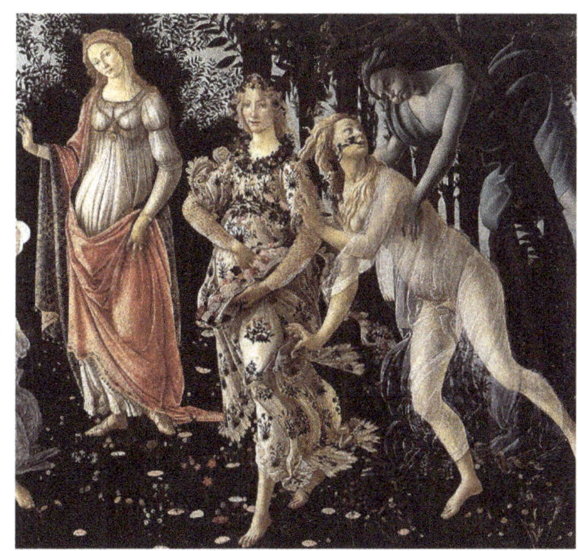

Fig. 53: Sandro Botticelli, *La Primavera*, detail. Uffizi Gallery, Florence.

The figure to her left with the floral gown doesn't share in her apparent distress, but simply prepares to scatter a handful of the flowers which she has gathered in the fold of her dress. The green-leafed vine with pink flowers that emerges from the first girl's mouth merges with the flowers of the other girl's dress and appears again in the garland that she wears in her hair. Also, if you look closely at the nymph's hands, you'll see that there are places where the flowers of the dress grow over her hands and other places where they are visible through them. All of which—in this age before morphing technologies—suggests that the first girl precedes and is mysteriously transformed into the second.

In fact, when we look at the three female figures as an ascending series, we notice a variety of progressive changes:

- The first figure is virtually nude, wearing only a filmy gown. Her hair is loose and undressed. Her feet are bare.

- The second figure wears a flower dress and sports a floral necklace; her waist is girdled by a flowery vine (which, like the necklace, may be part of the dress). Her hair is loose, but dressed with a garland. Her feet are bare.

- The third figure is dressed in tailored clothes. Her robe of red and blue shows detailed workmanship in the fabric patterns and the decorative bordering along the hemline. She wears gold jewelry. Her hair is carefully braided, and she wears a jeweled headdress. Her feet are shod.

The first figure tries to run away; the second walks purposefully; the third stands and presides. The sequence invites us to think in terms of three aspects of the feminine or three stages in the life of woman: the innocent nymph, naked and unfettered; the fruitful, flowering young mother; the mature woman: poised, self-possessed, sophisticated.

Scholars who believe they have found the mythological sources of these mysterious figures identify them as Zephyr, the wind god; Chloris, the nymph whom he pursues; Flora, the goddess of springtime and flowers; and Venus, the goddess of love and beauty. But one of the things that's marvelous about Botticelli's image is that we don't really need labels: the figures already show us who they are. In the ways that they move, dress and carry themselves, they embody the play of energies that reference to the classical myths merely confirms.

As we move left, the dance continues. Over the head of Venus/Aphrodite, a blindfolded Cupid gets ready to shoot a fiery-tipped arrow at one of the three graceful dancers. If you carefully follow the line of the arrow, you'll discover its intended target. It's the

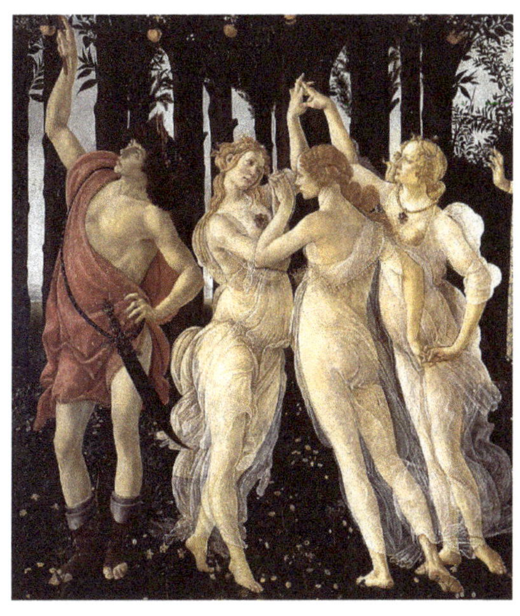

Fig. 54: Sandro Botticelli, *La Primavera*, detail. Uffizi Gallery, Florence.

middle dancer, the one whose shoulder is bare, her buttons all undone. The other two are holding their bridged hands over her head like a canopy. She stares intently at the young man off to her left who is poking around in the clouds. We're left to imagine, now that he's caught her eye, what will happen once the arrow strikes.

The young man on the far left is draped in an elegant fabric; his feet are shod and his sandals have wings. He carries a sword and wears a sort of helmet or crown. In his right hand he holds a caduceus, a wand around which two snakes intertwine. The caduceus is associated today with medicine and healing, but formerly would have been recognized as a sort of magic wand. Our young man is using his tool for exploring the mysteries of the heavens where his gaze and his attention are fixed. We're reminded of Aldous Huxley's definition of a genius as someone who doesn't think about sex all the time.

Note the perfect symmetry between the couples who frame the dance before us. We begin with an aerial creature who is pulled downward by hunger and desire while the nymph he grasps flourishes and flowers. And we end with a maiden about to fall in love with a young man of noble bearing whose

thoughts are fixed on celestial things. If we think once again about the education of Lorenzo's nephew, we might imagine him learning about how love
hits us wildly from below, then transforms us, and ultimately carries us to the
threshold of sublimity. The male entering Aphrodite's realm dives in head-
long but exits standing upright, marveling at the heavenly majesty of it all.
The woman is startled and apprehensive at her initiation into the mysteries
of the body, but she then moves gracefully through them and is ultimately
lured beyond them.

Part of the inexhaustible fascination of the image is the sense of a world
where all is as it should be; where art, beauty and love are in perfect harmony;
where the dance of earthly desire is revealed in its correspondences to the
cosmic cycle of renewal. In this pagan dream of the Renaissance, we stop to
marvel at the sophisticated embrace of eros in all its differentiations from lust
through graciousness. And it makes our own dominant conception of sex as
an animal need or "instinctual drive" seem almost barbarous by comparison.

BOTTICELLI'S
Birth of Venus

When we shift our attention to the *Birth of Venus*, we recognize certain elements from the *Primavera*: the winged figure with blue cape and puffed cheeks; the nymph with the wild, wavy blonde hair who now appears to be his mate; the profusion of pink flowers; a floral dress with flowering vine around the neck and the waist; the grove of trees. Things are similar, but somewhat different.

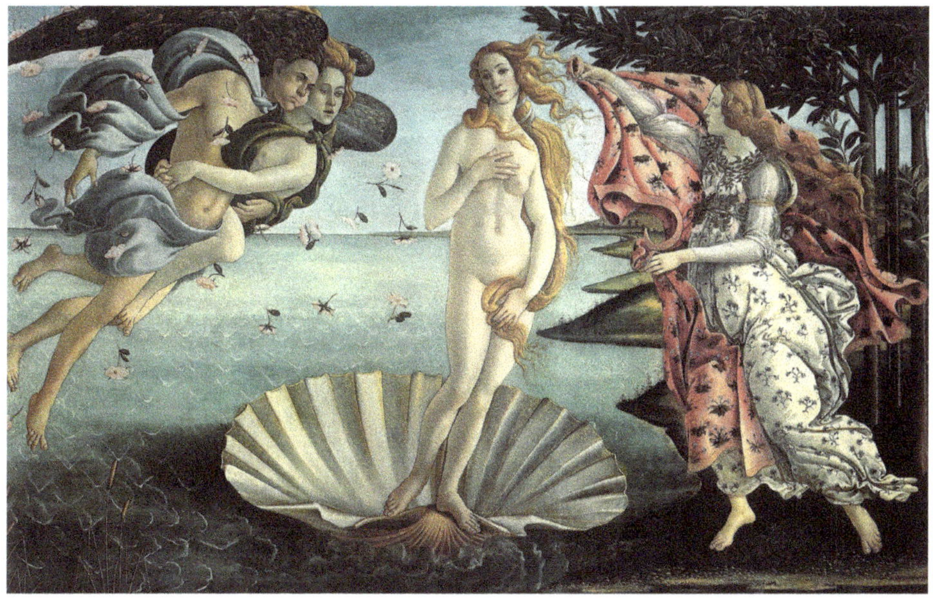

Fig. 55: Sandro Botticelli, *The Birth of Venus*. Uffizi Gallery, Florence.

The winged figure and the nymph that clings to him are now in a very differ-ent phase of their relationship than the one we saw in the *Primavera*. He is no longer blue all over; his skin now has warm flesh tones. Given his line of work, his cheeks are still puffed, but his face has lost that desperate intensity. The relationship appears to have infused him with new vitality.

The nymph who leaned away from him apprehensively in the *Primavera* now trusts him enough to let him transport her through the air. She holds on to him like a young girl on the back of a motorcycle clinging tightly to her boyfriend and enjoying the ride.

Anyone can see that these two are now a couple. In fact, with her body wrapped all around him in the way that it is, they are so coupled that it's hard to tell whose legs are whose. If you look closely, you can see the breath stream coming out of her mouth as well as his. The energies of their coupling with its huffing and puffing and fluttering are providing the motive force that brings Venus ashore.

The couple on the left are bringing a host of pink flowers in their wake. It's as if traveling in a cloud of flowering pink blossoms were the "objective cor-relative", or external mirror, of their inner state of being. Meanwhile, the maiden on the right rushes forward to drape Aphrodite in an elegant pink floral cape. The flowers on this garment are woven and designed—as distinct from the "real" flowers brought by the couple on the left. Like the cape itself with its elegantly embroidered hem, these flowers are a product of art, rather than of nature.

All of this suggests that Aphrodite is fed by nature on one side and culture on the other, and that she is, herself, the matrix in which they are united. Like her hair which runs from head to loins, her gesture and stance echo this union of higher and lower. One foot stands flat and honors gravity, the other lifts up and suggests ascent. And, after we lift our eyes above her breasts, we may notice that her right hand is gently placed over her heart while she holds her left hand over her pubis, and seems to reflect on the mysterious relation-ship between these two domains.

You may remember that Venus is born from the severed genitals of Uranus after they are tossed into the sea. This is a very difficult image for us to connect with the loveliness of the goddess. But this aspect of the myth forces us to recognize that the sexual organs are Aphrodite's essential foundation in earthly life. Indeed, the birth of Aphrodite from male genitalia reminds us of the fact that we have all entered this world of flesh and blood through the same gate.

Botticelli's image offers us a chance to see the birth of Venus, not as an all-at-once event, but, rather, as a process. If you look closely at Aphrodite's face, you can see that she is still dreaming, still coming into consciousness and not yet fully awakened. She's only now arriving at the shore where she is about to receive her floral cape. Unlike the branches in the *Primavera* that are full of fruit, the trees here are still in their first flowering.

Aphrodite is naked, with barely a tie in her golden hair, while the maiden who comes forth to receive her is beautifully dressed, with elegant braids in her carefully coifed hair. The couple on the left has provided the energetic impulse to get Aphrodite ashore, but the maiden who receives her provides the accoutrements of civilization which will complete the birth. They will allow Aphrodite to be transformed from a windswept ingénue who's out at sea to a regal figure who's come into her own. If we imagine Aphrodite ashore, elegantly dressed in her new cape, and the trees in the grove grown heavy with fruit, we're not far from the world of the *Primavera*.

During the Middle Ages, after centuries of suppression of pagan culture in Christian Europe, the images of the pagan gods were virtually lost. It was only after the Renaissance humanists began excavating antique statues and matching them to their textual descriptions in classical literature that the gods and their images were united once again.

By the late 15th century, this work of cultural archeology had reached a high level of sophistication, and Botticelli's painting draws on it extensively. Venus was associated with gold and jewelry, with flowers, with pink, with dawn and dusk. Also, much of the classical phenomenology of Venus, as the goddess of love and sexuality, links her with the sea. She was associated with the sea smells of sex, the languorous movements of love and the ebb and flow of desire, the sea-foam, and particularly with the shoreline, where the rhythmic movement of water meets the land, sometimes lapping gently, sometimes plunging forcefully.

Aphrodite was also associated with creatures of the sea like oysters and mollusks and anemones. Based on scent, texture and appearance, and perhaps also for the way they suddenly clam up when stressed, these creatures were considered evocative of the female sex. The next time you visit an aquarium look around for the jellyfish and observe the rhythms of their fluttering veils. As you do so, remember the fluttering of the gowns of the three Graces in Botticelli's *Primavera* and you'll catch a glimpse of the way in which the classical world experienced the presence of Aphrodite.

Botticelli has carefully introduced all these elements into his depiction of the realm of Aphrodite—the clamshell touched with gold, the pink flowers, the shoreline and the sea, the wild eros of young lovers flying through the air, and, of course, the goddess herself in a pose reminiscent of her appearance in classical statuary. But what is, perhaps, most amazing about his painting is the way that it affects us: Botticelli's magic invokes the presence of Aphrodite, and we feel it when we stand before his painting. After an absence of a thousand years, the Florentine Renaissance lured Aphrodite back from the archetypal realms to dwell among us for a while...

This is certainly magic enough, yet there's still one thing more. Botticelli's image takes one of the dominant metaphors of Western mythology and stands it on its head. We have learned both from Moses and from Aristotle that our spiritual energies are "higher" and our physical desires are "lower." But look carefully at this birth of Venus one more time. The erotic couple on the left, the huffing and puffing lovers, are winged, aerial creatures, and they are blowing *down* their energetic bounty from above. Meanwhile, the flowering, flowered earth maiden on the right stands on her tiptoes and reaches upward to bring her embroidered cape to Aphrodite.

Here in 15th century Christian Florence, we are invited to imagine Heaven descending to bring its gifts of erotic desire. And, perhaps even bolder, we are invited to recognize the intelligent, civilizing energies of the earth rising seamlessly from the soil and trees through the flowering maiden to the exquisite artistry of an embroidered cape. Sustained by these forces, and standing upon the waters like a column connecting heaven and earth, Aphrodite brings ashore the gifts of the sacred feminine: love, beauty, compassion and wisdom.

BOTTICELLI'S
Annunciation

N ow that you've been immersed in Botticelli's pagan mythologies, you may be surprised to discover that he is no less skillful, earnest or profound in his exploration of Christian themes.

Botticelli's *Annunciation* imagines the meeting of Mary and Gabriel as a meeting of earth and air, spirit and flesh. The angel seems no less awed at being in Mary's presence than she is of being in his. Look beneath the angel's wings at the way that the gossamer veil over the angel's gown flutters in an imagined breeze while he bends low close to the ground. Then look at Mary. Think of the angel as air, and of Mary as earth. Doesn't the stem of her body look like the calyx of a bulb, newly risen from the earth and slowly opening to the light?

You may remember from our earlier discussion of Annunciations that, in paintings

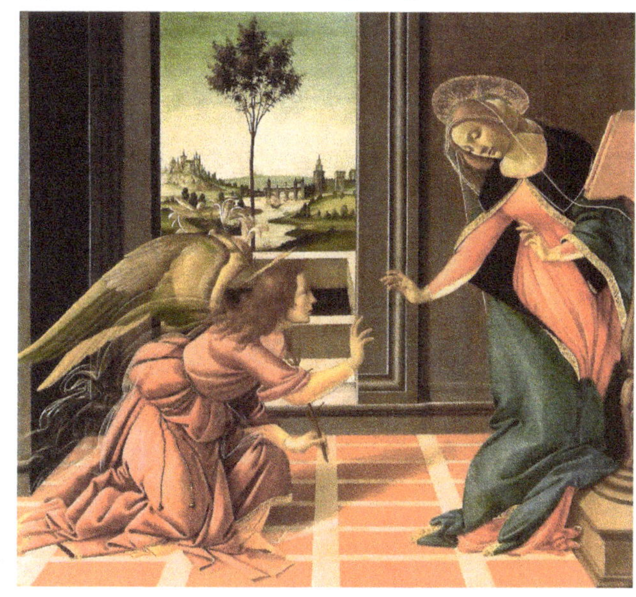

Fig. 56: Sandro Botticelli, *Annunciation*. Uffizi Gallery, Florence.

of this type, we typically find some kind of barrier or division that separates Gabriel and Mary. In Botticelli's painting there are several lines of demarcation between the angel and Mary that are crossed on the way to her acceptance.

Botticelli looks at the moment when Mary is first saying, "Yes." And this silent "Yes," conceived in the soul before being expressed in words, is subtly and beautifully depicted through the various ways in which the boundary lines between Mary and Gabriel are being crossed.

Note the vertical line that comes right toward us in the middle of the painting. The tip of the stem of the angel's lily reaches this far, and the rest of his body remains behind this line. Except, of course, for his right hand which reaches across to the edge of the windowed space as his fingertips extend ever so slightly beyond it. This door frame divides Mary's interior space from the greater world of rivers and mountains and cities that provides the backdrop for the angelic visitor.

Mary's space is delimited primarily by the rightmost vertical running between the tiles; her pink dress touches it while her blue cloak falls just beyond it. The door frame has an ornamental element that looks like a reversed "L," and, at her furthest point of extension, Mary's hand just crosses this line, almost meeting Gabriel's. Their palms are already turned toward each other, and the whole drama of the painting focuses on bridging the small distance that remains between their hands.

The reversed "L" design is an ornamental motif that you can still see in the *Ospedaledegli Innocenti*, the foundling hospital, that Brunelleschi designed early in the 15th century. In the image before us it serves to draw the eye down from Mary's hand toward the angel's, and it heightens the sense we have of them reaching toward each other despite the obvious hesitancy that each exhibits. And it's the exquisite tension between their modesty and reserve, and that unseen force we sense pulling them toward each other, that gives this image much of its remarkable poignancy.

While this all takes place, the most significant boundary crossing occurs almost unnoticed. It's the angel's shadow which actually extends all the way into Mary's space. Its significance is confirmed by the Latin words painted across the predella of the painting which translate in the King James as: "The Holy Spirit shall come upon thee, and the power of the highest shall overshadow thee."

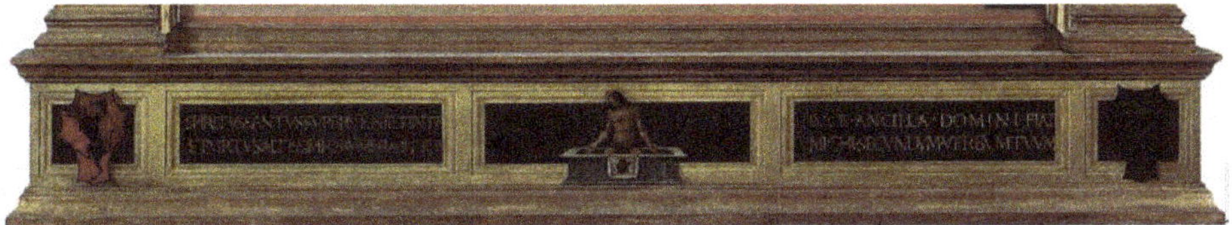

Fig. 57: Sandro Botticelli, *Annunciation*, predella. Uffizi Gallery, Florence.

These are the final words that the angel speaks to Mary, and they conclude his visit just as the "Ave Maria" begins it. They indicate the actual or immanent completion of the angel's mission, much as the words inscribed here on the frame beneath the image of Mary indicate her willingness to become the servant of the Lord.

Through the window in this painting, which is open to the elements, you can see earth, air, and water. We are invited to supply the missing fourth by imagining that spark of divine fire that passes between their palms.

Meanwhile, the doorway that opens out into the wider world shows us the consequences of this fateful meeting. The thin stalk of the lily that Gabriel holds seems to grow into a sturdy tree. From this most private encounter in the Virgin's chamber, Christianity emerges as a world religion.

* * *

In his later years Botticelli had a difficult time holding together the reverent paganism and passionate Christianity that seemed to blend together so seamlessly during the earlier part of his life. But, in this respect, he simply mirrored the divorce that was happening between these two cultural streams in the larger world.

In the time of Cosimo the Elder, the mystical Christianity of San Marco thrived alongside of Cosimo's deep love of classical learning and esoteric philosophy. By the time of Lorenzo the Magnificent, Cosimo's grandson, the alliance was over, and San Marco's Prior, the monk Savanarola, regularly denounced Lorenzo as a tyrant and an irreligious soul. After Lorenzo's death in 1492, Botticelli came strongly under Savanarola's influence and was even persuaded to cast some of his paintings into the infamous "Bonfires of the Vanities," which were to meant to purge Florence of its decadence.

The attempted reconciliation of the Judeo-Christian and Classical traditions ended in failure, and the marriage was annulled. In the year of Lorenzo's death, the Most Holy Catholic monarchs of Spain sent all their Jewish poets and enlightened Sufi masters into exile. Shortly after in northern Europe, bands of Protestant zealots went through the churches smashing statues, and scraping frescoes off the walls. Catholic Italy retrenched and, after the Council of Trent, began to enforce strict adherence to Church doctrine in all representational art. Lorenzo de' Medici's Platonic Academy, where Pico studied Kaballah in Hebrew and Ficino translated Greek philosophy, was replaced by Duke Cosimo's court. In exchange for 50,000 pieces of gold and an agreement to put the Jews in ghettoes, young Cosimo was granted the title of Grand Duke by the Pope. In both northern and southern Europe the common people went off looking for twigs to help the Churches burn the millions of witches who had been hiding among them. And in place of the exciting experiments in conjoining disparate elements, dreams of Purity and Power became the motive spirit of the new era.

APPENDICES

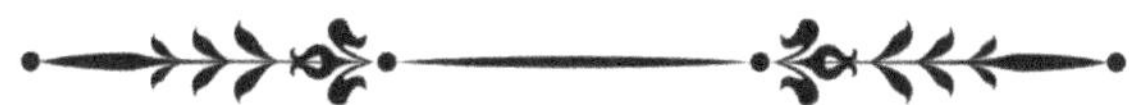

Rather than burden the art essays unduly with arguments about hermeneutics, I have collected various thoughts about images and interpretation and placed them here at the tail end. Readers who are interested in learning more about the critical approach taken in the body of this work will find here a succinct overview of "Image Work" in the form of three brief essays.

Also included is the transcript of an early experiment in imaginal dialogue with a Renaissance fresco that may be of interest to some of you.

IMAGE WORK:
ART HISTORY VS. ART APPRECIATION

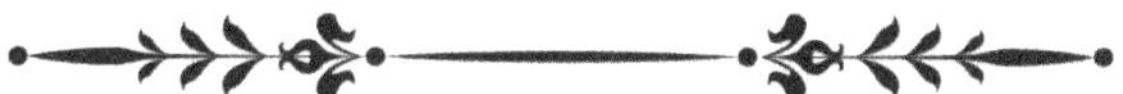

Having come to the end of our journey through the early decades of Italian Renaissance art, I would like to conclude the polemic I began in the Introduction with a few thoughts about method. My own way of working with paintings and sculptures is based on an approach called "Image Work" which I learned from my mentor, Professor Gordon Tappan, at Sonoma State University when I was a student there in the late eighties.

To begin with, we should consider that different kinds of questions may be asked when we stand in front of a painting. Not simply different questions, but different *kinds* of questions. The first kind may be described simply as questions regarding matters of fact. Who painted it? When was it done? Where was it painted? To these may be added additional queries about patronage, initial installation, restorations, and so forth. Here we find ourselves in the realm of right and wrong answers: such questions may be answered definitively and unambiguously, at least in principle, if the appropriate documents can be uncovered.

Now the situation changes dramatically when we begin to address the Why and What sorts of questions: What are the themes of the painting? Why did the artist always paint Madonnas in a certain way? Why are certain kinds of painting done at certain periods in history? What is the relation between the image and the events of the day? Why do styles and conventions of representations change, or not change? Why do similar themes reappear at different times in different places?

All such questions are speculative and unavoidably engage the imagination in the search for answers. Here we legitimately enter the realm of myth-making. All possible answers are always provisional, and can never be either conclusive or definitive. We can neither now, nor ever, answer with any finality what the meaning of a poem or a painting may be. Yet this does not mean that our interpretations ought to be entirely free of any constraints. The ground rules, the constraints we observe, must be set by what scholarly studies have established to be the facts of the case about a given image. If we learn that the saint crossing the river is St. Christopher, and that the painting was executed in Bruges in the 16th century, we are not at liberty to treat the work as a medieval Italian painting of St. Francis.

Certainly one of the greatest cultural achievements since the Renaissance has been the discovery and development of research methodologies which strive to distinguish fact from fantasy. Although epistemological debates about how much is given as opposed to how much we contribute to perception will no doubt persist to the end of time[107], we have learned, in principle, that research of any value must begin by distinguishing the essential facts from what we wish, hope, or believe to be the case. Vasari's depiction of Andrea del Castagno as a darkly jealous artist who murdered his rival, Domenico Veneziano, was believable until a study of death certificates showed that Veneziano died several years after his purported assassin. Indeed, I would suggest that the crucial difference between legitimate attempts to re-vision history and the vile trash put forth by propagandists, Holocaust deniers, and their ilk is largely the degree of willingness on the part of the writer to respect the known facts in telling his or her story.

D.C. Allen's marvelous study of Renaissance man's approach to historical studies, *Mysteriously Meant*, shows us plainly how far we have come since

---

107 Through what must have been an inadvertent omission, Dante does not appear to have provided a place in Purgatory for epistemological philosophers.

the Renaissance in these matters.*108* In Renaissance essays on history, the facts are always gingerly subordinated to the objective of the essay. If the writer wishes to show that the Egyptian sage, Hermes Tristmegistus, is more ancient than Moses, he avails himself of all the ingenuity at his command. He looks for coincidental similarities in names, he cites opinions of other worthy wise men of old, he weaves the most fanciful etymologies, he makes bald assertions of how things must be, he turns to other fables as evidence of historical fact, he notes formal analogies between things and derives causal relations from them—and upon this foundation of sand he builds his house.

Between then and now we have learned how to separate reasoned assessment of evidence from fanciful speculation. And in our delight at having discovered the realm of objective fact and the laws which pertain to it, we have tended to denigrate and dismiss the imaginative powers of the soul. The understanding, after millennia, that fantasy is not a substitute either for measurement or for careful, reasoned inference, has been generalized inappropriately, and our speculative energies have been largely excluded from *any* legitimate role in the study of the humanities.

If the first goal of art historical research is to establish factuality, the goal of Image Work is to use that factual bedrock as a point of departure for animating images. Perhaps if we could be clear that the work of animating images is distinctly different from the work of preparing a basic monograph or a *catalogue raisonné*, we could make room for both fastidious research and inspired Image Work under the greater rubric of art studies. Is it not time to recognize that both fact-gathering and myth making are valid and valuable activities, that they are inter-dependent although their methods and aims are quite different? I am hopeful that a clear distinction between art historical research proper and the mythopoetic activity which I'm calling "Image Work" may eventually help us to have both siblings dwell again under a single roof, but without the collusion and confusion over boundaries that previously prevailed. Indeed, such clarification and distinction of methods and goals might

---

108 D.C. Allen, *Mysteriously Meant: The Rediscovery of Pagan Symbolism and Allegorical Interpretation in the Renaissance* (Baltimore: Johns Hopkins Press, 1970). See especially chaps. II & III for examples of Renaissance "historical" writing.

even allow art historians some greater latitude to explore and express the love for images which drew them to their work in the first place.

This erotic aspect of relationship with images lurks unacknowledged in the background even of some of the most sober, scholarly attempts to elucidate images. If we observe with an imaginal eye some of the battles, say, over readings of Botticelli's *Primavera*, we find that we can only really account for the intensity of the discussion by recognizing that scholars establish relationships with images through their interpretations, that they are loathe to surrender their interpretations because these are their erotic bonds with the image. When we watch scholars like E. H. Gombrich and Erwin Panofsky draw forth, from the almost unfathomable depths of their erudition, the widest array of learned reference to classical texts in a variety of languages, all for the sake of establishing the plausibility of their own reading of the image, are we not witnessing two knights battling for the love of their lady?

The Dutch historian, Johan Huizinga, wrote an intriguing study of the play element in human society called *Homo Ludens*, Man the Player.[109] Huizinga's *Homo Ludens* is both a survey of the role of the "play impulse" in the historical development of various cultural forms as well as a plea for recognizing the continuing value of play in the elaboration of our present cultural life. Specifically, he points to the relation between the play impulse and the activity of mythopoiesis, or myth-making.[110] I would suggest further that mythopoiesis is the play element in criticism; it is what enlivens it. While it has no place in factual studies, it is the soul of interpretive work, its *raison d'etre*.

Can we not make a bit of room for *Homo Ludens* along side of his wise, serious minded brother? If we could let go of the notion that there is a right answer to true interpretive questions, then ambiguity would no longer pose a problem. And we could actually begin to enjoy the mythopoetic aspect of the elegant game of interpretation, to find delight once again in the variety and multiplicity of the soul's response to animating images.

---

109 Johan Huizinga, *Homo Ludens* (Boston: Beacon Press, 1966).
110 Ibid., p. 136ff.

Further Notes on Image Work

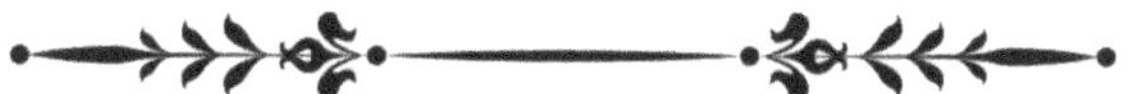

So, how does the present approach to images differ from other notions the reader may have regarding a "psychological" approach to art? Let me first offer a brief sketch of the method which is here called "Image Work" before proceeding to distinguish it from certain other psychological approaches that I have studiously avoided.

A maxim attributed to Rafael Lopez-Pedraza that is often quoted in the literature of archetypal psychology states the cardinal rule plainly enough: "Stick to the Image!" In these essays the attraction of the image has been treated more as a kind of magnetism than as a type of glue. Taken too literally, we could get stuck in the image in the way the New Critics did in the 1950s and 1960s where the act of interpretation became constrained by the pretense that an image has no relation to anything external to it. The goal here is not to apply a pure formalism. We want to see the image against a multitude of worldly contexts, but as we venture forth into the realms of iconography, social history, or patronage studies, we do so for the sake of the image, to enhance its visibility and intelligibility. So we allow the magnetic pull of the image to always draw us home after our peregrinations: we leave the image for the sake of a richer return to the image.

To say it another way: we don't use images for the sake of illustrating our assertions about sociology or biography or even about the developmental patterns of art history. Quite the opposite. We are free to explore Greek mythology, Biblical typology, or Renaissance mysticism, we can go anywhere we like, "all times and all worlds shall be used."*111* But our focus, the hearth from which we depart and to which we always return, remains the image.

* * *

I believe that many past efforts at psychological inquiry have been of limited value for appreciating art precisely because, while they purported to reveal the work of art unto its innermost depths, they were, in fact, merely appropriating the image for other purposes. Chastened by these failures, the three cardinal sins which I've sought to avoid in pursuing a psychological engagement with art are here identified as *reduction, displacement,* and *projection.*

The first of these, *reduction,* may be described as the effort to "decipher" images by subordinating them to a more fundamental, explanatory framework. When the critic tries to account for the image by revealing it to be no more than the "expression" of underlying factors, e.g., wish-fulfillment, homoeroticism, unconscious parental rage, astigmatism, latent psychosis, etc., he is inviting us to look past the surface of the image to see more deeply into the sources which generated it. What makes this kind of work so dull is that it routinely achieves what it attempts: its reduces the apparent multiplicity of images to a few, basic underlying forces. Though he believed wholeheartedly in the value of this style of work, Freud himself noted the drawbacks:

> [T]he matters dealt with are few in number, whereas the symbols for them are extraordinarily numerous, so that each of the few things can be expressed by many symbols practically equivalent. When they are interpreted, therefore, the result of this peculiarity gives universal offense, for in contrast to the multifarious forms of its representation in dreams, the interpretation of the symbols is very monotonous. This is displeasing to everyone who comes to know of it: but how can we help it?*112*

---

111 From "Bénédiction" in Charles Baudelaire, *The Flowers of Evil and Other Works,* trans. by W. Fowlie (New York, Bantam: 1964), p. 25.

112 Sigmund Freud, *A General Introduction to Psychoanalysis,* trans. and ed. by Joan Riviere (New York: Washington Square Press, 1967) p. 161.

How can we help it? We might begin by being attentive to the phenomenology of the image, noting its detail and specificity as well as its family affiliations. We could approach the image with basic courtesy, respecting its self-presentation as its most appropriate form, and not as some sort of disguise. And, rather than seeking to explain away the image as a recurring symbol, as an expression of something "deeper," we could cultivate an appreciation of its particularity, noting the marked differences between a dull knife, a slippery black snake, and a pink marble column—before cracking them open to find the phallus hidden within.

The sin of *displacement* is the practice of using images for the purpose of illustrating or establishing truths in other domains of knowledge. This practice is a sin only from the vantage point of Image Work. It is perfectly valid as a tool for other purposes. So, for example, for anyone writing about clothing and styles of dress in the fifteenth century, painted images can be a very useful source. But while the information gathered may do much for our understanding of Renaissance costume, it typically does little to help us appreciate particular images.

In psychological writing about art, Jungian-inspired work has been especially prone to depotentiate images in this way. The presence of water in an image leads us immediately into a discussion about the nature of the unconscious, the presence of fire to a discussion of transformation, and so forth. By leaping immediately from the details of a particular image to generalizations about the archetype, this style of work displaces the focus of attention from the image. The image is then used either to contribute to our repository of general knowledge, or it becomes an occasion for illustrating the truths of Jung's observations about the psyche.

In a series of important and influential essays written for the journal *Spring* in the late seventies, James Hillman tried to formulate a set of critical principles which, if followed, might allow images to regain some of their psychic potency.[113] One of his primary objectives was to correct the abusive use of

---

113 James Hillman, "An Inquiry into image", <u>Spring</u> (1977), 62-88; "Further notes on images" <u>Spring</u> (1978); 152-82, and "Image-sense", <u>Spring</u> (1979), 130-43.

Jung's technique of amplification, the process of moving all too quickly from the specifics of the image to pontification about its archetypal components. To keep the analyst from making this facile move toward generalization, Hillman took the radical position of arguing that there were no archetypes, only particular images. If we dreamed of a dead white swan with five arrows in its breast, only the image itself could disclose its meanings. Source books about swan symbolism and general reflections about the meaning of "swan-ness" were not to be substituted for a direct encounter with the particularities of the image.

Much as there is of value in Hillman's suggestions and in these essays in general, I think that they over-correct the problem of displacement and lead us ultimately into certain untenable positions. In seeking to champion the image apart from all other contexts which might distract or detract from it, Hillman ignores the figure/ground relationship which is operative whenever we contemplate images. We always see images against a background of associations and contexts, whether we bring our own or whether a critic or analyst helpfully provides them.

When we encounter a swan in an image, we bring to it the experience of our encounters with live swans, the fairy tales about swans we may have read as a child, the lore about swans which we have acquired either casually or deliberately by studying ethology, other images of swans in paintings which we have seen, the swan pillow that used to be on grandma's couch, and so forth. The swan in the image reverberates against the backdrop of all contexts which I bring to it, consciously or unconsciously. It is only against the backdrop of a general familiarity with swans which I bring to the encounter, that I can even begin to discern what is unique about the particular swan in the image before me.

The correction for *displacement* is not to protect the image against the claims of all external referents, but, rather, to use them, deliberately and artfully, for the sake of the image. Indeed, various elements in the image only become visible when we provide the appropriate context. Donatello's *St. George* becomes more interesting when we learn about the tradition of magical animation of statues, when we contrast this St. George with his traditional representations, when we learn that the figure was commissioned by the Armorer's Guild. We begin to notice the tension between earthly and unearthly beauty in Filippo Lippi's Madonnas when we are reminded of the transition from imaginary to actual models in *Quattrocento* figure painting. And it is when we explore the conventions of the genre of Annunciation, or turn to Dante's tales of spiritual questing, or consider the fresco in relation to its physical placement at the top of the stairs, that we are enabled to appreciate more fully the complexity of Fra Angelico's San Marco *Annunciation*.

The work of animating images requires that we recognize the figure/ground relationship between the image and its contexts, and that we strive to display the image against the backdrop of those contexts which reveal it most fully. If the work of authenticating, restoring, and accurately dating paintings may be compared to gemology, Image Work may best be compared to the jeweler's craft. The image is placed in a setting which has been crafted to show it off to best advantage. And just as different settings may display the beauty of a jewel in very different ways, the various contexts which may be appropriate to an image each help us to appreciate it in a different light.

Rather than subordinating the image to the pursuit of general knowledge, Image Work requires that we use our knowledge of various disciplines to provide the relevant contexts which may illuminate the image. And so long as we utilize art history, sociology, Biblical typology, or comparative religion for the sake of the image—and not vice versa—we avoid the displacement of attention and the depotentiation of the image.

The final psychological sin which I have tried to avoid is that of *projection*. As a psychological term, *projection* doesn't necessarily have negative connotations; it simply describes a situation where something has provoked us to externalize our interior fantasies. Quite often, however, we do hear the term pejoratively used, as in the phrase "mere projection", when someone wants to distinguish plausible assessments from wishful thinking. An almost equivalent term of disdain which art historians reserve for work that needn't be taken seriously is "impressionistic." By this they mean that, rather than building a case from the known facts, someone has chosen to bypass research altogether and has preferred simply to wax poetic about the virtues of an artist's work. In other words, rather than "discover" something, the writer has merely "projected" his or her fantasies and opinions.

In my approach to topics in art history I, too, have tried to avoid "mere projection" while continuing to practice the "unmere" variety. I've done so because I am persuaded that just as we cannot use projection instead of analytical thinking when we try to establish the facts of art history, we equally cannot experience the power of images unless we allow them to engage the psyche. So, on the one hand, I have familiarized myself with historical, social, and critical perspectives and used these to guide my readings. Yet, while respecting established knowledge about images and their contexts of meaning, I have tried to remain open to the psychic stimulus of the image. Rather than attempting to extirpate projection from my critical responses, I have worked to qualify and to focus it by grounding it in careful knowledge of the image, both its phenomenology and its contexts. That experience of psychological animation which we sometimes attain through the contemplation of images ultimately depends upon a willingness to allow the image to stimulate the imagination. And through some strange process which I do not pretend to understand, the imaginative response seems to grow stronger as it comes closer to, not farther from, reality, as if it prefers to build with real materials than with mere wisps of dream.

Imaginal Dialogue

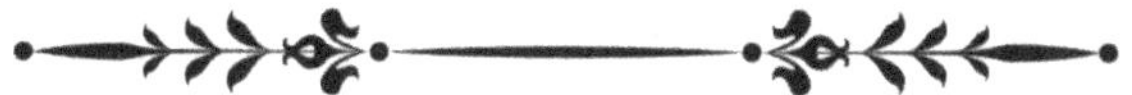

The Art of Imaginary Conversation

Imaginal dialogue is one of the practices that I have found fruitful in my efforts to animate my own encounters with images. It is a technique of inquiry which is well known to practitioners of depth psychology but is rarely utilized by art historians in their approach to reading images. Apart from its usefulness in enlivening our engagements with images, the phenomenon of imaginal dialogue itself raises all kinds of interesting and important questions about the act of creation and the art of interpretation.

Rediscovered by Carl Jung in the early twentieth century, the practice of active imagination, or imaginal dialogue, requires a suspension of disbelief in the "unreality" of imaginal figures and a willingness to engage in conversation with them, or, at least, to let them speak. Since they are discarnate entities, we need to share our vocal centers with them so that they may give voice to their side of the conversation. This requires, beyond the mere suspension of disbelief, a willingness to step aside, as it were, and to give permission to the voices that present themselves to express themselves freely through us.[114]

In Dostoevsky's novel, *The Brothers Karamazov*, one of the brothers carries on a conversation with a devilish figure whom he treats initially as a hallucination. He is convinced that, being a hallucination, the devil merely represents a portion of himself and, hence, could not possibly know anything

---

114 Jung's account of the origins of the process of active imagination is given in Chapter 6 of his autobiography, *Memories, Dreams, Reflections*, ed. by A. Jaffé and trans. by R. and C. Winston, (New York: Random House, 1965), pp. 170-199.

that he himself did not know. But when the devil begins eventually to tell him things beyond his own experience, the brother runs screaming from his house. In a similar vein, but without the panic, Jung discovered in dialoguing with the imaginal figures he encountered in dream and reverie that they began to tell him things that he himself did not know. In fact, it is through the dialogues and the exercises of active imagination during this period immediately following his break with Freud that Jung substantially differentiated his vision from Freud's and defined the parameters of his own work. Using an alchemical metaphor, Jung referred in his autobiography to the fecund material which emerged during this period as the *prima materia* of his life's work.

In certain popular therapeutic practices derived from Jungian thought, we are invited to treat all of the characters of our dreams and fantasies as "parts of ourselves." This, unfortunately, tends to depotentiate the imagination by implying that its inhabitants are merely allegorical representations of the ego's problems and desires. Jung himself avoided this reductive personalization of the imagination by stressing the quasi-independence of imaginal figures. He treated them as "semi-autonomous" figures who lived in the psyche, and he worked with the assumption that the psyche was that greater sea of Self in which the ego was only an island.

Jung's practice of active imagination continues to be used today not only in Jungian analysis, but, also, in various other therapeutic approaches influenced at least partially by Jung's work, ranging from art therapy to drama therapy to hypnotherapy.[115] My own encounter with active imagination first occurred in the context of a weekly dream group hosted by a Jungian-oriented therapist. Like many of those who experiment with imaginal dialogues, my experience of the process was one of astonishment, even bewilderment. My own assumptions about the characters in my dreams were often sharply challenged by these same characters when I invited them to speak. How could these characters, whom I had dreamed up myself, have their own opinions about the events of the dream and about my life, opinions which were often

---

115 See, for example, Shaun McNiff's discussion of imaginal dialogues in his art therapy salons in *Art as Medicine*, (Boston & London: Shambhala, 1992); for dramatic/narrative therapy, cf. Alida Gersie & Nancy King, *Storymaking in Education and Therapy* (Stockholm: Jessica Kingsley, 1990); and for hypnotherapy, Hal Stone, *Embracing Ourselves* (New World Library, 1989)

   IMAGINAL DIALOGUE

unfamiliar and startling to me?

One comes away from such encounters with a sense of the ego's voice being only one among the many voices of the psyche. And I suspect that this potent, experiential confirmation of Jung's ideas about the Self is one of the more common ways in which some of us become interested in Jungian thought.

USING IMAGINAL DIALOGUES

"This willing suspension of disbelief does not imply the adoption of a set of beliefs. As long as the approach to the dialogue is "as if", there is no necessity to explain what is happening. The question "Was Philemon real?" distracts from a consideration of whether Jung made discoveries, whether Jung, through his active imagination dialogues with Philemon, was able to imagine more fully what was under consideration between them. Clearly Philemon became an agent for Jung to enlarge the scope of his imagination. The critical question is always what was made available, not theorizing on how it came about."[116]

~ Gordon Tappan

Let's turn now to the question of how we might use active imagination in the context of looking at paintings or statues. How might we plausibly transport this procedure from its native soil in depth psychology and use it to deepen our appreciation of art? What shifts in our orientation and approach are required by the change of context? And what exactly might we hope to gain if we are successful?

To begin with the last question: imaginal dialogue is one of the most potent tools for enlivening our relationship with an image. It can involve us emotionally with the image and lead us into a deeper engagement with the fictive world which the image has constellated. Though not without its perils (which we will come to in a moment), the act of dialoguing with the characters and/or the elements in a painting has been, at its best, an "Open Sesame!"

---

116 Gordon Tappan, "Active Imagination with Images of the Dead", unpublished paper, 1987.

which has led me from casual acquaintance to profound intimacy in my relationship with certain images.

And, by sidestepping the habitual perceptual approaches of the spectator's ego, imaginal dialogue can sometimes bring new perspectives to our conscious attention, revealing aspects of the image which have hitherto escaped our critical awareness.

* * *

If we keep in mind the multiplicity of the Self which imaginal dialogues presume, the dethroning of the ego has important implications for the ways in which we conceive of the roles of both the creator and the viewer of the work of art. In the world of literary criticism, until it was challenged by the New Critics in the mid-twentieth century, the prevailing assumption underlying a great deal of critical commentary was that an artist's opinions or biography held the key to understanding the work of art.[117] If historians of early Renaissance art have never been accused of "the intentional fallacy," it's probably because so little is known about the actual lives and personalities of the artists themselves. Not easily deterred, however, scholars have argued that since the early Renaissance artist was merely a skilled craftsman hired under contract, creative responsibility rested more in the hands of the patron than the so-called artist. And, so, a good deal of attention has been given by contemporary historians of Renaissance art to questions of patronage, and to the search for patron's "programmes" in the hope of arriving at definitive answers about the meaning of given works of art.[118]

It is not the relevance but the *privileged status* of patronage studies (or of biographical studies) which is challenged by depth psychology's polycentric model of the Self. Here the commanding ego's voice is seen as only one of

---

117 E.g., W.K. Wimsatt, I.A. Richards, et al.

118 The gold ring chased by patronage studies: if we can find out what those who paid for a work of art expected it to be, we have our surest guide to its objective meaning. Here we have the tantalizing prospect of a method of inquiry which will finally free us from the vagaries of subjectivity and permit the gradual establishment of a definitive body of knowledge about art, thus allowing art history to move, albeit belatedly, out of the quagmire of speculative impressionism and to take its place proudly among its sister sciences, etc., etc.

several imaginal figures involved in the creation of the work of art. How many authors have described the experience of writing a novel as one of allowing the characters to tell their own stories? A psychological view of the creative act requires that we entertain the notion of a multiplicity of personages, some real and some imaginal, all involved in the creation of the work of art. The patron's intent may be heard only as one of the voices in the psychic

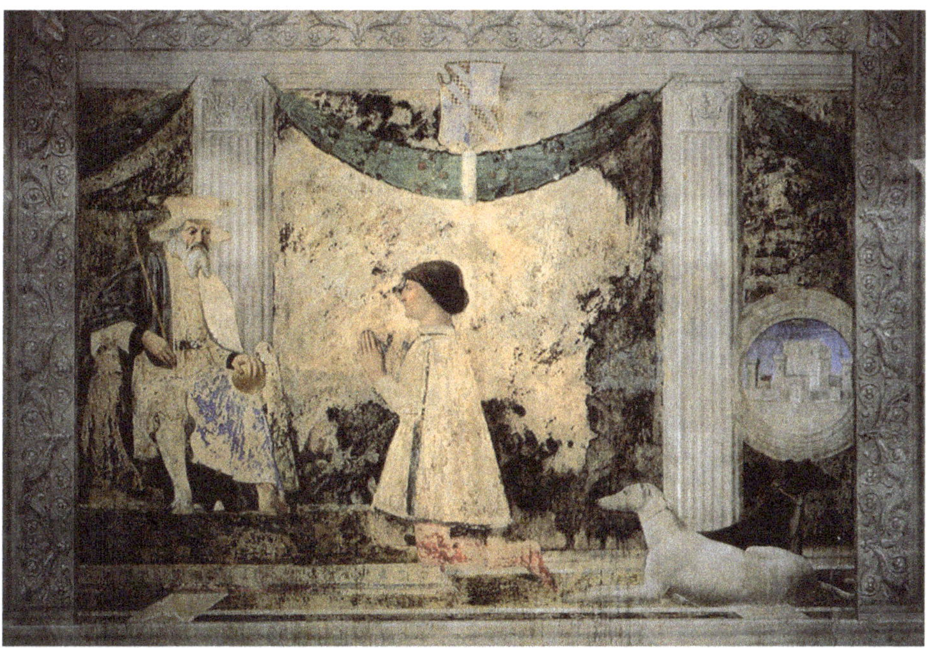

Fig. 58: Pierodella Francesca, *Sigismondo Malatesta Before St. Sigismondo.* Tempio Malatestiano, Rimini.

polyphony which constitutes the work of art.

Let's take a relatively straightforward example of a commissioned painting to draw forth the implications of this argument more fully. While he was at the court of the Sigismondo Malatesta, the tyrant of Rimini, Piero della Francesca painted a fresco of the lord of the city in his temple kneeling at the feet of his patron saint, San Sigismondo.

Regarding the character of this man, Jacob Burckhardt's summary should suffice:

It is not only the Court of Rome, but the verdict of history, which convicts him of murder, rape, adultery, incest, sacrilege, perjury, and treason, committed not once, but often.[119]

Yet we know that Sigismondo Malatesta was also a man of some learning and an active patron of the arts. And it seems reasonable enough that he would want a propitious image of himself with his namesake saint executed by a great painter like Piero della Francesca. The documented date of the painting is 1451, and we know that Piero lived for several decades afterwards. So, clearly, this fresco must have met the expectations of the patron tolerably well. In any case, it did not incite him to murder the artist, which we must assume he was quite capable of doing.

Yet if we look at the image we notice certain interesting details. First of all, the presence of hunting dogs, greyhounds most likely, in a temple in the presence of a saint is highly uncommon in paintings of this sort, and not a little strange. We may assume that Sigismondo was a man who loved his dogs and was only too happy to take them anywhere, hence his indulgence of their presence in this portrait of him and his saint.

The two pillars which appear on either side of the room frame the Saint on one side and the dogs on the other with the tyrant posed midway between them. The painting's diagonal axis, which runs from the Saint to Sigismondo to the dogs, again situates the tyrant in a midway position between the Saint and the animals. Also, Sigismondo's outstretched hands echo the outstretched paws of his dog, and, taken in conjunction with positioning and posture, we can say that he is in relation to his Saint as his dog is to him.

Of the two dogs, one faces toward the Saint, while the other has turned his back on him. Is it merely coincidental that it is Sigismondo's black dog which has turned its head away from the Saint? And isn't it interesting that it is directly over the head of the black dog that we see, as if in a dream of power, the crenellated walls and fortified battlements of the city? While he kneels before the Saint, the thoughts of his black hunting dog are clearly focused elsewhere.

---

119 Jacob Burckhardt, *The Civilization of the Renaissance in Italy*, trans. by S.G.C. Middlemore, in 2 vols. (New York: Harper & Row, 1958), p. 442.

There is, I am suggesting, a depiction of the tyrant's character in this image which he himself obviously did not notice. Does that mean that we, too, must remain oblivious to it because we can not reasonably assume that the patron intended this meaning for the painting? And what if the artist swore by all that is holy that he had no intention of disparaging his patron in any way? Shall we then deny what we can see with our own eyes?

* * *

From the viewer's side of the equation, there are distinct implications to the polycentric view of the Self implicated in imaginal dialogue. Just as there are multiple points of view which combine in the creation of the image, so there may also be several places, psychologically speaking, from which an image may be perceived. An image may appeal to us on multiple levels, inviting us to respond in distinct, even contrary ways. One of the virtues of imaginal dialogue is that it "loosens us up" just enough to permit our various internal voices to participate in the act of engagement with the image. Though we may have a dominant perceptual style through which we typically and habitually respond, imaginal dialogue makes room for some of our secondary, normally suppressed modes of awareness to become activated and expressed in our responses to the image. These marginalized, subliminal voices occasionally reveal to us certain aspects of an image that had previously escaped our awareness.

For example, in certain *Quattrocento* paintings we may find ourselves looking at what appears to be a conventional religious image. But perhaps there is something slightly amiss, an undercurrent of mild distress or tension that seems inappropriate if we notice it at all. We tend to pass right over these minor tremors when we simply trust the dominant voice that tells us what we may reasonably expect to see. But when we give some latitude to our own secondary voices in dialoguing with the image, we may find them leading us in some interesting and unforeseen directions. Particularly in working with certain of Filippo Lippi's paintings this style of investigation has led me to stumble across certain complex cross-currents in which an image seems to play different perspectives against one another.

At its best, imaginal dialogue invites an engagement between a multidimensional image and a multidimensional self. On the one hand it requires a certain psychic receptivity to the different energies present in the image. On the other hand, it requires a sufficient degree of psychological flexibility to permit one's own responding subselves to inform consciousness of their perceptions. The apparent One to One relationship of self and image ultimately reveals itself to be a dance of the Many with the Many. At the heart of the interplay, there is a strange confluence of what moves us in the image and what we contribute to the dance, but there is no need to analyze that dynamic. The important thing is always to appreciate "what was made available, not theorizing on how it came about."

* * *

Having set forth some of the potential benefits of imaginal dialogue with art images, let's look finally at some at the potential liabilities and misunderstandings of the process. For those who are familiar with the technique of imaginal dialogue from art therapy or dreamwork, it's important to the bear in mind that the purpose of using the technique in this context is not therapeutic. We don't want to use the image like a Rorschach ink blot or a Thematic Apperception Test simply to draw forth our psychic projections. We are not trying to stimulate the imagination for the sake of externalizing inner conflicts, either to diagnose or heal. For the individual contemplating a painting or statue, imaginal dialogue offers a means to achieve deeper engagement and a greater attentiveness to the image. Although the psychological impact of this practice can occasionally be quite powerful, it must remain a "secondary gain" of this style of work, never its objective. As soon as therapy becomes the goal of the work, the image is depotentiated and the process of animation loses its focus.

Although I engage throughout these essays in a running polemic against certain limiting conventions of art historical inquiry, I want to reiterate the indispensable importance of scholarship to Image Work. The facts that art historians labor diligently to establish define the playing field and provide the ground rules: we ignore them at our peril when we approach a Renaissance artwork. It is either arrogant or naive, or both, to assume that we can respond meaningfully to images created centuries earlier by another culture without an understanding of their very different context. If we fail to carefully qualify our psychological enthusiasms with factual knowledge, we wind up with little more than florid fantasies growing wildly in the fields of our ignorance.

Art historical research gives us the keys to the intelligibility of historical images. Apart from names and dates, scholarship provides an understanding of the stories that give meaning to the images of the past. The study of social, cultural, religious, and historical contexts adds richness and complexity to the encounter with the image and allows one to discern and appreciate the multiple realities in which the image lives.

There is no substitute for this kind of knowledge when dealing with other people's images—just being "psychological" is not enough. To see Michelangelo's statue of David without knowing the Biblical story, without having familiarity with any of the earlier Davids of the 15th century, and without knowing about the traditional local identification of Florence with David, is largely to have missed the boat. David without historical roots and cultural contexts is just an imaginal immigrant who has stepped off the boat without papers, speaking a language that no one understands.

Transcript of the
Trinità Dialogue

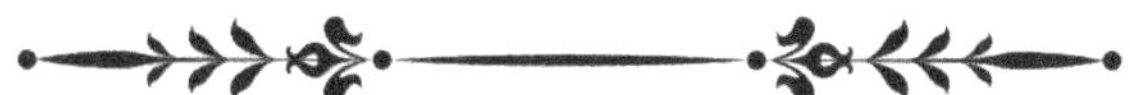

For those of you who have never attempted an imaginal dialogue with a painting or statue, it occurred to me that you might be interested in seeing a concrete example of this sort of conversation. So, I have provided a transcript of my own conversation with Masaccio's *Trinità* recorded in Santa Maria Novella in the fall of '93.

The method of imaginal dialogue along with caveats and qualifications has already been discussed. Here I would remind the reader only that in these dialogues we need to let go of our ideas about how the characters "ought" to speak, given their religious identity or functions. We should recognize that we are not talking with Christ or with God Almighty, only with an imaginal figure who may be playing that role within the circumscribed world of a specific image. These are psychological encounters, not statements of theological belief. We need only step aside and give the figures their say.

In such dialogues, shadow aspects of personality are typically engaged. My own "other voices" are frequently cynical and sarcastic, sometimes funny, sometimes blasphemous and irreverent, and occasionally insightful. The opinions expressed are not necessarily those of management.

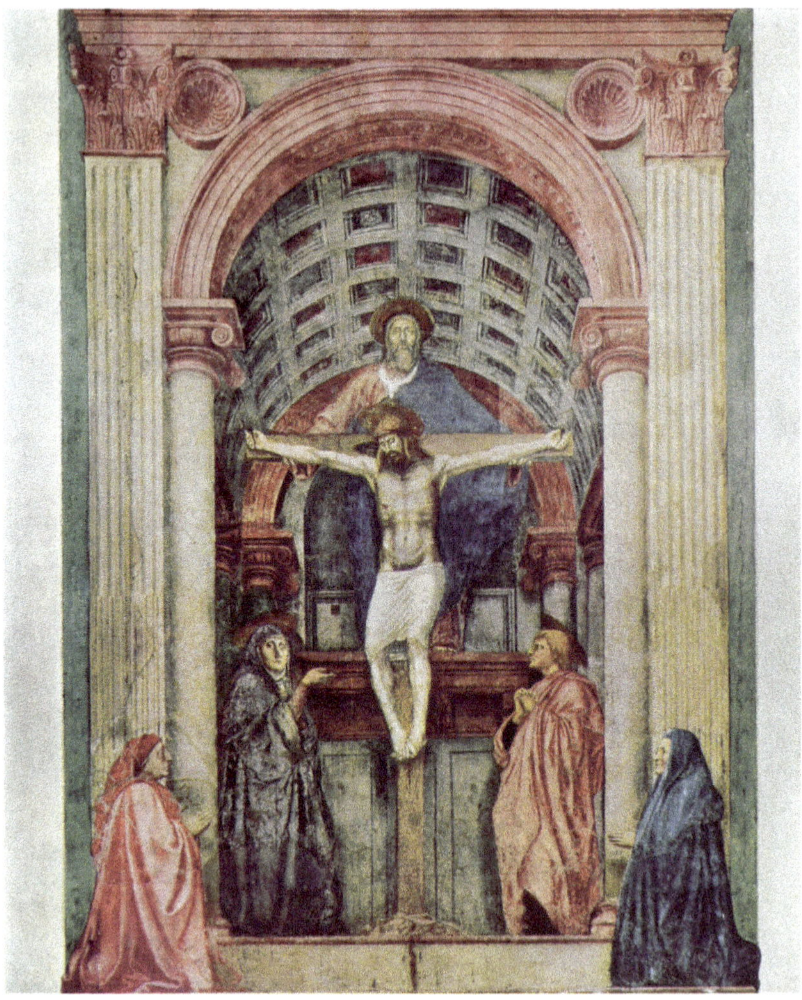

Fig. 59: Masaccio, *Trinità*, Santa Maria Novella, Florence

Sam: (Invocation): "In this image Mary stands, an older woman with an enigmatic expression on her face, holding her hand out, look-ing out toward the viewer. She is the one who directs her atten-tion to our space. She looks out toward us and, with her right hand, gestures towards the body of Jesus on the Cross. And in a totally curious kind of way, like... OK, let's let Mary talk..."

Mary: "You want to look. Look at this, here he is. Here he is. I raised him, I took care of him. And here he is nailed up on this thing. What are you doing, standing out there gawking? What are you looking for? We've got our reason for being here, what's yours? Where are you coming from? You think there's something special, you think this is some kind of a show or something? Is that what you think? I mean, this was my son! And here I am. Standing here like this..."

Sam: "OK, now, there's a figure on the right who has his hands clasped and he's gazing off into the distance. Let's let him talk..."

St. John: "Oh Jesus, I hold you before my eyes. I contemplate your sacrifice and the goodness that you brought into our lives. Oh, I stand here so reverently and allow myself to be morally enlightened, and my soul led to salvation by contemplating the image of your death and your sacrifice."

Sam: "All right. Now we've got a couple folks who are kneeling outside the archway of the Crucifixion. They are looking more or less at each other, toward each other. Let's see if we can shed some light on the subject here. (Sound of clinking of change in the machine that illuminates the painting for 500 Lire.) They're also kind of looking up slightly. They're not looking at Jesus. They're sort of just kneeling in prayer."

Mourners/Donors: "We're simple folk. We've just come here to pay our respects. We're a little bit outside of the main event. You know, we're not saints, we're not holy people. We're just here to take a look and see what's happening... We're trying to kneel and pray in a sacred way."

Sam: "All right, let's talk with God here who is over Jesus' arms."

God: "Hi, this is big G. himself, talking to all of you, here, from behind the Crucifixion. I'm here to lighten the boy's load. He is carrying a heavy load for all of you. And we've got this incredible stage set here. Look over my head here, we've got one, two, three, four, five, six squares of beautiful marble set behind me indicating the depth of dimension here and one, two... eight rows across the archway. That makes forty-eight squares if my calculations are correct. And you ought to realize what that means. I'm in blue and red. Other people are in either blue or red. And, there is a cosmic mystery which I hope some of you will follow, although probably most of you won't. But, you know, that's OK. I've got plenty of time. Those of you who want to figure out what's going here, you're welcome to. If you just want to stand and stare at the boy, then by all means you're welcome to do that also.

"Mary down there--see her?--that's my wife. She's not all that pleased with this whole thing. Frankly I thought we did an incredible job. But she's hard to please. For her money, the fact that our kid is up here nailed to this cross is an indictment of the whole thing. Whereas for me, I mean, you know, you have to see the grand architecture in all this. I mean the interplay of the human and the divine, you know, the pathos of it all and the incredible order and geometry and the mathematical purity to the whole schema of the myth. You can't just get caught up in this kind of literal-minded, 'Hey, the guy got hurt and died brutally.' That just kind of trivializes it all, but she just keeps being stuck in that 'Look, look what they did to him. Look at this. Look!' Kind of pitiful..."

Sam: "OK, let's talk with the architecture in the painting."

Architecture: "Well its about time you finally got to us. Obviously, we are the important element in this picture. We are the background against which this event is enacted. The figures in the foreground--they all have a little piece of the action. But we are the monumental backdrop, the eternity of logical beauty against which all these events are taking place. We have volume, mass, depth, poise, perspective, and our massiveness dwarfs the events taking place beneath us. Look well on this image and feel the

impact of these pillars, the archway, the columns, the massiveness of scale of this building. Do you see the way it dwarfs the
two little people outside it? How small they look in comparison
to my massiveness and my bulk? Events come and go in this
little alcove, but I'm here forever. I'm like the church that you are
in which will be here for centuries. Its columns will not move, its
spaces will not change, its fixed proportions remain immutable...
I am far more important than these puny figures beneath me.
They don't realize it, they think that they are what's important
here but (hahahahaha) they are not the reason that people come
and look at this picture. They look at it to see *me*. They admire
me. My perfect proportion. My absolute geometries. Look at
how the figures are arranged. They're trying to imitate my perfection. They're symmetrically balanced. They make triangles,
they make geometrical patterns that try to approximate my own
formal perfection. Look at those two poor pious fools kneeling outside; they're not even inside my framework. They're just
stuck on, on the outside. They are a step below what's happening
inside. Things move from them to Mary and the Saint, to Jesus
and then to God himself and then finally to the beauty and perfection of my archway, which is the real theme of this painting."

Sam: "Hmmm.........Mary wants to talk again."

Mary: "He went through all of this, for *this*. Look at this, look at that...
(shouting) *Look at him!* Look at his damn suffering! For what?
For *this*? For *THIS*?

Sam: I hear you, mother. I hear you. I will tell people what I saw... I
see your bitterness. And I see your disillusionment, and it breaks
my heart. And I am sorry for you."

* * *

Tourists wandering through Santa Maria Novella that day may have been
somewhat perplexed to see a middle-aged man with a microphone and tears

in his eyes making his way around talking to paintings.

But the experience completely changed my understanding of the *Trinità*. I realized that in his *Pisa Altarpiece Crucifixion*, Masaccio was capable of creating an image of terrible anguish. Here he was up to something very different. And here I am, years later, honoring my promise to an imaginal Mary to tell people what I saw.

BIBLIOGRAPHY

Leon Battista Alberti, *On Painting*, trans. J.R. Spencer (New Haven: Yale Univ. Press, 1971)

D.C. Allen, *Mysteriously Meant: The Rediscovery of Pagan Symbolism and Allegorical Interpretation in the Renaissance* (Baltimore: Johns Hopkins Press, 1970)

Michael Baxandall, *Painting and Experience in Fifteenth Century Italy* (Oxford: Oxford University Press, 1988)

Bernard Berenson, *The Italian Painters of the Renaissance* (New York: Meridian, 1958)

William Blake, *The Complete Poems*, ed. Alicia Ostriker (London: Penguin Books, 1977)

Giordano Bruno, *The Heroic Frenzies*, trans. P.E. Memmo, Jr. (Chapel Hill: University of North Carolina Press, 1966)

Jacob Burckhardt, *The Civilization of the Renaissance in Italy*, trans. S.G.C. Middlemore, in 2 vols. (New York: Harper & Row, 1958)

Ornella Casazza, *Masaccio e la Cappella Brancacci* (Florence: SCALA, 1990)

Keith Christiansen, *Gentile da Fabriano* (Ithaca, NY: Cornell Univ. Press, 1982)

Bruce Cole, *Masaccio and the Art of Early Renaissance Florence* (Bloomington & London: Indiana Univ. Press, 1980)

Cole, *Italian Art: 1250--1550* (New York: Harper & Row, 1987)

Henry Corbin, *Temple and Contemplation,* trans. P. Sherrard (London: KPI Limited, 1986)

Dante, *The Divine Comedy,* trans. Allen Mandelbaum (New York: Bantam, 1983) in 3 vols.

Gloria Fossi, *Filippo Lippi*, trans. L. Pelletti (Florence: SCALA, 1989)

Sigmund Freud, *A General Introduction to Psychoanalysis*, trans. and ed. by Joan Riviere (New York: Washington Square Press, 1967)

Northrop Frye, *The Great Code: The Bible and Literature* (New York: HBJ, 1982)

Helen Gardner, *Art Through the Ages,* rev. by Horst de la Croix and Richard G. Tansey (New York: HBJ, 1986)

Joseph Gutman, "The Sacrifice of Isaac in Medieval Jewish Art" in *Artibus et Historiae* vol. 8/16 (1987), p. 70

Frederick Hartt, *Italian Renaissance Art* (Englewood Cliffs: Prentice Hall, 1987)

Hartt, "Art and Freedom in Quattrocento Florence," in L. F. Sandler, ed., *Essays in memory of Karl Lehmann* (New York, 1964)

Philip Hendy, *Piero della Francesco and the Early Renaissance* (New York, 1968)

James Hillman, "An Essay on Pan", in *Pan and the Nightmare* (New York: Spring Publications, 1972)

Hillman, *Re-Visioning Psychology* (New York: Harper, 1977)

Hillman, *The Dream and the Underworld* (New York: Harper, 1979)

Hillman, *Healing Fiction* (Barrytown: Station Hill Press, 1983)

Hillman, "A Note on Story", in *Parabola*, Vol. IV, #4 (1979), p. 44

Hillman, "An Inquiry into image" in *Spring*, (1977), pp. 62-88

Hillman, "Further notes on images" in *Spring*, (1978), pp. 152-82

Hillman, "Image-sense" in *Spring*, (1979) pp. 130-43

William Hood, *Fra Angelico at San Marco* (New Haven & London: Yale Univ. Press, 1993)

Johan Huizinga, *Homo Ludens* (Boston: Beacon Press, 1966)

Carl Jung, *Memories, Dreams, Reflections*, ed. A. Jaffe, trans. R. and C. Winston (New York: Random House, 1965)

Thomas Kuhn, *The Structure of Scientific Revolutions* (Chicago: University of Chicago Press, 1970)

Stephen K. Levine, *Poiesis: The Language of Psychology and the Speech of the Soul* (Toronto: Palmerston Press, 1992)

Lauro Martines, *Power and Imagination: City States in Renaissance Italy* (New York: Random House, 1980)

Mary McCarthy, *The Stones of Florence* (New York: HBJ, 1959)

Shaun McNiff, *Art as Medicine* (Boston & London: Shambhala, 1992)

Millard Meiss, *Painting in Florence and Siena After the Black Death* (Princeton: Princeton University Press, 1951)

R.B. Onians, *The Origins of European Thought* (Cambridge: Cambridge Univ. Press, 1991)

Erwin Panofsky, "The Neoplatonic Movement and Michelangelo" in *Studies in Iconology: Humanistic Themes in the Art of the Renaissance* (New York: Harper, 1965)

Ginette Paris, *Pagan Meditations*, trans. G. Moore (Dallas: Spring Publications, 1986)

Walter Pater, *The Renaissance* (New York: Random House, 1873)

Jaroslav Pelikan, Mary Through the Centuries (New Haven: Yale University Press, 1996)

John Pope-Hennessy, *Fra Angelico* (Florence: SCALA, 1981)

Silvia Ronchey, *L'Enigma di Piero* (Milano: Rizzoli, 2006)

Jeffrey Ruda, *Fra Filippo Lippi: Life and Work* (London: Phaidon, 1993)

Gertrude Schiller, *Iconography of Christian Art*, trans. J. Seligman (Greenwich, CT: N.Y. Graphic Society, 1971)

Jean Seznec, *The Survival of the Pagan Gods* (New York: Harper Torchbooks, 1961)

John Shearman in *Only Connect...: Art and the Spectator in the Italian Renaissance* (Princeton: Princeton Univ. Press, 1992)

J. Webster Spargo, *Virgil the Necromancer: Studies in the Virgilian Legends* (Cambridge: Harvard Univ. Press, 1934)

Leo Steinberg "How Shall This Be? Part I" in *Artibus et Historiae* vol. 8/16 (1987), pp. 25-44; Samuel Y. Edgerton, Jr. "How Shall This Be? Part II", pp. 45-53.

Giorgio Vasari, *Lives of the Artists*, trans. G. Bull (London: Penguin Books, 1988) in 2 vols.

Jacobus de Voragine, *The Golden Legend*, ed. Christopher Stace, trans. Richard Hamer (London: Penguin Books, 1998)

D.P. Walker, *Spiritual and Demonic Magic* (Notre Dame: University of Notre Dame Press, 1975)

Frances A. Yates, *Giordano Bruno and the Hermetic Tradition* (Chicago: University of Chicago Press, 1964)

About the Author

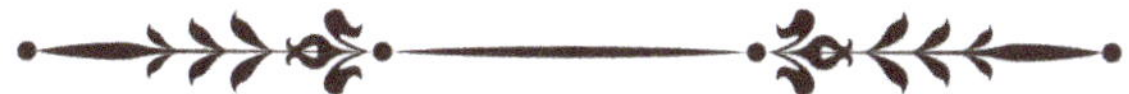

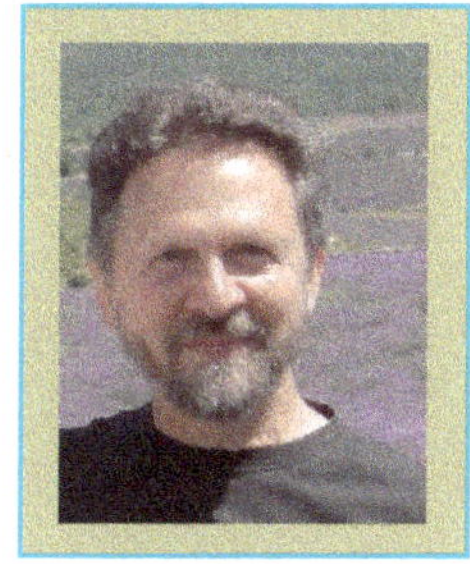

Sam Hilt's earlier works include a guidebook to Florence's Uffizi Gallery (*The Uffizi Gallery*); an entertaining account of his family's experiences in relocating to Italy (*Turning Tuscan: A Step-by-Step Guide to Going Native*); and a brief introduction to the art of travel planning (*Paradise Now: How to Plan the Perfect Italy Vacation*). All titles are available on Amazon.

While teaching part-time in the San Francisco Bay Area for several years, Sam and his wife began organizing summer art seminars in Florence for American travelers. Their avocation gradually became their primary activity, and they have been busy for these past ten years developing cultural travel adventures throughout Italy and France. Their travel company is on the web at www.TuscanyTours.com.

Sam Hilt was born in Munich, Germany, and grew up in Newark, New Jersey. He studied Comparative Literature (English, French, Russian) at Brandeis University (B.A.) and at the University of Toronto (M.A.). He also holds a Masters degree in Psychology from Sonoma State University in Rohnert Park, CA, and a Doctorate in Psychology from The Union Institute in Cincinnati.

www.ingramcontent.com/pod-product-compliance
Lightning Source LLC
Chambersburg PA
CBHW052358030726
47599CB00014B/1117